NURTURE GROUPS IN SCHOOL

NURTURE GROUPS IN SCHOOL

Principles and Practice

Marjorie Boxall

P·C·P

Paul Chapman
Publishing

To
Randolph
and all those who have nurtured us

© Marjorie Boxall 2002

First published 2002

Apart from any fair dealing for the purposes of research or private study, or criticism or review, as permitted under the Copyright, Designs and Patents Act, 1988, this publication may be reproduced, stored or transmitted in any form, or by any means, only with the prior permission in writing of the publishers, or in the case of reprographic reproduction, in accordance with the terms of licences issued by the Copyright Licensing Agency. Inquiries concerning reproduction outside those terms should be sent to the publishers.

Paul Chapman Publishing
A SAGE Publications Company
6 Bonhill Street
London EC2A 4PU

SAGE Publications Inc
2455 Teller Road
Thousand Oaks, California 91320

SAGE Publications India Pvt Ltd
32, M-Block Market
Greater Kailash - I
New Delhi 110 048

Library of Congress Control Number: 2001135449

A catalogue record for this book is available from the British Library

ISBN 0 7619 7342 7
ISBN 0 7619 7343 5 (pbk)

Typeset by Dorwyn Ltd, Rowlands Castle, Hampshire
Printed in Great Britain by Athenaeum Press, Gateshead

Contents

Preface

When nurture groups were introduced in the Inner London Education Authority (ILEA), they were ahead of their time. They were based on inclusive principles at a stage when rolls in schools for maladjusted pupils were rising rapidly. The concept offered an explicitly educational response to a set of problems that were often seen exclusively in terms of psychiatric or sociological constructs. It was a cost-effective initiative during a period when expenditure constraints in education were not as restrictive as they are now. It trained qualified teachers and unqualified classroom assistants together to create classroom teams long before the need for such training was generally recognized.

The abolition of the ILEA almost brought the Nurture Group project to an end. But the perseverance of a number of primary schools and the strong support of a handful of other local education authorities (LEAs) have sustained the project through very difficult times. It now looks like an approach whose time has come – inclusive, targeted, systematic and intellectually coherent, with a well-defined curriculum and clear programme for parental involvement. The appearance of this book, the first comprehensive handbook on the nurture groups, is therefore timely. The problems that Marjorie Boxall observed in an earlier generation of schoolchildren are no less prevalent now. This publication challenges us to respond to the children's needs with the commitment and clarity of vision that her approach expresses.

Tony Cline

Professor of Educational Psychology, University of Luton

July 2000

History

Nurture Groups had their origin in the 1960s in an area of East London that was in a state of massive social upheaval. Families had been resettled there following slum clearance, migrants from other parts of the UK had moved in, and there was a large recently arrived multicultural immigrant population. The schools were overcrowded and under enormous stress. Children were being excluded from school within weeks of arrival and unprecedented numbers were referred for psychiatric help, virtually all described as violent, aggressive and disruptive. The child guidance clinics modified their work in an attempt to engage with the problems, but the origin and nature of the children's difficulties were outside the conceptual basis of their work.

The children's difficulties seemed related to stress on their parents, historical or personal in origin. This had impaired the nurturing/learning process of the earliest years, and at the time of school entry there was a serious mismatch of child and school. 'The mother is the child's first teacher'; in normal circumstances her intimate involvement with the child provides his or her first learning experiences and is the model for the work of the nurture group.

The aim of nurture-work is to provide a restorative experience of early nurture in the children's neighbourhood school. Two experimental nurture groups were set up in 1970, in an infant and a junior school. They were successful and subsequently spread throughout the ILEA. The Department of Education and Science (DES) watched with interest, delegated Her Majesty's Inspector (HMI) John Woodend, to liase with the work, and subsequently funded statistical work on the Diagnostic Developmental Profile. This is an assessment instrument, then used internally and now, with permission, re-published by the Association of Workers for Children with Emotional and Behavioural Difficulties (AWCEBD) and titled *The Boxall Profile* (*Handbook*, Bennathan and Boxall, 1998). In 1974, the ILEA circulated internally a pamphlet 'The Nurture Group in the Primary School', (essentially chapter 2 of Bennathan and Boxall, 1996), and more groups followed.

From the beginning the work that developed was an attempt to ameliorate a desperate situation in the schools and to help the large number of children who were facing a disastrous future. It was a service to the schools and was not research orientated, though much basic data was collected and evaluated. The more formal work undertaken was a response to needs expressed by teachers, assistants and headteachers, and was a collaborative effort. Nor did the principles on which the groups were based derive from an attempt to work with existing theories, though over the years the connections have become apparent. Our concern was to build in experiences appropriate for the baby and toddler. At this stage they are structured and constrained by the child's physical and physiological development. When we modified the children's experience accordingly, many showed baby and toddler behaviours and the adults responded as they would to a child at this stage. Some attached themselves as babies. Others attached later as the adults used as their model the normal developmental progression from birth. The learning process followed.

This book is based on the collated experience from 1970 to 1989 of more than 50 groups in the ILEA, supplemented by information in relation to current practice in Enfield, where all the groups are in infant schools, and are established in strictly defined circumstances. They are within the structures and objectives set out in the 1993 Education Act and meet the requirements of the National Child Protection Guidelines and Enfield LEA Health and Safety regulations.

Following the practice in Enfield, the group is assumed to be in the infant school in a classroom of sufficient size and adequately resourced. These conditions are prescriptive in Enfield but, although desirable, in practice enthusiasm and need may drive schools to make do with accommodation that is far from satisfactory.

In the ILEA the situation was more flexible. 'Official' groups were well resourced, but good work was done without special funding in dingy, small, makeshift places, sometimes with very meagre equipment. Unsatisfactory conditions, however, are acceptable only when there is pressing need for a group and it has the unequivocal and enthusiastic support of everyone and no alternative is available. Similarly junior school groups are viable when there is informed and active support, but the long-term goal should be 'nurture education' at the earliest stage possible, logically as an induction-to-school class. Modifications of practice in difficult situations and in junior groups are available.

It is hoped that this co-ordinated past and current experience will provide guidelines for other LEAs to develop their work within their particular parameters and future national requirements.

For information about screening assessment and monitoring materials and for existing and projected written material, application should be made to AWCEBD Publications, The Administrative Office, Charlton Court, East Sutton, Maidstone, ME17 3DQ.

Acknowledgements

This book is based on the experience of many nurture teachers and assistants in the ILEA, and owes everything to their commitment, generosity and creative practice, and to the support, advice and encouragement of their headteachers. I am grateful to them for their readiness to share their practice and views, and for receiving me so cordially on my visits. It is not feasible to acknowledge them by name but I am particularly indebted to those who gave sustained observations over a long period of time and who provided carefully considered written material. Videos were made in 1978 in two junior schools and two infant schools. They led to extensive discussion with Iris Bounsall, Janet Crawley, Liz Doak, Sylvia Lucas, Joan Miller, Jo Richardson, Barbara Saltmarsh and Sarah Temple. I am grateful to them for the learning experience this provided, and to Alan Gifford and his team for their sensitivity and skill in making the videos.

I am greatly indebted to the small group of headteachers who met regularly over a period of many years to discuss issues arising. Their steadfast support, lucidity and wisdom has been invaluable and inspiriting. They are Liz Doak, Peggy Hall, Sylvia Lucas, Barbara MacGilchrist, Margaret Routledge, Liz Smith and Barbara Temple, and over a shorter period Pete Saunders made valued contributions.

Beyond the schools, I have valued the encouragement in the 1960s that came from the Woodberry Down Child Guidance Clinic where I was based, and led to work in local schools with the parents. This work was initially undertaken by Win Roberts and Gill Gorrell-Barnes, Psychiatric Social Workers, and was continued by the schools. Lastly, we were greatly encouraged by the enthusiastic endorsement of the collective Inner London Child Guidance Clinic staff who came to a general meeting at the end of the first year, in 1971.

We greatly valued the encouragement and support of John Woodend, HMI, and the hands-on practical help with mathematics provided by Edith Biggs, (retired) HMI. I am indebted to Brian Foss, who at that time held the Chair of Psychology at Bedford College, University of London, for his interest and support, and for his memorable remark that the nurture groups were turning the teachers into psychologists. And to Tony Cline, then an immediate colleague and subsequently the Principal Educational

Psychologist, who gave unstinting time, attention and clarity of thinking to issues that arose. He continues to be a never-failing support.

I greatly appreciate the key role played by Eva Holmes a one-time immediate colleague who, as Principal Educational Psychologist in Enfield, established nurture groups there in the mid-1980s and ensured that they were part of official policy and had integrated support. She continues to give unstinting time to the furtherance of nurture-work.

More recently Marion Bennathan, Chair of the AWCEBD initiated and has tirelessly followed through a sustained drive to spread awareness of nurture groups. This issued in the formation of the Nurture Group Consortium, now the Network, and led to the appointment of Ray Arnold and Eve Boyd, both formerly Senior Advisors in Enfield, to a shared Research Associate post at the school of Education, Cambridge.

Eve Boyd, Eva Holmes, Joyce Iszatt and Pam King, all closely involved with the Enfield Groups, have given much appreciated advice on current procedural requirements and changes in primary schools over the past few years.

The continuing survival of the nurture groups owes everything to the enthusiastic commitment of all these colleagues, and the dedicated work of the new practitioners who have the joined the Network is helping to make nurture groups more widely known.

I am grateful to Eve Boyd, Tony Cline, Eva Holmes and Sylvia Lucas for their valuable comments on the penultimate typescript.

Finally, a big thank-you to my computer literate young, and not so young, friends who came so rapidly to my rescue at times of crisis.

Marjorie Boxall

Author's Note

In the text which follows the teacher and assistant are referred to as she/her because most, though not all, are female, and the child is referred to as he/him because most, though not all, are male. This has been done to avoid ambiguity and to ensure ease of reading.

All cultures are represented in the nurture groups. Specific information is not provided because pressures on different groups, and the ensuing difficulties, have changed over the years. Without an outline of the changing sociological context this would be misleading. Suffice to say that the same problems are seen today, and now, as then, boys are markedly overrepresented.

In line with the Department for Education and Employment (DfEE) publication 'Curriculum guidance for the foundation stage' (DfEE, 2000), the term 'mother' refers to the primary carer and 'curriculum' to everything children do, see, hear or feel . . . both planned and unplanned.

By 'earliest learning' we mean everything the baby and toddler absorb through their close, mutually responsive relationship with the carer. It includes trust in being cared for and valued; the security that comes from predictable responses and routines; intimations of a sense of self; interest in the immediate world and eagerness to investigate and explore; basic perceptual and motor experience, and some understanding of how things happen. It is implicit learning that becomes part of the child's core being, and is the central strand running through all later learning.

In the ILEA the furniture included a small bed. With increasing concern about child protection issues, this may no longer be acceptable and a divan or sofa may have to take its place. Anecdotes relating to the bed have nevertheless been retained because they demonstrate so clearly the needs of the children concerned. For the same reason prams remain in the text, though since the 1980s they have been largely replaced by buggies.

1

Overview

Nurture groups are an in-school resource for primary school children whose emotional, social, behavioural and formal learning needs cannot be met in the mainstream class. Their difficulties are markedly varied, often severe and sometimes lead to exclusion from school. They are of major concern to their teachers, but when referred for a psychiatric opinion are rarely considered appropriate for psychotherapy. Usually they are referred on to a resource within education where more personal relationships can be made, and emotionally expressive outlets provided. Typically such children have grown up in circumstances of stress and adversity sufficiently severe to limit or disturb the nurturing process of the earliest years. To varying extents they are without the basic and essential learning that normally from birth is bound into a close and trusting relationship with an attentive and responsive parent. Normal educational provision traditionally has been based on an implicit assumption that this first stage of the learning process has been adequately secured. It was therefore expected that new entrants to school:

- would quickly feel secure, and would trust their teachers to be kind and helpful, and concerned about their well-being; They would be responsive to them, and biddable, and would approach and respond to the other children;
- had experienced a normal environment, and had some understanding of immediate cause and effect;
- would be eager to extend their past experience, and could tolerate the frustration and disappointment of not succeeding;
- would find the school day stimulating but not overwhelming.

This has never been the case for all children, and their numbers are increasing. Disquiet became more evident in the 1960s, and at the beginning of the new millennium is a national anxiety as school exclusions rise. The purpose of nurture groups is to bridge this gap. The aim is to create the world of earliest childhood in school, and through this build in the basic and essential learning experiences normally gained in the first three years and so enable the children to participate fully in the mainstream class, typically within a year. The process is modelled on normal development from birth and the content is the essential precursor of established foundation stage education for 3- to 5-year-olds.

The children's difficulties: nature and origin

The children's difficulties in school are often severe, and sometimes seem bizarre. They range from autistic-like behaviour at one extreme, to antisocial behaviour at the other that may involve physical violence leading to disruption of the class and sometimes exclusion from school. Although not always immediately apparent, many of the children have not reached the developmental level of the normal 3-year-old, and are in difficulties from the time they enter school. They undermine the teachers' skills and cause enormous stress and despair, and sometimes negativism. They are not usually felt to be suitable for psychotherapy because to varying extents all aspects of their development have been impaired: their experience is limited, poorly organized and has little coherence, and their concepts are imperfect and their feelings confused. They are without a sufficiently organized and coherent past experience from which to develop, and there is no clear focus for intervention.

The parents, too, are often difficult to engage. Many of them live under extreme and disabling personal stress. If referred to a mental health resource because of their children's difficulties in school, they have the burden of finding their way to an unfamiliar place to face a bewildering discussion and even more problems. It all seems of little relevance particularly when their situation seems beyond repair. Their feelings are too chaotic to disentangle, or are submerged under anger or depression. They have no mental space in which to think and the visit can be counterproductive. Many first appointments are not kept, and if kept are rarely sustained.

The origin of the children's difficulties

The children's difficulties seem related to the stage in the earliest years when nurturing care was critically impaired, and the aspect of development most affected. In some families external pressures caused unmanageable stress, in others deprived and dysfunctional parents were without the resources to provide adequate nurturing care, in others again there was a discontinuity of experiences and behaviour management between home and school.

Nurture children are functionally below the age of 3, and all have considerable emotional, behavioural and learning difficulties. For historical reasons, these were relatively clearly defined in the 1960s in the area concerned, and it is from this experience that the thinking and practice of the nurture groups derive. Some were without adequately normal experiences from birth. Their difficulties resemble those seen in the Romanian orphanage children described by Rutter et al. (1999). Features seen to differing extents were: use of inappropriate objects to chew, smell; intense preoccupation with an excluding, limited often bizarre routine; poor language development and inappropriate utterances, often repetitive; fixation on a single aspect of experience; and 'following' behaviour. Others, after a satisfying baby stage, experienced restrictive or punitive management when they were beginning to explore and establish an identity. They were robust children, eager for experiences but overstimulated by the riches of school, and were without the competence to use these opportunities constructively. Typically, they plunged in and created havoc: 'He's like a bottle of champagne with the cork out' (a teacher). Others seemed dazed and functioned minimally.

More usually, stress on the families was more pervasive, and to varying extents there was a generalized and continuing impairment of nurturing care. In extreme cases this was sometimes in the context of severe social stress and often mental disturbance in the parents. Some children had been brought up in disorganized and chaotic homes, without structure, order and consistency of experiences or management, and with little or no opportunity to make trusting attachments, to immerse themselves in experiences and to learn. Others had grown up in homes where limits were rigid and uncompromising. Their experience was unusually limited and they could not bridge the gap between home and school.

Although these difficulties varied in nature and origin, all seemed related to developmental impoverishment and loss in the first three years. It followed that an effective approach to a wide range of difficulties stemming from deprivation of many kinds was to create the world of early childhood in school and so provide a broadly based learning experience, normally gained in the first three years.

Children who need nurturing were also successfully placed in nurture groups but were not 'nurture children' as already described. They were emotionally disorganized, but were not without the basic learning of the earliest years. We refer to them as 'children who need nurturing', and other forms of provision for emotionally and behaviourally disturbed children with an equally non-specific designation meet their needs. The conceptual basis is usually different, and they do not necessarily give explicit emphasis to structure, routine and organization, nor are domestic experiences and family-type relationships always an intrinsic part of the child's day, though they often are.

'Children who need nurturing' have some functional experience of the world about them and relevant skills, and to some extent are able to control their own behaviour and reflect on experience, but destructive and distorting experiences, and in some cases harmful separations, have interfered with their personal and social development. They are disturbed and disorganized by stress and anxiety. They need support and reassurance to function adequately, and 'space' to express their hurt in play or verbally. The organization, routine and ambience of the nurture group provide support and security, and lead to a closer attachment, a more personal relationship, and an emotionally relevant and reassuring experience. The children become better organized and function more effectively.

Over the years, changing historical forces have led to a different distribution of the more clearly defined difficulties, and those that are more generalized have markedly increased and over a wider social spectrum.

Varied difficulties but shared needs

The difficulties of children in the nurture groups are complex and varied but the teacher and assistant work within this complexity without needing to understand how it came about. They rarely need to know the nature of the past stress on the child, and attempting to understand the dynamics of the particular family and the child's perception of himself and his world is not feasible and has little relevance to practice. Although the difficulties vary so widely, the children share a history of early developmental impairment and loss, and their common need is for restorative learning experiences at a pre-nursery level.

The children's needs are usually multiple

The difficulties of virtually all children in nurture groups are multiple, and a disproportionate number, compared with the general school population, have complicating features such as motor co-ordination difficulties, impaired hearing or sight, or ill health. In the ILEA, difficulties of motor co-ordination were the most striking.

The basis of nurture-work

Nurture-work is based on the observation that everyone developmentally ahead of the baby and toddler seems biologically programmed into relating to them in a developmentally appropriate way. This is the intuitive response that the teacher and assistant bring to their work. This is so important that when a course was instituted in 1972 a headteacher cautioned: 'A course might destroy the spontaneity.'

The model

The model is the attentive, interactive process of mother and child in the earliest years within a structure commensurate with the physical and physiological development of the infant and toddler. This is shown in 'Earliest learning: a summary chart', which follows.

Earliest learning: a summary chart

EARLY NURTURE

attachment

identification with ····> interaction and sharing ····> developing autonomy

concepts, skills, controls

THE CONTEXT OF EARLY CHILDHOOD EXPERIENCES

The baby/toddler in the home	Re-created structures in the nurture group
The baby is emotionally and physically attached from the beginning, is physically dependent and needs protection.	Close physical proximity in the home area in a domestic setting facilitates emotional and physical attachment.
His experiences are determined by his developmental level (mobility, vision, interest, attention), and mother's intuitive response to his needs.	T/A (teacher/assistant) select basic experiences, and control them. They emphasize developmentally relevant features and direct the child's attention to these.
His waking day is short, slow-moving, broken up by rest and routines. There is a clear time structure. His physical needs determine the rhythm of the day.	The day is broken up by slow-moving interludes and routines. Everything is taken slowly, and there is a clear time structure.
The mother provides simple, restricted, repetitive routines and consistent management from the beginning, and manageable learning experiences through appropriate play materials and developmentally relevant interaction.	The teacher establishes routines, emphasizes order and routine; ensures much repetition. She achieves/conveys her behavioural expectations by clear prohibitions and limits. Toys and activities are developmentally relevant, and the adults' language and interaction is appropriate for this level.

The situation is made appropriate for an earlier developmental level; simpler, more immediate, more routinized, more protected. Restrictions and constraints provide clarity of experience and focus the child's attention; he engages at this level, his attention is held and there is much repetition. Basic experiences and attachment to the adult are consolidated. The child experiences satisfaction and approval, and attachment to the adult is strengthened. Routine gives security and he anticipates with confidence and pleasure.

Growth promoting patterns are established.

THE CONTENT OF EARLY CHILDHOOD EXPERIENCES

'Mother's lap'
Attachment and proximity: earliest learning

Food, comfort, holding close; consistent care and support.	Food, comfort, close physical contact; consistent care and support.
Cradling, rocking; sensory exploration; touch in communication.	Cradling, rocking; sensory exploration; touch in communication.
Intense concentration on mother's eyes and face. She communicates her mood/feelings in her face/voice; spontaneous exaggerates her response.	T/A draws children's attention to her eyes and face. Makes and establishes eye contact. They deliberately exaggerate their facial expression, and tone of voice.
Closeness; intimate interplay; shared feelings/satisfaction. Mother's verbal accompaniment reflects pleasure, and child's loveableness and value. She makes frequent positive acknowledgement of her child.	There is closeness; intimate interplay and shared feelings/satisfaction. The T/A's verbal accompaniment reflects pleasure, and child's loveableness and value. They make frequent positive acknowledgement of each child.
She has age-appropriate expectations; accepts asocial behaviour but controls events and provides manageable constraints and alternatives.	T/As have developmentally appropriate expectations. They tolerate asocial behaviour but give purposeful direction, control events and provide manageable constraints and alternatives.

'Mother's lap'
Attachment and proximity: earliest learning

The foundations of trust, security, positive mood and identity are built in through continuing support and shared basic satisfactions in the context of adult–child emotional attachment and physical proximity. Feelings are communicated and shared, and there is close identification and empathy, the one with the other, and an empathetic response to subtle non-verbal signals. Shared experience, registered in language, leads to an understanding of basic attributes and properties of materials, and of objects and their relationships, and cause and effect.

and

'Mother's knee'

The child has already internalized the security that comes from attachment to a reliable, attentive, comforting parent and this security is reinforced through the continuing repetition of the simple routines of his daily life. These become a familiar and meaningful sequence of events, and through them the child gains a sense that the world about him is stable, orderly and predictable. In the course of physical maturation in an appropriate environment he has acquired basic competencies. He has also experienced adequately consistent management of his behaviour, achieved and conveyed by explicit setting of boundaries.

From this secure base the parents help the child to personal autonomy through a complex process of letting go and bringing back. He is 'let go' into experiences that the parents control and ensure are manageable, and where support is provided when needed, and he is 'brought back' to the security of close contact with the parents when the situation is overwhelming and he can no longer cope. Because the parent is sensitively involved and intervenes when necessary, new experiences are manageable and the child is able to assimilate and consolidate them.

Letting go and bringing back: developing autonomy

'Mother's day'

Child does things with mother, or with mother nearby. There is frequent contact and reassurance and expression of pleasure and approval.	Children do things with T/A or with T/A near; are collected together frequently with calmness and reassurance and eye contact is re-established.
Child shows spontaneously arising need for 'transitional objects' providing comfort, support, control.	The T/A make 'transitional objects' available to provide comfort, support, control, and may introduce them.
S/he gives attention to simple experiment and repetitive play and of own accord persists at	They introduce, demonstrate, and share early play, with experiment and repetition.

Continued on next page

Continued from previous page

this level. There is much experiment and repetition.

Support, encouragement, pressure help them to persist at their developmental level.

S/he engages in simple investigation and exploration, and because this is limited by his/her physical development and mother's intervention, frustration is tolerable.

Teacher selects basic experiences for investigation and exploration; She controls and directs these, anticipates and avoids unmanageable situations; diverts attention. Unnecessary frustration is reduced.

Mother gives help with basic skills, procedures, and provides information, suggestions, ideas.

T/A gives help with basic skills, procedures, provides information, suggestions, ideas.

Mother helps/intervenes when necessary; often plays with child for mutual enjoyment. They share experiences, learn together. Mother responds with pleasure to each new achievement.

T/A helps/intervenes when necessary; often plays with child for mutual enjoyment. They share experiences, learn together. T/A gives immediate praise for each small gain.

Relationships are individual. Mother intuitively identifies child/object/task by name, and provides a developmentally relevant running commentary.

Requests/instructions to the children are at first individual, never general; child/object/task specifically named, and there is continuing verbalization.

Child's development is gradual, and simple experiences, in the course of physical maturation, come before complex ones. Mother prepares her child for new experiences; anticipates and describes events and feelings in simple language.

Everything in incremental stages, simple before complex; situation structured; essentials highlighted; complex instructions broken down. Detailed preparation for each new experience; feelings anticipated and described.

Sharing, choosing, come in manageable stages. There is enough play space. Mother supports/controls co-operative play with other children;

Need to share is deliberately limited at first (enough for everyone).Grabbing is controlled. Sharing/choosing are built into manageable

anticipates problems, averts, intervenes; identifies with and shares child's feelings.	stages; Play space is respected. Co-operative work/play is not expected, but is encouraged, introduced, controlled. T/A anticipates problems, averts, intervenes; identifies with and shares child's feelings.
Child needs/demands order. Mother meets own and child's need for order by providing routine and orderliness. She involves her child in orderly routines such as tidying up, sorting out and putting away.	Routines structure the day. Sorting out, and tidying up and putting away are stressed. T/A shows them what to do.
Mother provides simple consistent basic training. Makes clear her expectations, demonstrates. Her approval/disapproval is immediate and evident. She gives help and reminders when necessary. Her verbal commentary and reinforcement at this early level are simple and basic and reflect the achievement.	Simple, consistent, unremitting basic training. T/A make their expectations clear and constantly stress them, with demonstration when appropriate. They give immediate and evident approval/disapproval and help and reminders when necessary. Their verbal commentary and reinforcement reflect child's level and achievement.

The situation is made manageable and support is there when needed; new experiences are assimilated and consolidated, and the child explores with purpose and confidence. He becomes personally better organized and realizes that he has some control over his environment. He learns to give and take and control his own behaviour, and makes constructive relationships that provide satisfaction and extend his horizons. He can now manage on his own for limited periods in a familiar situation and will soon be able to function without direct help in a bigger group.

The foundations of the child's autonomy are becoming established.

Growth, not pathology: the central tenet

The focus of intervention for psychotherapists is the children's difficulties, and their concern is to unravel knots in a tangled fabric of early experience. The thrust of the work of the teacher and assistant is on the process and content of normal early emotional, social and cognitive development, and the relationships, experiences and physical environment that support and facilitate this. They are concerned with weaving in and strengthening the strands of early nurture. Their perspective is forward looking from birth, not looking back from the present. The process is one of normal learning, but at an earlier-than-usual level. It is education, and the challenge is to build in the emotional, social and cognitive developmental experiences inherent in early nurture. The orientation of the work is not 'What has gone wrong?' but 'What has not gone right?' and provides a way of putting it right. With this the mood in the school changes from despair to optimism and hope, from being de-skilled to becoming empowered.

They need a broadly based experience

The children function well below their potential and the immediate objective is to try to realize this potential by providing a broadly based and progressing experience equivalent to that of the earliest years. The process in the nurture group, as in families, is based in and through attachment, and is mediated within and through a secure relationship. It is a complex process, but under benign circumstances it happens during the course of normal parenting, intuitively, without much conscious thought. To restore this process in the nurture group, it is crucial that the children become attached. Their needs then become apparent and the teacher and assistant respond accordingly. The learning process follows. Those children who do not attach and respond need more than the nurture group can provide on a time-limited day school basis, or different provision. Becoming attached, and all that follows from this, depends on re-creating the structure as well as the content of the earliest years.

The model is normal development and normal parenting

The nurture teacher and assistant provide a normal learning experience of the earliest years by responding intuitively to the children, as parents do. They build up incrementally their experience of themselves and the world, and positive relationships with others. The process is structured overall by an explicit awareness of the nature and content of development, the context that is essential to it, and its direct relevance to the work of the mainstream class. It is a total learning experience, and is the earliest stage of the normal developmental/educational continuum. Practice, intuitively and in conceptual analysis, is based on normal development in the first three years, structured in discussion and developed as a nurture curriculum leading into the foundation stage of the National Curriculum, its essential precursor, and seminal to it.

What is a nurture group?

A nurture group is a class, typically of ten to 12 children, staffed by a teacher and a learning support assistant. It is in the child's neighbourhood primary school and is an integral part of the school. The classroom is furnished to be both home and school, is comfortable and welcoming, containing and protected. It is big enough for a wide range of domestic and personal activities including ' breakfast' early in the day and needed experiences at a baby and toddler level, as well as activities that lead into and overlap with the foundation stage and Key Stage 1 of the National Curriculum.

Re-creating the process of earliest learning

The notion that they should respond intuitively to the child is usually attractive to teachers and assistants, and the term 'nurture' is likely to suggest a close, supportive and caring relationship. But there is another dimension. At this early stage in the home, experiences for the baby and toddler are determined and limited by their perceptual and motor development and physiological rhythm. In creating this learning process in school, the teacher must ensure that the child's day is equivalent to that of the first three years at home. It is slow moving and routinized, and experiences within this routine are basic, clearly delineated, frequently repeated, and carefully planned and controlled. The structure and content of the nurture group day are appropriate for an early developmental level, and in this modified situation most of the children are able to function, and to varying extents show baby and toddler behaviours. The teacher and assistant, in responding accordingly, engage the children's attention and direct their interests and physical energy forwards in an organized and constructive way. They verbalize what is happening in appropriate language and build up the children's experience in manageable stages, making causal connections explicit. When their experiences are monitored in this way the children give attention, register what is happening and begin to remember. They take in simple cause and effect and the relationship between events, and become able to predict a sequence of events. Secure expectations reinforce trust, and lead to the development of valid concepts and a sense of time. The teacher's first objective in starting this process is to engage the children's attention. She first ensures that they give attention to her face and takes them forward from there on a personal/social/cognitive interactive process modelled on that of the parent with the infant and toddler. It is a learning experience, but at an earlier-than-usual level and mediated through a closer relationship than is appropriate in the mainstream class. In the home it comes through the total participation of the mother: 'whole mother, whole child'. In school it comes through the total participation of the adult: 'whole adult, whole child'.

The nurture group thus provides a restorative experience of early nurture, normally integral to the home but increasingly needed in school as the first stage of the learning/educational process. As noted above, it is the essential precursor of foundation stage educational provision.

The working model

The teacher and assistant provide this complex learning experience of intermeshing emotional, social and cognitive developmental strands by being fully available to the children, as parents are. They respond intuitively to any behaviour that would be normal in a very young child. To make their task manageable a general principle was adopted from the beginning, and this continues to be a guideline for all the basic work that is done in the group: 'We will be and do for them as we would for our own, at whatever developmental level they appear to be.' This guideline leads directly to concerned identification with the children and an unconditional commitment to their well-being through which these developmental experiences are made possible. It gives confidence and provides a working model that generates management stratagems and learning experiences that are purposeful and of crucial developmental importance.

The term 'nurture'

The term 'nurture' was adopted for this form of provision because it has a specific, meaningful and purposeful connotation. It describes the children's needs, the nature of the help provided and the learning experiences involved, and places this provision within the mainstream of the educational process, but at an earlier level than hitherto. The class is therefore referred to as the nurture group but is known in school according to the system in use and, where class names are based on colour, is sometimes called 'rainbow class'.

The school and the parents

School is local, accessible and familiar, and has a welcoming unthreatening atmosphere. The staff make friendly supportive relationships with the parents, who sometimes ask for practical advice, and when distressed are given time and attention. They feel valued for themselves, not just because they are the parents of the children, and have a greater sense of self-worth. This is a positive factor in their child's progress in school and their well-being at home.

The nurture group is fully integrated within a supportive school

The purpose of the group is to enable the children to be fully part of their peer group within a year, or two years at the most. It is therefore important, in practice and in principle, that the group is based in and is fully part of the children's ordinary neighbourhood school. For this outcome to be realized it is not enough to build in the personal, social and cognitive experiences that foster emotional well-being and enable the children to achieve and relate productively to each other within the group. They also need help in extending their growing competence to situations beyond this. The group must therefore function as an integral part of the school. The children then see and make viable relationships in wider contexts and move outwards with confidence because they feel themselves to be at the protected centre of widening networks of support.

The teacher's responsibilities therefore extend to creating an integrated experience for the child that includes the world of school beyond the group. This leads to procedures within the school being modified to accommodate to the needs of the undeveloped child. School thus offers a nurturing environment that potentially includes all the teaching and non-teaching staff, and provides for the child a positive, reinforcing and sustained experience. The interacting and cumulatively developing process that is the substance of nurture work thus mirrors the normal human situation at social as well as personal levels.

The children must be in a group of medium size

The developmental needs of some of the children are not apparent in an individual relationship, and although individual work consolidates and reinforces an attachment, opportunities do not arise naturally to help them to separate and function autonomously within the peer group. Nearly all the children need to learn to give and take with others and to be self-directing, and so it is essential that they are in groups where they are required to respect the needs and attitudes of others. In the ILEA 12 children was felt to be a viable number.

Interdependent partnership of the teacher and assistant is essential

Two people are needed to run the group, partly for the mutual support and personal development this provides but also because the children need to see constructive interaction between adults. It is a relationship they can accept, even though on occasion it excludes them, and this makes it easier for them to share the adults with the other children. One of the two people is a teacher, the other a learning support assistant. They work closely together in a mutually supportive, interdependent partnership. There is considerable overlap of roles, but the teacher's key function is to structure the context of the work and to control the learning process, to take central responsibility for the child's academic needs and records of progress, and to liaise with others within the school and beyond, as appropriate.

Meticulous attention to detail

The model is one of normal learning in the pre-nursery years. The method is based on an intuitive sense of the child's early developmental needs and the parent–infant/toddler interactive process, within developmentally appropriate structure. This parallels the learning process from birth to 3 years. The teacher and assistant therefore ensure that experiences and events are relevant and are simple, unhurried, and carefully planned and controlled. They pay attention to sequence and consistency of routine, and provide a considerable input of developmentally commensurate language. They anticipate difficulties, are alert to give any necessary support and intervene immediately when problems arise. This meticulous attention to detail is essential at the beginning for it enables the children to use their experiences and to achieve. Their difficulties become less marked, their underlying needs are apparent and the teacher and assistant respond accordingly.

Tight structure is necessary

The nurture day is structured to be appropriate for the level of personal organization and control of a toddler: the tempo is slower, the structure tighter and the constraints more immediate and evident than in the mainstream class. This structuring is essential for unhurried early developmental learning. It also reinforces trust and security, underpins the purposeful direction of behaviour and events, and provides a context for the formal teaching of Key Stage 1 related work. Within this structure the children can be let go into 'mother's day' activities, or drawn back into an early attachment relationship.

The content within the structure

Within this structure, and through their relationship with the teacher and assistant the children gain the experiences they need, mostly during the course of 'mother's day', sometimes 'at mother's knee' and, in some cases, 'on mother's lap' or 'in mother's arms'. Some children are initially much of the time at a baby and toddler level, while in others these behaviours are less striking and are more sporadic. The context is supportive, and through a reliable relationship with concerned adults they gain:

- trust and security;
- awareness of their own feelings and those of others;
- visual and kinaesthetic awareness of themselves, leading to a more inte-grated and differentiated body image;
- increasing awareness of their own bodies in space;
- awareness of the sensory qualities of the things about them, and their relationships;
- appropriate and purposeful attention to their immediate real world.

These experiences are the essential underpinnings of all later development, that is:

- the capacity for empathy;
- control and management of their own bodies;
- attention-giving and achievement;
- a more coherent understanding of the properties of the physical world, and of sequence and process;
- constructive social relationships.

All this leads to more effective use of their formal learning op-portunities, increasing self-worth, and a sense of mastery and control of events.

The learning process for the teacher and assistant

The process begins in attachment and leads on to increasing separation as the children become able to function, personally and socially, in a wider context without direct support. The process has considerable learning potential for the adults, for they live through the experience with the children and at the same time are explicitly aware of the developmental content and its relevance to the requirements of the mainstream class. They are therefore intellectually as well as emotionally involved and gain theoretical insights as well as considerable personal awareness and enrich-ment. Their commitment and resourcefulness is at a high level, and they have little or no need to turn to others for support.

They 'feel into' the baby and toddler years

The teacher and assistant are able to initiate and foster this growth process by 'feeling into' the earliest years and identifying with the feelings and needs of the child. They interact with the child as a parent would, within a relationship of continuing care and support, intuitively following a pattern of normal development. It is a human response, and the most valuable source of help for the teacher and assistant is within themselves.

They draw on their own intuitive resources and each learns from the other. In discussion with other nurture teachers and assistants, they deepen their perception of themselves in relation to the children, and gain increasing understanding of the emotional and cognitive content of their work. They are reassured of the validity of their intuitive response, and begin to discipline this within a simple and clearly formulated developmental framework that leads, in concept and in practice, to the expectations and aims of the mainstream class. This approach dissipates the considerable anxiety and impotence generated by the children's difficulties, provides a helpful guideline, and frees the teacher and assistant to draw fully on their own personal resources uninhibited by the feeling that somewhere there are 'experts' who know better.

The teacher provides direction and controls the child's experiences

This process is crucially dependent on a close relationship with the children and an intuitive 'feel' of their needs, but there are reservations:

- The process for the developing child in the years before school is carried forward by an innate impetus for growth, but in the nurture group it is the teacher's responsibility to know where the process is leading and to provide direction.
- The pre-nursery child's experiences are determined and constrained by his developing physical competence and come to him in an ordered and incremental way with all aspects intermeshing. For the older child in the nurture group, the teacher has to provide the constraints, plan comparable experiences, focus the child's attention on them, and provide and support the necessary repetition. This presupposes that the teacher has sufficient faith in the rationale of the approach to be committed to the tight structuring that is needed.
- The teacher therefore needs, more than the interested parent, an explicit awareness of the nature of the developmental process, the circumstances that are essential to it, and its direct relevance to the work of the mainstream class.

The nurture group leads to a nurturing school

The work of the nurture group always involves the class teachers concerned, and in a committed school both teaching and ancillary staff are nurturing in attitude, have some understanding of the needs of the children in the group and actively support their development. In schools where there are considerable numbers of deprived and distressed children, the principles underpinning nurture-work become part of general classroom practice, and in some cases it may be more appropriate to have parallel classes, run on nurture lines, rather than a nurture group as such. Nurture provision is flexible, but developments of this kind are possible only when the nurture group is well established, and the underlying principles are accepted and their relevance to normal academic achievement is understood. The first step, therefore, towards a cumulatively reinforcing nurturing process in the school generally is to have a classic nurture group, running well. But an essential determinant of eventual integration of the children within the mainstream class is the initial and continuing involvement of the class teachers in understanding and supporting the work of the group. As with the development of the children, this is a circular, reinforcing and ultimately spiralling process. The onus for initiating and maintaining this process falls to the nurture teacher. But everyone must have patience, for it takes time for the many strands in this intermeshing and reinforcing process to come together and for the work to be seen as successful.

Outcome

The cost of nurture group provision, assessed by Enfield Educational Psychology Service and recorded in Bennathan and Boxall (2000: 56), was slightly less than one-quarter that of extra help for a statemented child. The success rate recorded (ibid.: 57), was 88 per cent. The ILEA evaluation was complex as follow-up ranged from one year to 15 years, and was not systematic, but the outcome was similar.

In one school the teacher and assistant had been in post long enough for some of their children to have left school. Of the 21 who called in to see them:

- three were in stable partnerships and had children, occupations not known;
- three were at college and had clearly defined ideas for the future;
- two were on holiday from the country of origin of their parents;
- seven were in full-time employment, and five of these were in work that required considerable self-direction and enterprise.

In this same school, 12 children over a four-year period had been recommended for special schools by the educational psychologist. They were placed in the nurture group for a trial period and all remained in the school and were felt unlikely to need special schools at the secondary stage.

The way forward

In all areas transitional home-school provision set up as nurture groups for new entrants to school, preferably 3- and 4-year-olds, though it is expected that children who are clearly at risk would be referred by health visitors. These would have a dual function:

- They would be multi-professional assessment centres for all children and would be diagnostic for children with special educational needs.
- They would provide a continuing nurture experience for fundamentally deprived children, and those with minor specific difficulties, who would remain there until they could be settled in their neighbourhood school in an age-appropriate class.

Experience might indicate a need for nurture provision in all schools, either as a special resource within the nursery or reception class, or as separate group in the school, according to the extent of the need.

- At a practical level, a course on nurture-work should include something on every special educational need. Conversely, courses for all special educational needs should include a component of nurture-work.

Breaking the downwards spiral of deprivation

Beginning at the beginning and making explicit the implicit learning content of earliest childhood led us into an area that was little explored at the time, and where little direct help to the schools was possible. The autonomous life of the nurture groups and the growth and health of the children within them therefore owes everything to the goodwill, generosity and selfless work of everyone involved in the schools concerned. Each has generated energy and enthusiasm for the others. Each has relied on a personal capacity to cope, but the knowledge that others were in the same testing position has provided support, and the shared problem-solving has contributed to the foundations on which everyone has built. The work itself is energizing. Although hard and demanding, it is implicitly an affirmation of a commitment to life and brings increasing self-awareness and the energizing sense of shared growth. All these things are found in good measure in the nurture groups, and we hope and have good reason to believe that the children and their families have gained as much from us as we have from them.

At roughly the time of the first nurture groups Sir Keith Joseph, then Secretary of State for Education, coined the phrase, 'The cycle of deprivation'. Now, in 2001, nearly two generations later, stress is more widespread and attitudes to responsibilities are more casual. The cycle of deprivation has become a downwards spiral, as deprived children within adult bodies become depriving parents, and with each generation the fabric of nurture becomes increasingly ill-woven and thin.

Deprivation is a downwards and inwardly spiralling process of despair and depression. Nurture is an upwards and outwardly spiralling process of hope and growth. Our capital of good nurture is diminishing fast and the fabric of society is at risk, for with each generation there are fewer people with the personal resources to provide good nurturing, and more children who have been deprived of it. It is of the utmost urgency to invest our capital of good nurture while we can, before it runs out. The processes of deprivation are cumulative and soon it will be too late.

All of us who have been involved with nurture groups over the years want it to be invested in nurture education, the first and earliest stage of our existing mainstream education, leading on to the 'stepping stones' of the foundation stage of the National Curriculum. It would be logical to make this provision available at the earliest age to all children at risk of personal and school failure, and the disastrous future that so often lies ahead.

PART I
NURTURE GROUPS IN ACTION

2

Structured Experience

Children who are without the personal resources needed for school are a major problem for the class teacher. To varying extents their past experience, personal organization and self-control are poor, and they have insufficient awareness and understanding of their surroundings to give purposeful attention. Some give their whole attention to anticipated attack, and become aggressive or have a tantrum if accidentally touched. Others are bewildered and inattentive and make no response to requests. Others again are confused, have no sense of self or purposeful meaningful action and hold back, not able to involve themselves. Others yet again are tense, tightly controlled and organized, but very restricted in what they can do, and are without spontaneity and initiative. Some sit awkwardly and do not spontaneously involve themselves, while a few seem out of touch with their surroundings and occasionally might rock. Many interfere with children nearby, indiscriminately and trivially. Others are exuberant with energy, stretch out, loll and roll about and disturb the others, and when an activity is initiated they rush in without waiting to grasp what is expected, and with no understanding of what they are to do. Another child might sit hunched up, half turned away. He is sullen and resentful and reacts negatively or angrily to all requests, and particularly if older is likely to be hostile and alienated, and has no wish or intention of being involved. Some do take part to some extent but are poorly organized and unhappy, restless and resistive; others are listless and without interest, and have no appetite for experiences. In general the children are not biddable and few spontaneously make eye contact, particularly at the beginning of the day. If they attend at all it is rarely to the teacher as a person, or purposefully to an object or event as a complete whole. They notice little of what is happening, other people have little relevance for them, and they do not engage purposefully with the situation or use constructively the toys and materials about them. And underlying these difficulties is a history of disappointment and failure, and the expectation of continuing disappointment and failure. The children are likely to remain inattentive and unsettled. There is no sense of group, no interaction with each other and no expectancy in relation to the teacher.

They are good candidates for a nurture group. What would happen there?

Attachment and support

The nurture teacher's objective is to attach the children and provide support for clearly defined and manageable expectations and goals. This enables them to achieve. Security and attachment is bound into this process and from simple achievements stem the development of basic skills and competencies that lead into the work of the mainstream class. Routine is the broad structure for this process. Procedures vary from school to school, but whatever the variant the same routine is followed in the same way, every day, in the school concerned and, except for unavoidable events, the same familiar people are in the same expected place, every day.

Reception into school each day

Whatever the arrangements for reception into school each day it is important that the children are 'held' in a network of support from the moment they enter the building. This extra support is important because many of the children are confused about their surroundings or are indiscriminately attracted by irrelevant events; they are poorly organized within themselves, have a high level of anxiety and are unlikely to have had a reassuring and supportive start to the day. Some children come to school late and cannot latch into the routine without help. Others come very early and face a locked gate or an empty playground. In schools where substantial numbers of children arrive before official starting time, the doors open early and arrangements are made for the children to play in the school hall or nurture group room as an alternative to the playground. More usually the children are welcomed and acknowledged a few minutes before school begins by the member of staff who is supervising in the playground and they go to the nurture group from there. The more competently functioning children stay to play and they line up with the others in an orderly way when the coming-in signal is given. For all of them, their first personal welcome is from the nurture teacher and assistant, at the school door as they arrive or at or near their classroom door, or when they are collected from their mainstream class if this is where they register. In schools where the children use a general cloakroom, the nurture teacher and assistant are waiting there, to help with the difficult task of finding the right peg and hanging up their coats. This first contact with the familiar and reassuring presence of the nurture teacher and assistant is the beginning of systematic and reinforcing support throughout the school day.

Registration

Registration in the mainstream class is the more usual practice as this provides a regular contact that is manageable for all but a few out-of-touch or particularly alienated children. They give in their dinner money there and wait until collected by the nurture teacher and assistant. This procedure provides a visible link with the class teacher and continuity of attachment. The nurture teacher and the class teacher exchange friendly appreciative comments about the children that convey their expectations. They collect the children in the same order every day and those in the classroom furthest away from the nurture group classroom are collected first. Children who cannot register in their mainstream class are received and welcomed by the assistant in the nurture classroom, and the teacher collects the others on her own. In some schools all the children come directly to the nurture group. The teacher and assistant are already there. One of them is available to chat with any parents who come and occasionally a parent stays on. The other is available for the children.

They walk in an orderly way

The first two or three children usually walk together. As their number increases they walk in line. The teacher leads and the assistant, if involved at this stage, brings up the rear. The children are 'contained'. They have the security of being led by the teacher, and being supported and protected from behind. A child particularly in need of support walks hand in hand with the teacher or assistant. The teacher chooses the order in which they are to walk, because at this stage they push, fight and argue if not given clear directives. They are reminded to walk well, and to carry their coats and other possessions tidily. Constant reminders are necessary because the children cannot regulate their own behaviour. They have not internalized order and initially need to have order imposed from without. The children wait in line at the door of their classroom in the order already established, without jostling each other. They are reminded not to rush and to go in only when everyone is quiet and still. Children who cannot register in their mainstream classes come directly to the nurture group; they do not have the stabilizing routine of walking to the group room in an orderly way and waiting quietly at the door before they go in. Others come in late, miss all the early routines of the day, and find it difficult to latch in. Some struggle in halfway through the morning.

The assistant helps them to hang up their coats

Another variant is for the teacher to take each group of children to the nurture classroom as she collects them. The assistant is waiting, welcomes them, and helps them to hang their coats on the right peg. This is a clearly delineated task that indirectly controls the child's behaviour by focusing his attention on himself and on the task of hanging up his coat. It also provides positive direction by preventing the disorganization and disruption that arises if he cannot decide which peg to choose, or wants a peg someone else has chosen. A useful practice is for each child's peg to have hanging from it a card in the colour of his mainstream class, with his name and photograph on it. This provides a link with his 'other' class, acknowledges his identity, and introduces him to symbolic representation. A procedure that began the day in one group and was enthusiastically adopted in others where the room was big enough, was to walk from the door of the classroom heel to toe along a line marked on the floor, the assistant going first. This concentrates the children's attention on themselves in a purposeful way, is ordered and orderly, and gives much needed practice in motor co-ordination and balance. It is a particularly useful beginning to the day because many of them have little awareness of their own bodies, and are poorly co-ordinated. Another practice is for the children to walk in on numbered footsteps painted on the floor, counting as they go.

The children wait quietly with a simple activity

If the first children to arrive are sufficiently competent it is usual to allow them to choose from a strictly limited range of structured quiet activities in the home area. Others are provided with a simple activity. Those too inexperienced to manage on their own are kept occupied by the teacher or assistant while the rest of the group is assembling.

They register again in the nurture group

Although in most schools the children will have registered already in their mainstream class, there is always a less formal registration in the nurture group. The procedure adopted is always the same each day and carries important learning experiences. For example, each child finds his name card, which in some groups has his photograph on the back, from a box of cards or from a scatter on the table, and puts it in the appropriate wall pocket. The pockets are in numbered order from left to right and he uses the next empty one, or he is required to put it in a pocket in the colour of his mainstream class, or the one with his name or photograph. This exercise provides an experience of sorting, identifying, matching and filing, and movement from left to right, and sequence. They get help with this basic task for as long as they need it.

This ritualized routine is manageable

The ritualized routine that begins the day is a simple manageable procedure that slows them down and calms them. Almost all the children can give attention to this, though some may need help. It is a recognizable beginning to the day, is remembered and becomes familiar and reassuring. It gives each child the satisfaction of a task achieved, and the satisfaction of approval for the task achieved. Putting his name card into the wall pocket is an objective representation that is both tangible and symbolic of his identity, his presence in the school and his membership of the group.

He is anchored firmly in the group, and the beginning of the day has been marked. He then moves over to the home area, also part of the routine.

In the home area

The children are now in the home area, facing the teacher. She controls where they sit and gives each child his designated place on the carpet, thus avoiding arguments. Some of them have a poor sense of their bodies in space, as though without sufficient experience of free movement, and are confused and poorly orientated. They are taken by the hand and guided to a place. Many have little or no structure of their own, no grasp of where the situation is leading or what is expected, and without this help continue to be confused and disorganized. Those who are particularly without experience and volition, and remain passive and unresponsive, may need individual help to sit appropriately and comfortably on the floor in the required place; a verbal request is not sufficient. Others respond to instructions to sit in the required place and one or two are able to find a place on their own. In some schools the children sit in the home area on personal cushions arranged beforehand in a circle.

Learning to give attention to the teacher

Some teachers ask the children to sit with their legs crossed, arms folded and hands tucked away, lips together and their eyes on her. They associate this requirement with giving attention to the teacher, and because everyone is doing the same thing everyone's attention is reinforced. And because they are concentrating on self-control they are less likely to fidget and interfere with the others. They know they have these four things to remember. Teachers have stressed the value and importance of this procedure. Others require the children to be contained and attentive, sit still and wait. If there is enough room, the assistant sits with the children and the teacher faces them. The children feel supported because the assistant sits with them and joins in the activity.

It is time to begin. The children are in the home area, sitting on the carpet or on chairs or cushions, facing the teacher. She is alert to potential trouble and so positions the children carefully and might lift a child and place him closer to herself, or move another child to a different place in the group. Many of them actively dislike the close proximity of another child; they seem alert to possible attack and if touched only slightly are liable to erupt. They are therefore placed well apart to reduce the possibility of provocation by poking and hitting. A particularly undeveloped, dependent child who passively clings and is not involved in the activity at all, is likely to be with one of the adults, probably on her knee, while an unrestrained, potentially out-of-control child is close to the other adult, a restraining hand put out when needed. The children least able to follow what is happening, or who are very restless, are usually in the front. Some seem incapable of independent coherent action, but if they appear to want to take part they are shown individually what to do, and the action is performed with them. A child who makes no attachment and does not relate to the group, is left on the divan or sofa with a soft toy. Group time in the home area means nothing. The child will be passively contained within the structure of the day and will get his individual time later, when he will learn to look at the teacher and make and accept touch. At first he might sit propped against the adult's legs for long periods, either because he flops without support or needs to feel contained and 'held'.

Learning to make eye contact

The children have been brought together in the carpeted area and have been helped to sit without touching each other, with their legs crossed. Everything has been taken slowly. The teacher faces them. They are all in a position where they can see her. She speaks very quietly and slowly and draws attention to herself. The children have difficulty giving attention. She asks them to look at her and names them one by one. The child's name comes first, to attract his attention, and the request to look at her follows. Eye contact is thus made individually. The children get recognition and approval for this, one by one. They wait, and get approval for waiting. They have been helped to sit and helped to look at the teacher, and have a sense of approval. The teacher looks round the group and acknowledges the children and shows her pleasure as she makes eye contact. She repeatedly addresses them individually by name, making positive comments. Helping the children to establish and maintain eye contact is very important, for in making eye contact they acknowledge the possibility of a relationship. Attention is therefore given to this from the beginning, and in both junior and infant groups continues to be given. Quiet insistence brings eye contact in most cases, but the process is very gentle for children who find this distressing.

The teacher does not intrude if a child is passive and unresponsive, or actively avoids eye contact or averts his gaze, or whose eyes wander because he is distractible and cannot involve himself. Eye contact is encouraged later, when he is alone with the teacher or the assistant; the teacher usually makes touch first, tentatively, though this might not be acceptable to the child for a long time. When the child is used to this, the teacher or assistant might gently take both his hands in hers, and later his face in her hands. She looks at him at eye level, and might blinker him with her hands to encourage eye contact, and gently insist: 'Look at me, look at my eyes.' A big smile of pleasure follows when their eyes meet. Children who are resistive and resentful are more likely to respond at the 'breakfast' table when food is being handed round, or when a situation lends itself to humour, and the first eye contact, albeit indirect, may be when child and adult look at each other in the mirror. The teacher continues to direct their attention to what is required, and asks them to look at her. Her requests are simple, direct and positive, and if necessary are repeated until the contact is acknowledged. These details are important because few children heed the teacher and are not biddable and responsive without this help. They have little sense of personal identity, and so their existence as individuals, and the relationship with the teacher that is expected, has to be stressed.

There are special difficulties for children who have been brought up in cultures where eye contact with the adult is avoided as a mark of respect or contrition, but teachers and assistants are sensitive to this, and modify their approach accordingly.

The children have been encouraged to look at the teacher and making eye contact is their first achievement.

Learning the meaning of non-verbal signals

Many of the children pay no attention to the expression on the teascher's face or the tone in her voice, though a few stare fixedly, apprehensively vigilant for any indication that they are doing wrong. These non-verbal signals are initially beyond their experience and mean nothing to them. Often communication at home is not a mutually adaptive and progressing interaction but is a statement of the mother's caring or control, shown in a caress or a smack, or it reflects the feelings of her thoughts and is not relevant to the child's needs or behaviour. The meaning of these non-verbal signals and their alerting function, the feelings and wishes they indicate and the response expected, is their next learning experience.

So the teacher next draws their attention to her face and voice. She asks them to notice the expression on her face and the tone in her voice, and she links this with her feelings: 'Look at my face' (indicating); 'Look how pleased I am'. Few of the children register her expression, so she exaggerates this and many times during the day will say, 'Look at my face', and indicates. In the relaxed peacefulness of the home area some children for the first time become aware of the teacher's face and expression, her gestures and tone of voice and what all these mean. Later, when they are more secure and are more aware of themselves and each other, the teacher comments on the expression on their faces, and might send them to the mirror to look. She interprets their feelings from the expressions on their faces, and develops games centring round the interpretation of facial expressions.

A slow pace and simple language

The children have been helped to make eye contact and to give attention but are likely to have difficulty in maintaining this and following through what is said to them. The teacher therefore continues to draw attention to herself many times, perhaps by doing no more than speaking the child's name, very quietly. She verbalizes what she is doing, and what she expects. She talks very slowly and deliberately, in short simple sentences, because the children have difficulty in following complex language, and in sustaining attention beyond the first word or two. Everything is taken slowly, for only in this way are the children able to settle, attend and listen. It may take them a long time to settle, but the teacher accepts this without anxiety because it is an important and essential part of the day and comes before everything else. At first it is enough for them to sit where required and to give their attention momentarily, and in this calm, quiet and relaxed setting most of the children do begin to settle, give attention and wait. Later the requirements are increased, but nothing starts until everyone is quiet and is purposefully attending.

The children are restless: they need directives

Some of the children remain restless. Others sit passively, are unresponsive and give no attention, or are sullen and resistive. Occasionally a child hits out at another sitting nearby. The children find it difficult to sit still, but no comment is made and no disapproval is shown. If several are particularly restless the teacher might ask all of them to put their hands in their laps. They are able to give attention to keeping their hands in their laps if told to, otherwise they fidget with them or poke each other. They are able to sit still and concentrate when given a specific detailed instruction. They need to be told exactly what to do.

They identify themselves and each other

When all the children are reasonably well settled, the teacher might say, 'Who is here today?' and she answers the question by looking at each child in turn and identifying him by name: 'Yes . . . is here today. Good.' Then: 'How many children are here today?' When this has been established: 'Who is not here today?' 'How many children are not here today?' 'How many boys are here today? How many girls?' How many more boys than girls?' This interchange draws the children's attention to the others in the group. They notice them and recall their names, and reminders of the ones who are away evoke a memory of what they are like, and sometimes a sense of concern and caring. All this reinforces a sense of group. And incidental to this is an experience of basic number. Each time the teacher gives back to the children in a short simple sentence the information elicited. Then their names are written down to affirm their presence in the group. The children continue to wait, their eyes on the teacher. Purposeful waiting is a basic learning experience, and they are able to wait, sit still and give attention because they are given explicit direction. After one or two interested observations by the teacher, perhaps her pleasure at the calm way they came into the classroom, the day's more formal work begins.

They learn that time is structured

The day of the week is established. It is Tuesday and followed on from yesterday, the day that was Monday. At this point they might chorus the sequence of days and clap when they come to the right one for 'today'. Sometimes shakers and clappers are introduced, or the teacher holds up cards, one by one, showing the days of the week, and the children tell her when she comes to the right one for 'today'. 'Yes. Today is Tuesday. What do we do on Tuesdays? We do PE (physical education) on Tuesdays. Today is Tuesday and we do PE today.' The card showing Tuesday is slotted into the wall chart. Later on, when they are secure in their knowledge of the days of the week, the month also would be recorded, though it might be enough at first to learn that days have names. Friday is given special note because it is the last day of the school week, and the weekend follows, and on Monday they are reminded that Monday is the first day of the school week, and comes after the weekend. These concepts, and the language that denotes them, are built in slowly, one at a time, and are reinforced daily for as long as needed. Even for some junior age children it is a novel idea that there is something called a weekend, and that the weekend is different. Many of the children have disorganized lives; basic events are without pattern, and they have no experience of sequence from which to predict. It cannot be assumed that when Friday comes they know that they do not come to school the next day, and on Monday some may not recall that they did not come to school the day before. One confused child went home at playtime, thinking it was the end of the day, and even junior children have asked 'Have I had my dinner?' when the routine was changed. For most of them, life is without meaningful form; they have no sense of sequence and pattern, and the way time is structured has to be learned.

Gaining a concept of group

One child might now be chosen to count the name cards on the wall chart, from left to right in order, and then he goes round the group, counting the children. He touches each child as he counts; usually this is acceptable because the reason is clear and the contact is anticipated and limited. The teacher asks again: 'How many children are here today?' This leads on to: 'How many drinks/straws/biscuits will we need?' They are reminded to add two. This reinforces the sense of group and the teacher and assistant as part of the group, and they are associated with the satisfaction of the milk and biscuits to come. Interest is heightened, and attention-giving. Once again, they have had an experience of basic number.

Personal chat: reminders of class procedures

An informal chat might follow, about their clothes, the weather, any happenings of immediate interest, or any theme that meant something to them and was within their everyday experience. One or two might be eager to give their personal news. Others have nothing to say: they cannot recall what has happened immediately before; their perceptual world barely impinges, experiences are not connected and events go by unrecognized. They are reminded of the baking they did yesterday and step by step anticipate what is going to happen today: 'We are going to have breakfast again today.' Imagery and expectancy is evoked, and the concept of the 'family breakfast' is consolidated. The teacher reminds them of class procedures, thereby establishing a sense of order and the notion of limits.

Action songs relieve restlessness and have considerable learning content

If the children are particularly restless, teachers find it useful to launch them into an action song. This focuses their attention on themselves. It is something they can do that is directly linked to the teacher and channels their energy. She therefore asks them to look at her, and to watch what she does. The request is gently repeated and specifically addressed to any child who has not responded. The teacher again asks them to look at her and watch what she does and to join in if they can. The action song might involve no more than the child touching, exploring and naming different parts of his face, but the experience makes an important contribution to body awareness and identity. The action songs can be done loudly/softly and quickly/slowly, and the words that accompany the actions extend their basic vocabulary. Stopping and starting, waiting and taking turns, contribute both to self-control and to a sense of periods of time. The teacher speaks slowly. Her language is simple, every step is specified, and she provides an immediate and visible model of a simple action. The children respond to varying extents, some not at all even though they may have taken part in this activity often in the past. Others watch and try to follow, though might quickly get lost. Others, again, take part with zest and enjoyment. A child who rushes in without restraint is likely to need direct help. If he has been put at the assistant's side, she might take his hand or gently hold him, to restrain him, or lead him individually, showing him in action and telling him in words what he is to do. If necessary the activity would be stopped because of this child, and when everyone was still they would start again, with reminders of what to do. No pressure is put on those children who do not take part. Some sit and watch at first, and begin to take part of their own accord by shadowing the others as their confidence grows, or they begin to feel reassured that it is permissible and might even be fun and tentatively join in. Others take no part, and later will have time with the teacher or assistant individually. Those who could take part but will not, also are left till later. A child who is only tenuously attached in the group, remains by the teacher or assistant at her feet, holding her hand, or he lies in her lap. If he wanders off, the assistant follows him and stays by him, and might involve him in a simple activity involving physical contact; or she would keep an eye on him from a distance, if this seemed more appropriate.

This physical outlet in body-centred activities is important. It channels the children's restless fidgeting into simple motor activities that are relatively easy to master. They are teacher centred and teacher controlled – songs, rhymes, finger and hand games – and interest most of the children and engage their attention. They give them intense pleasure and their competence is a source of pride and achievement. They are more manageable than giving news, which requires recall, verbalization and the ordering of ideas, and presupposes that events were registered at the time. The children are not at the stage of interacting constructively with each other but are able to take part in a simple group activity because they are linked through this to the teacher and experience her approval. These activities are part of the basic routine. They become a class ritual, a source of security and well-being, and engender a sense of group. An important dimension is the special pleasure of a shared pleasure, and the positive group feeling that flows from this. When the children settle well, these activities are developed into something more complex, or lead on to something requiring more concentration. But if the children remain restless, the teacher introduces a routinized activity that is even simpler and more basic, one that will draw them back to an awareness of themselves and will strengthen the link with herself, and will settle them: 'Show me your fingers. Touch your nose.' And the children are brought back to the security of these simple familiar routines when too much has been expected of them and they have lost their way.

These games also have intrinsic importance because they provide the pleasure of the rhythm of the rhyme and the satisfaction of the repetition of the rhythm and the rhyme, and contribute to a sense of pattern and organization. Hand and finger games contribute to an awareness of body and body image and give a sense of identity, physical wholeness and containment, and for some of the children a sense of existence as they touch themselves and each other. Many of them seem unaware of their bodies and the relationship of one part to another, and cannot appropriately direct their movements to indicate as required. In these games the children become aware of their own bodies and their own skin, and establish their body boundaries as they make skin contact with others. And for all the children there is, sooner or later, the enjoyment of finding and naming the different parts of their bodies in games, but many of them first of all have to learn the names, and what the names stand for.

Trust is being built in

In these games in the home area the children begin to respond to the teacher as a person, to follow where she leads, and they experience satisfaction and well-being in the achievement, and in her responsive pleasure. Attachment and trust are being established through the shared pleasure and achievement. For some of the children the games are important also in that they help them to establish physical contact in a way that is acceptable. Many of them do not immediately accept this, and may resist touch of any kind, and even accidentally brushing against another child sometimes triggers a tantrum. Some of those who at first hold back want to make physical contact, and gradually draw closer and might lean towards the teacher and assistant and touch them, and children who are even more timid begin to draw close and want to touch them. They become part of the group and begin to tolerate the close proximity of other children. Some are particularly reluctant to make physical contact during the course of these games. They make no response to a natural and spontaneous overture from the adult, and may resist or reject it, though seem to want it. Some are self-aware and may not want to be noticed making physical contact except during the course of an incidental game. Others are overtly hostile, and resent and reject any form of contact, as they resent and reject a relationship. Most of the children, however, respond to physical affection and the comfort and close physical proximity and intimacy of the home area fosters easy and natural physical contact. The children begin to sit closer together, and build up attachment and trust for each other, as well as for the adult.

Activities with more complex content

All the games usual in a nursery or infant class are later introduced in the home area: feeling objects in a bag and guessing what they are, simple hiding, finding and remembering games. They are introduced very gradually, and particularly inexperienced children are made familiar with the objects beforehand, individually with the teacher or assistant. These games are done again and again until the children understand what is expected and can join in, however inadequately or tentatively. Variations are introduced with a comment such as 'We will do it this way now?', because the children have not sufficient experience, understanding and flexibility to cope at this stage with even a slight change, unless they are told that it *is* a change. The next step is to make the activity or game slightly more formal by building in simple constraints in the form of rules.

Everything stops if they are not paying attention

Before beginning anything the teacher waits until everyone is quiet and still, and they are sitting as required, without talking. The assistant joins in. If the game or activity has started and there is any poking or pinching it is usual for everything to be stopped immediately. Often it is sufficient for the teacher to stop, for many of the children are totally dependent on the support gained from watching and following her actions. Gradually they are able to manage longer sessions that have more complex content, but if they become restless the activity is changed to something simpler, or they do something involving gross movement or, if particularly restless, are taken for a run-around in the playground.

The home area: the secure base

Group time in the home area is important, because the children are learning to relate to the teacher and to be physically part of a group without any requirement to be involved with the others. The teacher judges their mood and competence during group activities, and the extent to which she can expect to gain and hold their attention. She modifies the day's activities and her expectations accordingly, and spells out for them what they are to do and how they are to do it.

The day starts in the home area and it is to the security of the home area and its simple, quiet and slow-moving, familiar routines that the children are brought back many times during the day. This happens whenever the children are becoming fretful or arguments are breaking out, or the noise and excitement level is rising. At these times all activities are stopped and the teacher 'brings them back', as mothers do with toddlers, to reassure them that she is there and all is well; and then she 'lets them go' again when they are once more able to manage on their own.

Being biddable is reinforced

The home area is also the place where 'being biddable' is reinforced. Bringing the children together in the home area several times during the day maintains close reassuring physical proximity to the teacher, and encourages eye contact in a comforting and supportive situation. It also builds in the expectation that they will heed her wishes, and she reminds them of her pleasure in this before letting them go. Sometimes her wishes have to be demonstrated more visibly, for example, the children at the beginning of the year had quickly begun to meet the teacher's requirements at their regular milk and biscuits time, but were not otherwise readily biddable. The routine and ritualized occasion of milk and biscuits continued, but the teacher now gathered the children together two or three times a day, and they all had a biscuit. Her next step was to call the children together for a little pleasurable group activity and then disperse them again, without giving them a biscuit. In this way the 'being biddable' response was strengthened and extended, and became part of a growing relationship with the teacher.

Structuring the way ahead

Initiating activities

The children are now ready to be launched into their individual activities. This is more difficult, even for those who will get individual help, because they are no longer linked directly with the teacher and assistant but indirectly through the toys or equipment, and they are required to do something in relation to the toys or equipment. There are considerable problems in this, for few of them are able to use even simple materials without help. They cannot give attention and persist, predict, anticipate and plan, and have difficulty in understanding where the teacher's instructions are leading, or the practical consequences of even a simple action. Poor tolerance for frustration and inability to share and to choose also limit effective functioning, but direct specific attention to these things comes later. At this early stage they first of all need help in learning how to experience and use the materials, and are not expected to share and choose.

The teacher's support and control

It is usual for the children to be launched into their activities from the home area. This is where personal contact with the teacher has been established, and the support and control inherent in this is likely to be maintained when she is no longer close by. Some of the children are not involved in the happenings about them, but a few are expectant. They are waiting for a lead from the teacher, but nothing happens until there is peace and quiet, everyone looking and no one interfering, everyone still and attending. All the children need help with personal organization and behaviour control and this is borne in mind all the time.

The children are 'held': the way ahead is structured

But the teacher's first consideration is to 'hold' the children while she structures the way ahead. This is essential for those children who cannot wait but plunge in unheeding, and is a reassurance and support for those who are confused and unventuring, or fearful of failure. The teacher therefore continues to build in constraints, and her request might begin with: 'Sit very still. I'm going to tell you what to do. Sit still until I say your name.' In most groups at the beginning of the year, and always when management problems are severe or the children are very unformed, the teacher provides very limited activities and does not offer anything beyond the child's experience, or too exciting without an adult there all the time. She does not give access to paints or sand and water, and does not expect creative work. At this early stage the teacher might associate herself with the toys and equipment in a direct and visible way by sitting with them beside her, or she gets them one by one from the cupboard as required. She then hands them to the children individually, one by one. The toys and equipment thus carry with them the teacher's expectations, controls and support, and have enhanced value. Later on, when the children have more autonomy, they help themselves. This procedure avoids the confusion and overstimulation of making a choice, and reduces squabbling. Children who are very inexperienced and insecure are relieved when the teacher chooses the toy or activity, or offers a specified and named choice. She gives instructions in detail, to every child individually. She speaks quietly, in close physical proximity, with eye contact, and touch where appropriate. Everything is taken slowly in simple manageable stages because many of the children grasp only one thing at a time and find it difficult to follow through a simple verbal sequence. All stages of a request or instruction are specified in short, simple sentences, in clear sequence, without ambiguity, because instructions that appear to be simple may involve unfamiliar concepts and be linguistically complex, or may require an understanding of a novel situation. And the children are restrained stage by stage as needed. For each one, the teacher picks out the essential features of the activity, so that he gives attention to these as he plays. She stresses the sequence of events, and where this is leading, and gives reminders. This provides the help they need to manage on their own. The slow pace is a brake on the more impetuous children and reassures those who are unforthcoming. It also provides a sense of orderliness and containment. All activities and explanations continue to be broken down into simple manageable stages, and there is a great deal of repetition.

Restricted choice

Many of the children want everything they see, and grab, but they do not know what to do with the thing they have grabbed, and bang with it or discard it, or give up in frustration or have a tantrum. Others see no purpose at all in the toys and throw them about or kick them around. Others again roam about, momentarily glancing, briefly touching. A few settle initially but are highly distractible and do not persist. Others are listless and want nothing. Others are inert and do nothing. They need to have their activities chosen for them, and they need direct help from the adult in engaging with them. In terms of exploration the children are developmentally 'at mother's knee', some still in 'mother's lap'. They can do little on their own, and the task of the teacher, as with parents of pre-nursery children, is to so structure the requirements that they always know what to do, what is expected, and are never left without adequate help and support. This demands of the teacher a perceptive awareness of the complexity of the experiences offered in relation to the developmental level of each child, for even a simple activity may involve unexpected difficulty.

In an established group, those children who are familiar with the routine and have experience of the materials and toys, and are sufficiently competent to manage to some extent on their own, are sent off first. They are given a choice of the available activities only if they have enough experience and maturity to make a choice, for choice depends on the earlier assimilation of a wide range of experiences, and the memory of these experiences and the associated satisfactions. It also requires the discipline to forgo the things that are not chosen, and a sense of purpose and the will to take. The children sent off next would probably be given a choice from two familiar things offered by the teacher. They choose, but their choice is from the teacher's prior choice, and this would be only from activities they know and have fully experienced. If given a completely free choice virtually all of them would dither, or would become aimless and fights would start; or a child might choose the same limited activity over and over again. In time all of them can anticipate the possibilities and satisfactions of activities they do not know, because they can predict what these will be from their experience of other things, and when they have reached this stage they choose from everything that is available.

Teacher-controlled structured activities

At this stage of the day the only toys and activities on offer have inherent structure, are teacher controlled and have some relevance to foundation stage work, albeit at a very early level in some cases. For more 'advanced' children such things as inset shapes and pegboard patterns might be manageable. Some groups start the day with very simple, stylized teacher-controlled paper and pencil work but this is possible only when a separate table is available for 'breakfast'.

Most of the children are eager to begin. The more competent children are the first to be launched. As they cross the room and set out their things the others listen to the instructions given, and watch with interest and anticipation. This gives them a shadowy experience of *their* next step forward. They take in the choices available and the teacher's comments as she tries to help and direct each child, and the choice finally made by the child. Watching what the others do is an important part of the learning experience, for few understand what is required. Even a box of bricks is unfamiliar to some of them, and they may not know what to do with it. Waiting, too, is an important experience, and as they watch they are likely to build in imagery, and savour the experience vicariously in imagery.

Individual support

Eye contact is made with each child as he goes off. This slows him down and helps to maintain the relationship, and clear instructions at this point give him direction and an expectation of success, thus providing security as well as implicit control. The support given is individual to the child: his name, a smile, touch. Reassurance to a more capable child is given by the comment, 'I know you can manage on your own' or 'I'll come and help you later'. The assistant is there to receive any child who needs special help, and at the beginning of the year all the children would get this support. 'Go to Ms A' makes a verbal link from the teacher to the assistant, but a less competent child is taken to the assistant by the teacher, thus making a physical link. The comment that Ms A will show the child what to do orientates him to acceptance of the task ahead, and by implication indicates that the assistant is in control. This helps him to fall in with her expectations. Children who are poorly orientated to their surroundings are taken by the hand and helped into a chair. The children left till last are those who are least able to manage on their own, because they either are too inexperienced or are not sufficiently able to control their own behaviour, or both. The teacher chooses an activity or toy for each of these children and takes opportunities as they arise to acknowledge him when their eyes meet and to make gentle unthreatening contact through touch. Their first full involvement is very basic: rocking and cradling, baby games and nursery rhymes on the adult's knee, swinging and lifting, and a smile may be the child's biggest achievement.

The structure of the day

This teacher-controlled structured beginning to the day, when activities are quiet, individual and contained is commonly called 'first choosing', though the choice available is determined by the teacher. After this the children are drawn back to the home area where they are once again helped to settle and attend. The pattern of the day that follows varies with the timetable of the school, the developmental level of the children and the views and talents of the teacher and assistant, but all the groups are based on the same principles and the essential components are the same.

The teacher then describes step by step the event ahead so that the children are aware of the total experience. In some schools assembly begins the day, and because it demands of the children considerable self-control is usually followed by a short period of quiet, peaceful, undemanding teacher-centred and teacher-directed group work in the home area. Junior children, after assembly, might be launched from the home area into structured play activities such as Lego, chosen and controlled by the teacher. All these activities impose organization on children who have little organization of their own. They provide purpose, give security and are less demanding than undirected free play. The breakfast which follows is a relaxation and satisfaction, and a continuing support. Later, when the children can manage a period of demanding, concentrated formal work, breakfast is to some extent an acknowledgement of the achievement. Before the next event the teacher brings the children to the carpet, and introduces a hand game if they seem unsettled. Typically playtime comes next, but they go to the toilet first, in an orderly file, and afterwards wash their hands.

They have to be reminded to do this and every stage has to be described in detail, is treated as a separate operation and has to be demonstrated. An assistant: 'if you say "Push up the sleeves of your jumper", a boy wearing a shirt doesn't respond. He thinks it doesn't apply to him, so all relevant clothing has to be specified.'

Playtime is considered in Chapter 4.

After playtime, the children assemble on the carpet and the teacher comments on the way they behaved in the playground and how they came up the stairs, and she reiterates her expectations. They become so used to the ritual that they sometimes say, 'you didn't ask us how we came in'.

They now have directed formal activities at the table, possibly in two groups, the teacher leading one, the assistant the other under the guidance of the teacher, for games directly related to foundation stage work, though in some cases the connection, though real, is remote. They return to the carpet, go over the morning's activities, then an 'advanced' child might read a story he has written, or a story is read to them. They go as a group to the dining hall. There has already been a lot of discussion about this, what they have to do and the choice of food available, and breakfast in the classroom has made them familiar with sitting properly at the table and managing the cutlery. The teacher and/or assistant might stay with them at first, and later look in from time to time, but the supervising staff know that they might need extra help.

For the afternoon session they are once again sent off from the carpet, this time for 'second choosing'. They are now free to choose from activities selected by the teacher. It is helpful to mark these with a coloured 'flash'. When the group is stable, the activities available to the more experienced children involve more movement and co-operation, and extend to such things as sand, water and paint for those who can manage these materials, and house play. The teacher and assistant are actively involved, and take every opportunity to extend the children's language and mathematical concepts. Next comes afternoon playtime, followed by story and a review of the things they have done and learned.

The nurture group curriculum includes cooking, music and movement in the school hall, and computer work for the children who can cope with this. Out-of-school activities are slotted into the structure of the day, though not all are weekly events: visits to the library and the park, and from time to time to the zoo, city farm, etc. And they go to the shops for food, and other kinds of shops to see what happens there.

Helping the children with their activities

A characteristic of the children, irrespective of their developmental level, is lack of personal organization, and there are unexpected deficits of experience and understanding even in those who are more advanced. So irrespective of the children's immediate competence and long-term potential, no assumptions are made about the ability of any of them to use the simplest of toys and materials without help. Even though some have been through the nursery and have had these opportunities, they have not necessarily engaged with them. Few of them, whether juniors or infants, have the resources to use nursery level toys and equipment purposefully, or play together constructively. Their level of play is in many cases at the one or two year level and they need experiences at this level, and help in learning how to handle basic materials and simple toys. The activities available when they come into the group are therefore carefully monitored, and are provided within a controlled and restricted situation where they get a great deal of direct and continuing help.

They need opportunities at a baby and toddler level

Many teachers have said how difficult it is at first to gauge the needs of the children, and they find they initially pitch the activities at too high a developmental level. A frequent comment is that many nurture children of infant age, and some juniors, are not ready for cutting and sticking and painting, and certainly not for creative work. Activities at the toddler level or earlier are appropriate, and some junior children accept and enjoy baby toys. For such children it is useful to consider what would interest a child of 2 years of age or younger, and provide experiences accordingly, within a consistent routine. The children are able to give attention and persist at this level. Big blocks for building towers, posting boxes and building beakers are useful, and in some cases squeezy toys and rattles. The children need the basic perceptual-motor experiences these provide, and get satisfaction from the repetition. The teacher can sometimes very quickly lead these into memory and guessing games, and she develops informally but purposefully simple 'lessons' involving colour, shape and size. There is, however, a wide developmental range in most groups, and some children profit also from Key Stage 1 activities.

Individual help

Each child is introduced to his toy or activity by the teacher or assistant and continues to get individual help for as long as he needs it. No self-determination is assumed. The children may need to be taken by the hand and shown what to do because they cannot find out by themselves. They need to watch at first, and begin to help when they are able to. They need to be played with, to do things with the adult, to experience a sense of 'we' 'together' before they can do these things on their own. Children can only learn by discovery if they have had prior experience of earlier, more elementary discovery, have internalized simple basic concepts, and have a sense of self and purpose that enables them to use and extend these concepts in a new situation. These children have not.

Total support and direction for some

Some of the children function quite minimally and are likely to need total support and active direction. They may need to be told that they can touch the toy and hold it, can take the bricks out of the box, and be shown and told that the bricks are hard and they can build with them. They may need to be shown the right way up to hold the doll, and how to put on the clothes. Children who are poorly co-ordinated and oriented may need to be taken by the hand to the toy and shown how to sit on the floor in relation to the toy. Some of them sit with their legs wide apart, as though 18 months old. For them it is enough to learn how to open the box and take out the contents, and watch what the teacher does with them. Another child, who is excited, exuberant and eager for experiences, may well rush in without restraint. He needs to be slowed down, to be told to look and listen. The teacher might take both his hands in hers and ask him to look at her: 'No. Look at me. Look at my eyes.' If he stretches out for the toy before she has explained what he is to do, she holds it in both hands or keeps the lid on the box as she explains, and hands it to him only when he is settled and ready. Unless he is 'held' and then 'let go' gradually, he will rush in eagerly and within seconds will be 'aggressive and disruptive'. Other children are more advanced. They can pay attention to a wider perceptual field, can grasp what is required and remember what to do. When asked to notice and remember how the bricks are arranged in the box, and to put them back the same way when they have finished, they are able to do this.

They are shown how to play with the toys

When a child is new to the group or when anything new is introduced, the teacher or assistant always talks about it beforehand, and he tries it with one of them first. They might begin by attracting his attention with enthusiasm to a simple representational toy, which they identify by name. They describe its salient features, 'Look. It's a bus. It's red. It has wheels. Watch', and they develop the action in a simple way with accompanying words, verbalizing what they are doing as they show him what to do, and they register their actions and their feelings in language that is basic and is mother–baby/toddler in structure and quality. All new activities are introduced gradually and are built up slowly in simple manageable stages. Few of the children know what is expected, and they all need the pleasure of a shared activity, and the shared feeling that flows from this. This is a developmental need, and for as long as is necessary the teacher and assistant take part in these activities with the child. If he is new to the group sometimes the teacher and assistant spend time playing together, so that he sees how they play, how it develops, and where it leads. He also sees constructive interaction between the teacher and the assistant in a relaxed and happy family atmosphere, and he listens to their commentary on what they are doing and what he *sees* they are doing, and if hesitant realizes that it is permissible for him to try it too. It is important that he sees the end result before he tries it for himself, because he may not know what this should be. In a home offering normal opportunities a child would see activities taken to completion long before he had the skills to attempt them for himself.

The adults are watchful and give help as necessary

The children engage with their toys because they are appropriate and because expectations are at an earlier, more realistic and relevant level than in the mainstream class. They learn to play and explore with confidence, interest and pleasure because the teacher and assistant are fully involved and enjoy these experiences with them. And when the children are left to play by themselves the teacher and assistant stay nearby. They try to be alert all the time to possible difficulties, and intervene with help and encouragement. If they are busy they tell the child that they know he needs help and will go to him as soon as they can; and the children are repeatedly reminded to go to the adults for help if they are not able to manage. Problems arise because the children's tolerance for frustration is low. They get upset if things go wrong, and most have difficulty in sharing and taking turns. But even when they are familiar with the materials and toys, and can manage to play on their own without interfering with each other, and having a tantrum if another child interferes with them, they continue to need the support of doing things with the teacher or assistant. This emotional need for a shared satisfaction may persist for a considerable time. Even more advanced children continue to need a great deal of help, and the teacher and assistant involve themselves as needed, individually with a child or in small groups. They do things with and for them, showing them how to fit things together, how things work, verbalizing all the time, and all the time naming things, feeding in explanations, information, suggestions and ideas, and giving help with basic skills and techniques. They are alert to the complexities of all situations, however simple they appear to be. Difficulties, however trivial they may seem, are anticipated, and the children are told what to expect and with this extra help are usually able to develop their activities.

Verbal reinforcement

Verbal reinforcement and elaboration is very important, and is conveyed mainly through a running commentary. There is more of this than there would be in the normally supportive home in the earliest years because the children must catch up quickly. The teacher and assistant describe and explain, and with the more advanced children discussion and patient reasoning is possible. They voice their thoughts as they talk together, as though thinking aloud. They verbalize the nature of difficult situations, how people feel and behave, and they comment and share observations. This 'lesson' gives the children an experience of the way people think, how they reflect on what they are doing and how they work things out.

Persistence and repetition is encouraged and supported

A major and general problem with children taken into nurture groups is their inability to persist with an activity. The normally developing young child engages totally with an activity that is appropriate for his level of development, and of his own accord persists with it and repeats the experience. Following this model, the teacher chooses an activity that can be completed quickly. She urges and helps the child to persist, encourages and supports its repetition and provides it again and again so that he can fully master what is involved. Only then is a change of activity made, at the adult's discretion.

They know they have to persist

Each child knows that he has to persist with his activity for as long as the teacher requires this. Her expectations are realistic and she might provide support by showing him on the clock how much longer he has to go. But if he is becoming restless and is no longer able to concentrate, and it is clear that he has reached the limits of his persistence, she gives him something new to do. He is not allowed to change of his own accord because he would settle no better to anything else; he would merely flit from one thing to another, or would grab at the first thing that attracted his attention. The teacher's insistence that he persists, averts aimless and unproductive behaviour. Although the children may resist at first, they accept this requirement, and when restricted in this way become absorbed in their activity and seem very satisfied. And because the tempo is slow, and there is a lot of repetition, there is time for the experience to be consolidated and internalized. Later, when given a choice of activity, the children often return to these same simple things, and do so repeatedly. This is very like the behaviour of young children at home. They outgrow their simple toys but later go back to them, and play with them in a different way. Following this guideline, it is important to let the children go back to these simple activities and experience them again. They recapture the basic satisfaction and security they gained through this early play, and have the comfort of assured success.

The more advanced children also have to persist

Not all the children are at a pre-nursery level. Some come into school with a more adequate experience and are able to use materials and toys that are more advanced and have greater flexibility and imaginative potential. If they are able to choose their activity the teacher tries to ensure that it is within their capacity and attention span, and can be finished in a reasonable time, and that they will be able to tolerate any interference from a child nearby. They, too, are expected to persist with their activity and see it through to completion, and if they want to change they must have a good reason. One of their difficulties is dissatisfaction and restlessness, not settling and persisting, repeatedly seeking they know not what. Quietly setting limits helps to contain their restlessness and eventually leads to sustained interest in the task. Those children who have more autonomy are able to initiate change for themselves, but *all have to ask* if they want to start anything new.

Their play space is protected: the need to share is controlled

Another important function of the adult in the early days is to supervise and control each child's play space, and the behaviour of anyone who might interfere. Few of them are able to interact constructively with other children or even play alongside each other without interfering, whether by intent or accident. They need to play alone in their own unimpeded play space, and situations where space has to be shared are therefore avoided. Nor are they expected to share equipment. They need their own things, usually chosen by the teacher, and if they grab or fight the toy is taken away. They might pout, sulk or have a tantrum, but their resentment typically is short-lived and very soon they accept something else. At this stage they need to play repetitively and alone at a very simple level. They are motivated to give attention and persist at this level, and need protection from interference and distraction. Many of them, when helped in this way, quickly become engrossed in their activities and are increasingly able to sustain their attention. Later they are able to share space, materials and toys, and co-operate with another child. They need help, too, in extending their activity and co-ordinating it with that of another child. Later still, the teacher carefully controls and monitors an activity involving the physical participation of two or more children. For example she would take PE in a junior group slowly, step by step, specifying the activity of each child in turn, and waiting while this was accomplished before any attempt was made to co-ordinate these actions. Co-operative work of this kind is possible only when the children are able to acknowledge each other, however minimally, an with reminders can tolerate the frustration of holding back, waiting, sharing and giving way for others sufficiently well to keep the activity intact. As the children achieve greater competence, individual and class activities become more complex.

Experiencing achievement

It is important to ensure that the organization and structure of the nurture group day and the activities within it will 'hold' the children. The teacher and assistant are then free within themselves to tune in to each child, and respond to and acknowledge in a developmentally appropriate way any small feature of behaviour that is in a forward-moving direction. For a child who is unresponsive and barely functions, the aim of the adult would be to elicit a smile and encourage the slightest sign of initiative. His first achievement might be to empty a box of bricks of his own accord, and the warmth and pleasure of the adult's spontaneous and immediate appreciation, expressed in a hug or huge smile, tells him that it is permissible to do this. If he builds a tower he might need 'permission' to knock it down, and the teacher or assistant may have to knock it down first to reassure him that this really is permissible and 'safe'. They have the shared pleasure of the daring and the noise, and the child senses approval for having done it. Making a noise, daring to exist, is his achievement. For more advanced children, and perhaps for this child later on, being quiet when this is required might be the achievement, and the adult's approval would be more muted, perhaps no more than 'good boy' and for some children a smile of satisfaction. But inevitably there are times when an achievement is overlooked, and the tremendous step the child has taken goes unacknowledged.

The children are enabled to achieve

The teacher and assistant respond intuitively to the children's achievements, but it is vital that they formulate their needs in order to provide a situation which enables them to achieve. These are targets for their Individual Education Plans (IEPs). Many useful observations are made during group time on the carpet. The teacher and assistant notice how the children respond, and their mood, and what they can and cannot do, and where further help is needed. This is also a useful time for referring to their achievements, and commenting on progress.

Consolidation is important

It is important that each forward step taken is acknowledged, but consolidation of these gains is also important. When to re-experience an earlier stage, when to consolidate current learning and when to move forward may be particularly difficult issues in the case of academically able children. A single situation can, however, yield different kinds and levels of experience. Thus playing in the sand, where weighing and measuring would be extended by the teacher as a lesson, provides also a basic perceptual experience that might be much needed. The work developed by different teachers suggests that different experiences can and should go in parallel, though they are watchful not to expect too much, and resist the temptation to move the children on too quickly. It is a relief to think of the children as 2 years of age or thereabouts, for the adults can then relax, reassured to feel that their behaviour is 'normal', and that classroom achievements are not the immediate priority. But it is not easy to find the right balance. The children settle into the routine of the day and when they are calm and with the demands of the mainstream class in mind, it is tempting to move them on too quickly, but if they do, the situation could fall apart. The quiet, peaceful, slow-moving periods of the nurture group day are for consolidation. This is the time when the teacher and assistant relax quietly together, just as they would at home. The children are happy at these times. They like the feeling that the teacher and assistant are sitting quietly together. They draw close to them and sit quietly, too, touching them, stroking them. If the teacher and assistant sit still, they sit still. They seem to be taking in the attachment, the peace and the security, and a sense that all is well.

Teacher and assistant are alert to ensure success

For the children to experience achievement, the organization and conduct of the nurture group day must provide maximal opportunities for success, and must ensure that the teacher and assistant are relaxed enough to notice and acknowledge the success. They must be alert all the time, watching for the child who needs help and providing this before he loses heart or becomes frustrated, and intervening before trouble breaks out. They must also be aware of the complexities of all situations, however simple they seem, and break them down into stages. Each stage is manageable, the child's success is evident, and is reinforced by the response of the teacher and assistant. This is immediate and appropriate for the achievement concerned, whether a hug, or a touch on the shoulder with an exclamation of pleasure, or simply a satisfied supportive verbal comment.

Attention is paid to detail

Nurture groups work well when attention is paid to many points of detail. This sounds daunting but, as with families, it is the underlying attitude and general trend that is important. It is enough for a teacher and assistant new to this work to absorb the 'flavour' of the nurture groups and then get on with it in their own personal and spontaneous way. Losing some points of detail does not matter – it happens in all families – but if too many are lost the group will not provide a nurturing experience for the children. But the one thing that must be absorbed is the early level at which most of the children function. 'Think of them as 2; that's all you need to do.'

3

Internalization of Controls

Most nurture group children initially have no understanding of the teacher's role. They do not heed her but behave as they will, without direction and forward-moving purpose, unable to engage constructively in events about them. Some are without basic competencies and social skills, and inadvertently and unwittingly cause disturbance. Others are unhappy and fractious, resistive and rejecting, and are destructive in their hurt and anger. Others, again, have internalized negative attitudes and are destructive and disruptive in intent; they get relief from hurting and depriving others, and for some this is a satisfying pleasure. In many children primitive fear is readily aroused in normally unthreatening circumstances and they become aggressive and difficult to manage. The children's difficulties vary greatly in nature and severity, and often issue in 'destructive, disruptive and aggressive' behaviour. All are symptoms of frustrated purposeful growth, and in so far as the task of the nurture teacher and assistant is to promote normal growth, every aspect of their work contributes directly and indirectly to the alleviation of behaviour difficulties.

Normal development is based on a trusting attachment but this is rarely made immediately and the child's behaviour may negate attachment. The teacher's first objective, therefore, is for acceptable behaviour. She imposes her requirements. Attachment, and the attitudes, sympathies and experiences that stem from this and lead to self-directing behaviour, come later, when her control is established. Control leads to attachment, trust and the assimilation of constructive learning experiences. The process is reinforcing and cumulative, and begins with relevant structure and organization.

Relevant structure and organization

In establishing acceptable behaviour the teacher's first consideration is the organization of the nurture group day. In tempo and structure and the clear guidelines provided it is at an early developmental level. Experiences and events within this are carefully monitored and controlled. This is a major factor in the improved functioning of all the children, and it is usual for behaviour difficulties of most kinds to be less evident from the beginning and in some of the children the change is immediate and dramatic. They understand what is required, the expectations are within their competence and they get direct support and help when needed. They function more effectively, and energy which otherwise is aimless and undirected finds appropriate, constructive, satisfying and legitimate outlets. They feel secure, gain satisfaction and experience success and approval. Stress, frustration and provocation for and by all the children is reduced, and fights, tantrums and aggressive attacks on others are less likely to occur.

Level of organization is a crucial determinant

This initial improvement comes about because the child's day is organized for a developmental level where little or no autonomy is expected. This is of crucial importance. If a child's behaviour is still difficult to manage after the initial settling-in period, or he is fractious and has tantrums, the organization and conduct of the day must be questioned. Is it really at the earliest level? Is the situation too demanding? Is too much autonomy being expected? This is a particularly important consideration when new children are admitted to an established and well-functioning group, for the teacher has adapted to the children as they became increasingly mature and may forget how she began. Many comment ruefully on the salutary experience this provides.

In some groups, the constraints and self-control needed for successful participation in school are built in, as in a family, in a natural and unobtrusive way, and the teacher and assistant are then mainly concerned with widening the child's experience. Many who respond quickly are unventuring and fearful, disorganized and without trust, and their tantrums and fractious behaviour in the mainstream class seem largely a protest, and an expression of their unhappiness, aimlessness and stress. Some of the others need more direct and evident control, but they too settle in quickly. Typically they are robust children eager for experiences but unable to use them. They plunge into situations beyond their competence and become excited and out of control. They are not purposefully aggressive and disruptive but indirectly cause fights and upsets, mainly because they grab at everything in sight and disrupt and provoke the others. They, too, function better when their experiences are monitored and their behaviour is controlled. The aggression in some other children is more deliberate, and ranges from a sly physical jab at another child to vicious sustained attacks. This may be an expression of unhappiness, anxiety, fear and frustration, or the tension of energy that has no purposeful outlet. The approach is nevertheless much the same, and differs only in emphasis. Support, care and consistent management are within an ordered day. Strict limits are set, developmentally appropriate outlets are provided and the children are helped to gain legitimate satisfactions at their level of need and competence. Their energy is thus directed more purposefully, their behaviour is more acceptable from the beginning and any difficulties arising are more manageable. Food for these children expresses caring, and treats are a shared satisfaction and pleasure.

Limited opportunities at first

It is important that the experiences available to the children are very limited at first, with little or no choice, and no more put out than is necessary to keep all of them purposefully occupied. And whatever the nature of the toys and activities, their use is always carefully controlled, and the more difficult things are out of sight and reach of the less experienced children. The environment is orderly and organized, the rules are clear and frequently repeated, and the children are under constraints and are carefully let go into their activities. Many of them are without the resources or lack the organization to use a complex environment. They are overstimulated by the unfamiliarity and sudden richness of school and have no earlier experience to provide a basis for choice. They are easily distracted and want everything they see, and unless the situation is strictly controlled they alight on things at random and use nothing effectively.

Consistency within routine leads to security and trust

The consistency of everyday experiences within a broad routine enables the children to function in an organized and purposeful way, and eventually to predict. The routine is manageable, and familiar, contributes to a sense of trust and, after an upset, provides comfort and reassurance. And because the routines are constraining they slow the children down, and give them time to become aware of themselves in relation to others, and the implicit standards that have to be met, and lead to a sense of group identity. All the routinized group activities are important, but the routine of food is the most important of them all. Within the routine is ritual, a more immediate and personal routine giving comfort and reassurance.

Security, trust and acceptance of the adults' requirements

Within the structure provided by routine and organization is a complex web of experiences that builds up trust and a sense of the adults' caring, and leads to attachment and a wish to please. Discussion of feelings and behaviour becomes relevant, and through this the children gradually learn to regulate their own behaviour better and deal more constructively with their feelings of aggression. The role model provided by the teacher and assistant is important. The children are aware of them and begin to behave as they do, and the teacher and assistant therefore make explicit the constructive and supportive nature of their relationship.

Some change is apparent from the beginning

The essential dependency of the children is nevertheless usually apparent from the beginning, and attachment and response in all but a few is established fairly quickly, and in the younger children is sometimes striking. Accompanying this is an improvement in the children's behaviour, usually within the first three weeks in a typically developing group, and both adults and children are reassured that all will be well.

Lasting change comes about only with time

Although behaviour quickly becomes manageable when attention is given to detail from the beginning and the overall situation is carefully structured and controlled, fundamental and lasting change comes about only over time as different facets of the learning experience begin to reinforce each other. The process is cumulative and the learning content becomes part of the child's being. The teacher's requirements have now been internalized, and the child's behaviour is self-directing.

Behaviour control: general guidelines

Even when the nurture group day is modified appropriately for an early developmental level, aggressive, destructive and disruptive behaviour may nevertheless be the dominant and overriding problem for the teacher, and a worrying feature in the early stages. It nullifies everything she is trying to do, negates potential attachment, disturbs any group feeling that is developing and each child's difficulties preclude the possibility of progress for himself and all the others. It is also likely to provoke the other children, and an initially benign situation can rapidly deteriorate. In groups like this behaviour control is an urgent priority and is strict and unremitting at all times. It demands constant vigilance on the part of the teacher and assistant and is not at first an intuitive response within a relationship of trust, for effectively there is no relationship, and no trust. It derives from the strength of the adults' conviction that learning to meet basic social demands is a crucial stage in the child's personal growth, and from the strength of the knowledge that adult and child must endure a painful present for a more constructive and fulfilling future. It is through the adults' unremitting control, and the consistency and immediacy of their response, within a context of fairness and caring, that the children learn to trust, and become attached, dependent and biddable. They are responsive to the adults' responsiveness to them and begin to internalize the security and controls. In the words of an assistant in a very difficult group of first- and second-year junior children: 'They are all soft inside, really.'

Behaviour problems may be of a severe order

The impact of problems of this order on the teacher and assistant can be very great. The children have poor self-control, little sense of personal identity and no standards of behaviour, and when collected together at the beginning of the year show no real acknowledgement of the teacher, and there is no semblance of a group to which she can relate. After an initial period of disorganization, and sometimes wild excitement and aggression, the children begin to feel secure and usually settle down, develop and progress, with only minor recurring upsets. But particularly in junior groups when frustration, irritability, tension, anger and fear are at a high level, the children readily absorb each others' anxiety and aggression, and powerful formless feelings break through their fragile controls. In the words of teachers, the group becomes 'high', 'on the boil'. Any teacher control or self-control is lost, aggression rises and behaviour becomes destructive and disruptive. Fights or temper tantrums break out, and even when the group seems stable they sometimes erupt when one child looks at another. The fights may be 'nothing short of punch-ups' and, when in a temper tantrum, a child might 'go berserk'. When a situation disintegrates in this way there is no possibility of the adult exercising control. There is no relationship between adult and child, no acknowledgement of the existence of the adult, and any interaction between the children is negative. There is no sense of a group, and there can be no appeal to standards even were the children to listen because there are no shared values; and there is no response to the teacher's feelings because there is no shared experience of feelings. A commonly described high-risk period in a vulnerable group is at the beginning of the morning, particularly on Mondays, and the provision of a small 'breakfast' at about ten o'clock is dramatically stabilizing. The attention of the children is held by the food, and the teacher for the first time may be in control. Food at this stage, in groups like this, is not initially an expression of caring. It is a way of indicating the teacher's requirements, and is an agent of control.

Everything is 'writ large'

It is particularly important that the situation is geared at an appropriate developmental level and that there is meticulous control of the children's experiences. Everything, therefore, is 'writ large'. The tempo is slower, even if the children are juniors, there is more direct support from the moment they enter school, and individual help is given as needed. The limits set are very tight and are specified in detail, step by step. The essentials of what is required are made evident and are highlighted, and everything is repeated as often as is necessary. The teacher and assistant make their expectations and attitude quite clear, and their disapproval and the sanctions imposed are immediate. All this ensures that the children are successful. It also reduces the unnecessary frustration and provocation from others that lead to tantrums and fights.

Behaviour control centres on the teacher

In the early stages of a group like this it is helpful to direct the attention of the children exclusively to the teacher, for it is she who sets the general style of discipline and the expectations to be met. The assistant, who later works in a more balanced partnership with the teacher, supports her in making a viable group, and involves herself with the children only when they need support to do what is required. If both take initiatives at this early stage the children are likely to be distracted and confused.

The teacher and assistant reinforce each other's expectations

Within the framework established by the teacher, both adults are meticulously consistent in their management. They have the same standards where basic behaviour is concerned, and re-inforce each other's expectations in their individual ways. They make their attitude to the children's behaviour evident. They show their pleasure clearly, and say 'no' with implacable importance. In saying 'no' the adult might hold the child's hands and purposefully make eye contact as she says 'no'. Many of the children pay no attention at first, but if the adult claps her hands together before she speaks this sometimes alerts them, and for some is perhaps a symbol of the smack they might have had at home.

The most basic behaviour is dealt with first

The teacher's and assistant's requirements are directed initially to one feature only of unacceptable behaviour, and the developmentally more basic behaviour is tackled first. Swearing is therefore ignored if the children are still physically attacking each other, because it is difficult enough for them to control their fighting, and swearing is an outlet for their aggression. Later they are helped to say what is wrong, but as they learn to involve themselves in a more constructive and satisfying way they become less prone to yelling aggressively at each other, and to swearing. Similarly, not grabbing when the biscuits are handed round comes before not taking the biggest and the best. Later they can be helped to share and to give up their things for each other, and little courtesies and a polite manner are then encouraged.

The adults are vigilant, and their intervention is immediate

When behaviour problems are severe, a high level of vigilance and alert response is required of the adults. They must anticipate potential difficulties, constantly appraise and modify the situation, and whenever necessary have the will and energy for immediate intervention. They are watchful all the time for signs of distress and disturbance, and even when the focus of their attention is elsewhere never forget what the other children are doing, which child is with whom and what could happen. They constantly glance about, alert to any possible eruption of trouble, ready to verbalize what is happening and intervene with a reminder, or more actively if inflammatory squabbles and frustrations arise. They are strict and unyielding about very small details, for even trivial incidents are liable to disturb and distract the others and might escalate and involve the whole group. Most of the problems arise when the children are not able to cope with their activities or relationships, and so the need for help is anticipated. If the adult is occupied with someone else, she tells the child concerned that she will come to help as soon as she can. The comment that it is the other child's turn, or the removal of a toy, or the provision of an extra toy is sometimes enough to resolve the problem. Incidental passing help of this kind when the child meets difficulties in his play removes an obstacle to progress. It dispels the anger and frustration of not being able to achieve, and turns a potentially dangerous mood into interest and goodwill, or prevents a sullen mood turning to aggression. Even holding the child's hand when he is required to wait might provide any needed extra support. Often the child can be deflected from what it seems he might be going to do by the teacher or assistant saying what their expectations are in advance of his actions, or praising him before he does anything for the thing he was unlikely to do. In doing this they structure the way ahead, and the child usually falls in with this even if it was not his intention. Some of the children are not aware that they have been deflected in this way; others appear to get satisfaction from the realization that they are behaving as required.

Peace and quiet is re-established in the home area

If tempers and fights arise in spite of these efforts, or if the group is becoming disturbed and disorganized, all activities are stopped. The teacher draws the children into the home area, where they sit down, and she and the assistant wait quietly until they are calm and still. The children are used to being brought back to the home area many times during the day, and at times of stress the teacher introduces a simple ritualized activity, perhaps a familiar action song that was learned when they were relaxed, and which they associate with quietness and well-being. And before being let go again they are given a patient reminder of what to do when difficulties arise. Mothers of young children pick them up if they are crawling or toddling into a potentially destructive situation, and hold them close before letting them go and *putting* them somewhere else. The equivalent in the nurture group is for the teacher to draw the children to her in the home area, if possible before problems blow up, and wait for calm, before letting them go and directing them to something else. The small child is able to explore because he has within him the comfort and security of being nursed and protected in his mother's arms, and is aware of her presence close by. Correspondingly the home area in the nurture room is established as a quiet place of well-being and security, where especially nice things happen. It is where they are close to the teacher and assistant, are read to on the adult's knee, and at the beginning of the year it is where they have their treats.

Disruptive behaviour is often caused by grabbing

Although to the casual observer the aggressive and disruptive behaviour shown by the children may often seem unprovoked, it is rarely so. In the more controlled and carefully monitored situation of the nurture group it is often seen to be the outcome, directly or indirectly, of uninhibited grabbing. In the simplest case the child is attracted to something at a perceptual level, recklessly plunges in and grabs. An example is a 9-year-old boy, described as aggressive and disruptive, who wrought havoc in the dining hall when he grabbed at a shiny knife. Most of the cutlery was dull in finish but a few of the knives were shiny. He wanted the shiny knife, and he grabbed. Such children seem like inexperienced toddlers who are dominated by perceptual impulse and want all the attractive things they see. They grab, and in their excitement are aware only of the thing they grab. The situation disintegrates as excitement and anxiety rise. Excitement and anxiety turn to aggression. Unproductive behaviour escalates, particularly if one child is attracted by something bright or highly coloured that another child has claimed. He grabs, and the offended child clings on in a fury, and may become further inflamed because he experiences this assault as an attack on himself, and a violation of his space. Other children are attracted indiscriminately to all the things they see, though frequently settle to nothing. Others seem to have an insatiable need to grab everything for themselves, though some seem mainly concerned to deprive the others. Most of them guard what they have, fearing the depredations of others.

Greedy, grabbing behaviour

Unrestrained grabbing, which has the appearance of greed, is a theme in many of the groups, but the way it manifests itself suggests that the nature and extent of the underlying need varies greatly. It seems to be most marked in those children who have missed out on both experiences and constructive behaviour management, and characteristically these are the most aggressive children. It was particularly evident in the first junior group, and was described as remarkable. Left to themselves the children grabbed at everything to hand, not only food, and pushed and fought to get at the straws and milk, elbows jabbing and hands outstretched. They grabbed at a biscuit and with biscuit in mouth they grabbed for another. They grabbed at a jigsaw, a toy car or a crayon. They fought to open the door, or for the coat peg they wanted, they grabbed for something another child had, even if they did not want it or even know what it was, and would force open a tightly clenched fist to take it. They were greedy to be the first and have the advantage, greedy for the biggest and the best, greedy for the brightest and the shiniest. They were greedy for praise, to be acknowledged, to be the best, to be the most favoured, to be the most wanted; and greedy for attention and affection. They were greedy, too, in conversation. Each talked louder than the others and all of them were shouted down. During the first few weeks the assistant spontaneously described the 'aggressive' children as the 'greedy, grabbing' ones, and the 'withdrawn' children, who were not able to take anything and got left out, as the 'quiet, clinging, homey ones'. In her words: 'The quiet, clinging, homey ones don't grab but keep things to themselves and won't share; the greedy, grabbing children won't share, either.' The origin of explosive outbursts, otherwise, usually lies in the total involvement of the children with their own immediate interests, and anger when thwarted or provoked.

The situation is made manageable

The management problems are often considerable because many of the children are big and strong and can do damage. To control this, the teacher avoids situations which make demands beyond their level of competence, as she would with a younger child at home. If they cannot sit close together without digging their elbows into each other and pushing for more space, she keeps them apart. If fights start because they grab at a jar full of crayons, she gives them one crayon each, and if they want another colour they have to ask. She restricts the activities available to them by keeping most things out of sight in the cupboards. There is no need to lock these for it is unusual for children to go into them if told not to. She chooses each child's activity for him at first. Later he chooses from the alternatives she offers. Everything available is developmentally appropriate, is restricted in scope, and is provided in manageable stages. A new toy introduced is held back if anyone grabs. Children who are unwilling to take what is offered, or pay only scant attention to it, are given nothing else, and the cry 'I want . . .' is ignored. Impulsive behaviour, frustration and conflict are in this way controlled. The teacher and assistant praise the children who hold back, for with few exceptions the children want to be the best and get the most praise.

They learn to make a request

The children are trained to ask for what they want, and are taught the form in which the request should be made. If the child asks properly, the adult responds immediately; otherwise *she* makes the request and waits for the child to echo it. Should he continue to demand, challenge and swear, she appears not to hear, and makes no response. Many of the children seem to experience this social training as a lesson and are eager to succeed and to please. Quickly they begin to see a connection between the requirements of the adult and the satisfaction of their needs, and the sense of well-being that constructive interaction brings.

Food is a vehicle for basic learning experiences

The way grabbing is managed is to some extent determined by the attitude of the teacher and assistant, but more important is the extent of overtly aggressive behaviour in the group and the children's resistance to control. Some groups are dominated by children who are particularly aggressive and negative. They seem unmanageable and the provision of food is of crucial importance. It gives the teacher an opportunity to build in acceptable controls and is particularly important in the early days. For nearly all of the children food is of primary interest, though is not initially the valued expression of a satisfying relationship. It is something they want and at first may be the only thing to which they give attention, the first time that eye contact is established, and the only situation where they are motivated to wait, and can be helped to wait. Heightened attention is concentrated on the food as they wait, and thus on the teacher and assistant. They take in that the teacher is a giving person, they see themselves in relation to the giving person, and begin to get a sense of being attached and valued. The children learn to acknowledge the teacher and assistant. They develop an expectation of supportive, caring and consistent authority, and begin to attach themselves in trust.

'Breakfast'

In groups that are dominated by very difficult 'aggressive and disruptive' children it is particularly important to provide breakfast. Typically these children grab and use destructively anything in sight. Some seem dazzled by the riches of school and take indiscriminately. Others seem to be at a pre-social stage of instant gratification, while others again seem driven by infantile greed. A few are more purposefully destructive and are calculatingly antisocial. Whatever the origin of the child's grabbing, it is in many cases an important factor underlying his aggression, or behaviour which seems like aggression, and a family breakfast in school provides the teacher and assistant with a basic and powerful situation for modifying this behaviour. Breakfast may be no more than a biscuit or a piece of toast and jam, and a glass of milk or orange juice. But whatever the nature of the food the situation is a very simple one at first, every detail is carefully monitored and controls are built in stage by stage.

Food in a junior group

The following account is taken from the first junior group established. It included 9- and 10-year-olds. A high proportion of the children had serious behaviour problems: they were not biddable, readily attacked each other and some were big enough to be dangerous.

For breakfast at the beginning of the year everyone had exactly the same food and the same amount, and there was no surplus. The children waited at the table without touching anything while the assistant went to the cupboard. They waited while she took the biscuits from the cupboard, and while she counted them onto a plate; they waited while she put the plate onto a tray and returned to the table. And they watched her and what she did as they waited. When the children were quiet the assistant said, 'You can take your milk now'. The biscuits were then offered to each child in turn, and each child in turn took one. If any child was unable to accept this minimal requirement to sit down and be part of the group, he was allowed to have his milk in his own way and to wander about or sit in the corner, but he did not get a biscuit. When this happened the child concerned sulked. This is a common reaction, though very occasionally a child is consistently indifferent to sanctions of this kind. If the children generally were unsettled, even when this was because two or three children were paying no attention, no one was given a biscuit with their milk. The response was usually resentment, or a stunned silence, but the children accepted the teacher's conditions. These same children, when they took a picnic to the park early in the first term, 'grabbed everything that was going, and even when their mouths were stuffed with food still grabbed and wanted more'. On a later expedition to the park, no one was allowed to take a second sandwich until the slowest child had eaten the first. They ate much more slowly and some of the children refused a second sandwich.

Breakfast is important but is gradually faded out

Breakfast is an important feature of nurture group practice, particularly in the early days, and although conducted in a controlled and purposeful way, but the 'strictness' is rarely apparent. This is largely because of the relaxed attitude of the teacher and assistant, and an approach to the children that is sometimes spiced with humour. But breakfast does is not necessarily continue indefinitely. If most of the children are able to conform to basic social requirements it may be more expedient to dispense with a formal breakfast because it takes time more usefully put into other things.

Reinforcement of waiting and not grabbing is then made over milk and biscuits in the home area, or when the children are playing with their toys. A problem arises when one or two children only have a serious problem of grabbing at the food, but whether a family breakfast, or milk and biscuits in the home area, the procedure is much the same. The child who cannot tolerate waiting is the first to be given his milk already poured out, and he and all the others are allowed to drink it straight away. When the milk has been drunk and all the children are ready he is the first to be offered a biscuit, but is required to hold back, albeit momentarily, before taking the biscuit, and the demands are gradually built up as he becomes increasingly able to cope.

A child in an infant group learns not to grab

The following more detailed account concerns a child with severe behaviour problems who was admitted at the beginning of the spring term to a well functioning infant group. Breakfast had been discontinued.

> At milk and biscuits time John was the first to be offered a biscuit, because waiting even for the second turn would have been intolerable. When offered the first biscuit he was required to hold back, however momentarily, before taking it. He quickly learned to wait, and the pleasure of the teacher and assistant was evident. However, as soon as he had been given a biscuit he did as he pleased. A second biscuit was therefore handed round the group, and he did not get one. In this way the teacher demonstrated her requirements. He reacted with shock. At first he had tantrums and stamped his feet, but quickly conformed. The first biscuit was never withdrawn but he sometimes had it later on his own, and the teacher explained that when he could take his turn, as she required, he could have it with the others. In practice, he rarely had his biscuit later because he could manage to sit still for a moment, and the teacher's expectations were increased only gradually as he became better able to wait. Whatever her requirement, whether waiting for food or persisting with his work, a low level of achievement was accepted at first, but her expectations gradually increased, and each achievement was cherished. The teacher never insisted unless she felt he could achieve, but if she felt he could achieve she insisted. His experience and self-control, and her insistence, built up together. She was unyielding when she judged her demands to be within his tolerance for frustration and stress. And she always verbalized her expectations and her pleasure in the achievement.

John was being helped individually from the beginning. The caring constructive nature of the relationship is like that of a parent who is sensitively in touch with the pressures the child can tolerate, and yields or resists as s/he senses whether at that moment the child is able to take responsibility for his own behaviour.

Helping the children to learn to wait and not grab at the things they want requires delicate judgement on the part of the teacher and assistant. Although they build up their expectations gradually in small manageable stages, the procedure is not dragged out unnaturally because the situation would then be contrived and impersonal, and the children would become frustrated and negative.

Strength of mind and conviction are needed

The teacher and assistant need considerable self-discipline and resolve when the children are being difficult, for they must resist the temptation to overindulge them with food to keep them quiet. This aspect of the work, difficult though it is, is motivated by the wish to help the children. It is purposeful, not punitive, and the explicit aim is to foster in the children more constructive participation in the world about them.

Individual needs are formulated

Modification of the total situation is initially the teacher's main task. It makes possible achievement and satisfaction, reduces frustration, and is of immediate value in the alleviation of aggressive and disruptive behaviour. But if real and rapid progress is to be made the adults must be aware of each child's particular needs, and must be able to meet them. Awareness and involvement, sympathy and interest are the heart of their work. They identify with the child's feelings, see the world from his perspective, talk together about his difficulties and work on them, each reinforcing what the other says and does. They are alert to notice and acknowledge each small gain, and they try to be consistent in giving immediate recognition, directly related to the behaviour concerned and characterized by clearly demonstrated pleasure.

Achievements are acknowledged

The teacher and assistant acknowledge when a child of his own accord meets their expectations, 'he shared, how nice', and their pleasure communicates that it matters. When talking together they frequently refer to the achievements of the group, or particular children, and recall what they have done well. Even when an aspect of behaviour has become satisfactorily established they specifically refer to it from time to time,perhaps in the home area when they are having their milk and biscuits,or at the breakfast table, or when there is a feeling of well-being in the group.

Reinforcement throughout the day

Throughout the day the teacher and assistant take every opportunity to make clear their expectations. Repeatedly they say what is permissible and what is required, and frequently ask the children to echo back what is required. They use to the full every problem arising to demonstrate a social point. They constantly stress desirable behaviour and give simple explanations, re-inforced by demonstration and role-play when necessary and appropriate. They help the children to see a connection between the requirements that are being stressed and the personal and social consequences, and show them a more constructive way of behaving. Constantly the teacher and assistant make clear to each child the needs and feelings of the others and they highlight in their relationship with each other the awareness and consideration for others they are trying to develop in the children. They convey to them that they value this behaviour and the attitudes that underlie it, and in their insistence that the children meet these standards they by implication value the children, and acknowledge them as potentially well functioning members of the social group.

Basic needs are satisfied

Grabbing and keeping, and not being able to share, are closely linked with 'not having', but in the nurture group the children get the things they want and need: affection, attention, caring physical contact, early basic experiences and the reassurance that they are valued. They get them in manageable amounts and have time to assimilate them and be satisfied by them, and as these needs are increasingly met they become more able to share. The children have a keen sense of fairness at this stage but they learn that there is enough for everyone, and that the teacher and assistant are fair. They begin to understand the nature of group interaction, and that certain standards have general application and validity, are universal social demands and must be maintained. They quickly begin to accept the reality consequences of bad behaviour, and understand and help to maintain the standards that are being established. They take over the adults' attitudes and make clear to the others what is required, even using their words and tone of voice.

Imposed standards become internalized

At first the children conform to these basic requirements only because of the sanctions, but later these standards become more genuinely their own. This happens because of their close relationship with the teacher and assistant, and their consistent experience of being cared for, and the sense of well-being and purpose that comes from constructive relationships with other children. As affections develop between the children they begin to show concern for each other and are able to give up their things for each other. And as they become increasingly secure and satisfied they accept that the other children must have affection and attention from the teacher and assistant, and are more able to share this.

The timid children also benefit

The timid, inhibited children, and those who are 'frozen', gain security from the clearly defined structure, seem reassured by the firm and strict control, and begin to see what is acceptable. At first they hold back and are liable to get left out, but as they experience the care and support of the teacher and assistant, and the encouragement that follows any initiative they show, they become less fearful and begin to take, and may even begin to grab. Gradually they, too, learn to share.

Control is constructive

Usually within three weeks or so the children are orderly and are able to wait for their turn, though continuing attention to behaviour control may be needed for a considerable time, especially with older children. As behaviour in the group improves they become more trusting, and are less possessive with their things. They know that the teacher and assistant will ensure that they get a fair share, and so they give up for others when this is required, or share of their own accord. Firm control of behaviour is therefore constructive and caring for all the children, irrespective of the nature of their difficulties, and is the essential first step. Without intervention the children neither use their opportunities constructively, nor experience the satisfaction of the companionship of others.

4

Disruptive Behaviour: Nature and Management

An upsurge of uncontrolled feelings characterize tantrums, tempers and temper tantrums, but they vary greatly in the extent to which control is lost. Some outbursts are little more than an immature expression of distress or anger, in others the child is not in control of himself, may be out of control and is sometimes described as 'going beserk'. Fights, too, are an expression of uncontrolled feelings, but whereas tantrums and temper tantrums have a quality of impotence and distress, fights are more consciously purposeful. The child remains organized and relieves his feelings of anger by deliberately hurting or destroying the person who is the object of his anger. Children at a very early developmental level are not sufficiently aware of themselves and the world about them to get into purposeful fights. They respond to stress with a tantrum, and in distress and anger hit out. Similarly, children who are preoccupied with problems and unhappiness may have tantrums of distress, but are far less likely to fight. Other children never have tantrums, but are frequently involved in vicious kicking attacks and fights. They are beyond control, rather than in the out-of-control state of the temper tantrum. The motivation behind this behaviour is more complex; it is directed and purposeful and the aim is to destroy. Some of the children have temper tantrums *and* get into violent fights. These eruptions are commonly seen in children who cannot tolerate interference or having to share; they grab what they want or protect what they have, and a tantrum or fight ensues. They are also provoked by anything experienced as an attack or a threat. This could be an accidental touch or an ambiguous or innocent look, or the more straightforward name-calling. Jealousy or wariness of others is also sometimes indirectly the precursor of a fight.

Temper tantrums

Both mild and severe temper tantrums are characterized by rage, and are usually triggered by frustration. The child has an overwhelming need to take part, or do what is required, or achieve, but does not have the resources or confidence; or his own wants are urgent and he cannot give way to anyone else. Situations like this sometimes trigger an outburst of shouting, screaming, crying and kicking. A feeling of anger that might get out of control is being conveyed. The adult can sometimes avert a tantrum if she intervenes in time. If too late, but it is not escalating rapidly, she can sometimes prevent it from getting out of control. She holds the child's hands and sensing the origin of the upset, describes the sequence of events leading up to it and how he feels, clearly and in detail. She continues to hold him as he struggles and resists. She remains calm and she waits. A child in this state can be distracted relatively easily, and energy and angry feelings can be diverted, for example, by asking him to stamp hard with his feet, and when he has released his feelings in this way to stamp to the door and back. The teacher continues to involve him in simple energy-releasing tasks that take him further from the place where the upset arose. Most teachers try to manoeuvre the child into the home area and settle him on the sofa, and if he is still feeling angry he is left there to pummel the cushions. As soon as he is calm the teacher or assistant does what she can to make him feel wanted and valued, to re-establish the relationship. Usually he is quickly reassured. They talk about his feelings, and why he felt as he did, and what he should do about it. It is helpful for adult and child to look in the mirror. The child sees himself with the teacher and takes in that he has an angry face but hers is relatively calm. Seeing how angry he looks helps him to objectify his feelings and learn about himself. He begins to calm down. The teacher talks about how they look and the feelings they have, and when the child is himself again he sees how different he looks, and seems relieved. Teacher and child spend a long time looking in the mirror. They talk very quietly and it is very calm and peaceful. At no point is the child criticized or blamed. Episodes of this kind soon disappear. They were more common in children from homes where opportunities were limited, but standards of behaviour were strict and uncompromising and expectations for achievement were high.

Sometimes the temper tantrum escalates so rapidly that all communication is lost and the child becomes completely out of control. The cause may be the frustration of trying to establish and assert his identity, or excitement, or a surge of anxiety or even panic that breaks through his fragile boundaries, or he may need an outlet for unbearable stress at home, or all of these. Whatever the reason, these episodes are crisis points for the child. If handled well they are potentially the basis of a closer and more productive relationship because they demand from the adult close and total involvement. A temper tantrum of this nature is therefore accepted by the teachers and assistants as a necessary contribution to the child's immediate well-being, and his future progress. It may nevertheless be stressful and alarming for the adult involved because the child is awash with uncontrolled feelings that have swept away his precariously held identity. He has no boundaries, no structure, and the adult must provide them. It is therefore of vital importance that the adult does not lose control. If she becomes like the child, angry or frightened and filled with fear and panic, she will not be a secure identity against which he can define his own, and his fears and panic will increase. So he must be held, to contain and restrain him then, and to comfort him later when the storm is over. The other children too, must see that the situation is under control, otherwise anxiety spreads and sometimes panic. But holding the child is not always easy, for many are big for their age, are strong, slippery as eels and move with mercurial speed. Although these explosive outbursts are similar in quality to those normal at an earlier age, they are inevitably far more difficult to deal with, and a method of management has to be devised as soon as possible. Usually it is necessary for both teacher and assistant to be involved, and to act in concert.

Physical management of temper tantrums

The other children know what to do when a serious temper tantrum erupts because the teacher has talked about this when they were quiet and attentive. If necessary, she reminds them again. They move any chairs out of the way, and move away themselves taking their activity with them, and continue with whatever they were doing. If possible, they face away from the scene of action and take no notice. It is usual for the adult nearest the child to grab him. The other adult sizes up the situation, quickly removes any remaining obstructions or dangerous objects, and as soon as possible gets close to the struggling pair and does her best to remove the child's shoes, though this will not be easy. Events during a tantrum vary with the child's physical strength and the extent to which he is out of control. If the tantrum is severe, and the child is doing a lot of damage and is a danger to himself and others, it is advisable to get him into a safer place, usually the home area. This may be physically impossible if the child is big. An alternative is to take the other children outside, but this may not be feasible, as usually two people are needed to manage a serious tantrum. A compromise is to take him or the other children out when the worst is over and one of the adults is available. At this stage the child concerned is becoming more aware of himself, and separating him from the others spares him the shame of being seen in this state, and makes it easier for him to rejoin them when he is calm again. If not kept apart he is likely to feel self-conscious and become excited, fool about and have another tantrum later. By the time he is calm, and is with the others again, usually all of them behave as though nothing had happened.

Although often difficult to manage, a temper tantrum can nevertheless be helpful, for the others take in what is happening and realize that when they have a tantrum they, too, look like that. In spite of instructions to the contrary they stare and openly watch at first. As one child commented, some time after his own tantrums were a thing of the past, 'Miss, I used to be a bit like that', and the teacher remarked that he did not seem to like what he saw. The other children see how the teacher behaves and they realize that she is being controlled and considerate, not punitive or unkind, and this indirectly helps them when they are having a tantrum.

It is important that a child in a tantrum is held, and continues to be held. This is primarily because he needs to be physically contained when emotionally in disorder, but also he might run off and go out of school, and anywhere. So if he manages to free himself he is grabbed. Pursuing the child is whenever possible avoided, but the risk of him running into the road is too great. The other adult therefore guards the door and does everything possible to keep him in the room. Some teachers and assistants lock the door at this point. They dislike doing it, but a child in this state cannot be left on his own. Apart from the danger of being in the road, if he runs off there is no possibility of bringing the episode to completion and restoring the relationship. Later on, at a time when everything is peaceful, it is usual for the teacher to take up all the relevant points with the children as a group. The following descriptions give an idea of the broad sequence of events when a temper tantrum erupts, and the adult's management. The trigger is usually some form of thwarting. It may be 'no' to something the child demands, or restraint of something he is doing, or another child he experiences as a threat. Most tantrums are a direct response to experiences of this kind. In other cases the situation triggers pent-up anxiety and aggression, and sometimes the child seems subconsciously to be looking for a trigger.

If he is not completely out of control an experienced teacher copes calmly with the struggling child, and if necessary clamps his feet between hers for protection. She holds his wrists, partly to control the tantrum, but also to maintain his physical boundaries, for although he resists he needs to feel physically contained, needs to feel physically there even if in himself he has gone to pieces. Physical contact, whether restraining or comforting, is important. The child has 'lost' himself, has lost all communication with others, and physical contact is the first step in gaining his attention and restoring communication and calm. If the teacher is frightened or angry he experiences further loss of support. Still holding him, she tries to attend to any child who comes up to her, for the others in an established group totally ignore minor tantrums. This helps to maintain a matter-of-fact relationship, and with luck the struggling child gives partial attention to this, and might be momentarily drawn in. In other ways she tries to anchor the child in reality by making factual comments, perhaps commenting on the colour of his jersey, or she tries to develop as a conversation any remark he flings out, or coolly asks diverting questions: 'What would you like to play with?' The aim is to maintain contact with reality and, if possible, break into the mounting loss of control. She also comments factually on what is happening: 'You are feeling angry. I am holding your arms.' The child is probably screaming, kicking, biting. This is usual and is accepted as a stage in the development of self-control. The teacher's objective continues to be to keep the situation as 'real' as possible, and so at this point she might ask him to stand up. This deflects his attention and gives him something positive to do. Or she might ask diverting questions and if the moment has been well chosen he replies. If she succeeds in this she might try to limit his wild threshing about by telling him to use his hands, not his feet. The aim is to constrain, limit and channel his aggression, which is now being expressed in random hitting, while at the same time legitimizing it perhaps by offering her own hands for him to hit. This allows the child to show his anger and aggression and is the stage before turning the episode into a game. The teacher has provided an alternative outlet for the child and this has helped her to gain control. She also tries to limit the hurt and damage he could cause by attempting verbally to restrict and direct his physical outburst, and it is usual for a child in a tantrum of this kind to fall in with the teacher's suggestion, even while shouting out, 'No. No'. At this stage the teacher tries to make the situation increasingly 'real' by drawing his attention to her own existence, in the words of a headteacher: 'to recover the person that is lost'.

Ending a tantrum

The ending of a tantrum is important. The child must be helped to accept and forget what has happened, and to know that the relationship and lost self-regard has been restored. The following anecdote describes the way in which a tantrum was brought to completion by the teacher, and illustrates the relevance and importance of the many experiences that are built into a nurture group day. In this group, as in others, the teacher engages the children a great deal in simple hand games, which typically are introduced when the children are all together in the peace and quiet of the home area. The hand games are shared, intimate and enjoyable experiences in which skin contact and purposeful touch is made in fun, and is associated with a close and supportive relationship with the adult. This is important, because a child in a tantrum has to be held, and although this physical contact is initially resisted the earlier association with a secure and supportive relationship helps to make it tolerable and acceptable. These hand games are important also because a certain amount of aggression is allowed, but is controlled by the rules of the game. In one of these games the children in turn hit the teacher's hands, and she their's, in play. When one of the children in this group was having a tantrum, towards the end she offered her hands for him to hit. This distracted him, was a way of making skin and eye contact, and provided an alternative in movement that legitimized and controlled his aggression. It gave him something positive to do, and was a familiar activity associated with happy experiences and happy feelings in the home area. It was also part of a more elaborate game, and the teacher could lead him further into this game which, because of its greater complexity, diverted his attention from his angry feelings. So when the teacher extended her hands the child placed his on hers. He was familiar with this ritual and knew what to do. He clapped hard. This was allowed, as it was felt to be a legitimate way for the child to assert himself and maintain his self-regard. He then tried to run off but the teacher pulled him back. He was about to clap again, hard, but the teacher controlled his aggression by saying, 'One second. I'm not ready'. The pause was momentary, but this time he gently put his hands on those of the teacher. She was in control, and built in further control by saying, 'Slowly'. In this way, by introducing a familiar activity in which she, too, was involved, the teacher was able to impose manageable constraints and restore equilibrium. At the end of the tantrum episode the teacher and child raised their hands together, fully stretched out, and slowly lowered them again, a movement that demanded considerable self-control. Their eyes met. They were held together in eye contact. They were fully in touch and there was a strong bond between them. They walked quietly out of the room, talking softly. This way of ending the tantrum was idiosyncratic to the child and teacher concerned, but a ritualized ending is usual and teachers stress the importance of this and the comfort it brings to the child. It is important because he learns that it completes the episode, and so anticipates that the ending will come and that he will be attached to the teacher again.

When the tantrum is over

Tantrums typically are followed by a quiet period. If the child has not been completely out of control he is likely to be receptive to comments at this stage, and so the adult explains to him what has happened. She puts into words what it was that provoked him to explode, and helps him to understand why he was provoked. She comments on his feelings: 'You were angry.' Hand in hand they look at the damage, not in a mood of criticism, but for him to take it in. He is likely to be subdued and afraid. Another child may be more self-aware and more aware of the adult, and feels ashamed, embarrassed and guilty. He needs reassurance, perhaps by telling him that he is often good, but today he is angry. He cannot help feeling angry at times, and she does not mind when he is angry, but next time he is angry he must go where he cannot hurt anyone, and stamp and kick there. If her arms, legs or clothes showed signs of the struggle she might show him. Together they go to the corner and the adult stamps in good humour, and he stamps too. Finally: 'You were angry. Dry your tears. You feel better now.' The aim when talking about the tantrum afterwards with the child is to convey that she cares about him even though he has bad feelings and tantrums. At the same time she makes him aware of the consequences of his behaviour, and the reality of the damage he has done. He is not criticized, but there is the implicit assumption that he wants to grow out of the tantrums, and will. She might go on to develop the idea of give and take. She cannot always have her own way and has to do things she does not want to do, but if you have to do things you do not like you also do things you do like. Or two people might want the same thing and not be willing to share, but they must not get angry and grab. They have to listen to what the other person says and sort it out.

Very severe tantrums

Tantrums in which the child is completely out of control are more difficult to manage. Usually the same kind of simple frustrating incident triggers the outburst. In some cases this seems to provide a release for pent-up frustration and anger that has its origin beyond the immediate situation. The temper tantrum that ensues can be severe, and might go on with only short-lived lulls for an hour or more. The management problems are considerable. The child is extremely difficult to hold, seems completely out of touch with his surroundings and with himself, and sometimes goes berserk and destroys everything in his path. His kicks and bites have superhuman force and he screams, swears, scratches, shouts abuse and hurls anything at hand, frequently yelling, 'You all hate me'. If the tantrum is a very bad and aggressive one, the teacher or assistant attempts to take him outside. He is held, but struggles, thrashes around and probably knocks some furniture over. 'Let me go.' 'When you've quietened down.' 'Let me go.' 'If you stop struggling I will let you go.' If he shouts 'Yes. Yes', not necessarily indicating that he will stop struggling, he is trusted, but the adult lets go one arm only, talking to him all the time, saying: 'I am letting you go, but you must keep still.' If he renews his struggles when one arm is released, the arm is grabbed and held once again. This might be repeated two or three times. 'When you've quietened down, we'll talk about it. We'll talk about it and sort it out.'

Discussion is not helpful at this stage because the child is not capable of giving attention. It might be three-quarters of an hour before he quietens down but he eventually gives up, worn out and panting, exhausted, limp, and damp with sweat. He cries. At this point he might go into the corner, or sit in an armchair, screwed up, legs drawn up to his chin, perhaps sucking his thumb. After a tantrum the children want to be on their own for five or ten minutes. They are withdrawn and anti-everything. A frequent comment is 'I don't care;' but they seem sad and even while saying this might cry. 'Would you like . . . ?' 'No.' 'Would you . . . ?' 'No.' It is best to leave a child when in this mood, but very soon he is approachable, cuddles up and can be talked to. The adult mops his brow, a piece of plaster or a bandage might be put on, and on the adult too, as a reminder of the consequences of a tantrum and part of the process of reconciliation. Sometimes she dabs perfume on, or both adult and child have a wash. After a tantrum, they might go for a little walk around the school, looking at the pictures on the walls, and the adult keeps a conversation going by talking about them; or the child might cuddle up in sadness and exhaustion and go to sleep. Teachers and assistants like to keep the children with them until they are quiet, gentle and responsive, and then they might have a sweet together. Afterwards the wreckage is cleared up, but how this is done is a matter of judgement. If the child has no concept of himself the teacher would probably clear up by herself. Children who are more self-aware, and feel embarrassed and ashamed or angry also would not be expected to clear up. The adults or the other children would clear up leaving no physical evidence of the tantrum, rather than risk further humiliation or nega-tivism in the child. Often the most reassuring and comforting way, partic-ularly if the child feels guilty, is for the adult and child to clear up together when the upset is over and he feels calm, attached and dependent, though sometimes he feels better if he does it by himself, by way of restitution.

After a bad outburst, particularly if more than one child is involved, the children may not be in a state to take in any talk about what had hap-pened. The scene in the classroom may nevertheless be idyllic with chil-dren, who shortly before were totally out of control, sitting at the teacher's feet, drained of life and very dependent and loving. Later there is talk about what happened, what started it off, the feelings they had, and what they can do about it. Next time they suddenly feel full of these feelings they must pick up the cushion and thump that, or bang their fists on the floor, or clench them and say how angry they feel. If they want to they can go and tell the teacher or assistant how angry they feel, and what it was that made them angry. Bad language is accepted as the next stage in learn-ing self-control, but some teachers suggest something inconsequential and humorous for them to say.

Together they work out what happened

The precipitating cause of these outbursts is in many cases very simple, and the teacher works on it later. With older children, whether involved in fights or tantrums, more discussion is possible and it is usual for this to involve the whole group. The teacher helps the children with the words they need, and every child has a chance to say what happened. Gradually the children become aware of their behaviour, and try to control them-selves. They seem to know that the teacher is providing a learning experi-ence. After criticism, where before they would have a tantrum, they have said, 'I'm not having a tantrum'. This change happens because the teacher and assistant provide support and reassurance, put everything into words, and are consistent in their response. The children take in that the adults do not get angry and are not punitive. They accept their requirements and begin to learn to regulate their own behaviour. When this stage is reached they seem more aware of themselves: one child when seeing another in a tantrum said: 'Miss, it's a nice feeling, being good.' But anger in the adult can be helpful when the child is giving vicious vent to angry feelings, and knows what he is doing, and is capable of doing better.

Fights

The children who get into fights are more easily provoked and for less rational reasons than is usual for their age, and the situation holds for them fewer, if any, implicit constraints. Any controls they have internalized are not sufficient to contain their distress and fury, and it erupts into a fight.

Although fights frequently have their origin in distress of one kind or another, this is not always so. Some of the children, particularly if older, are well organized at a level of basic survival. They are alert to defend themselves from anything they sense as potential attack, forestall this by attacking first and retaliation follows. With lightning speed the whole group can be involved, bodies and chairs hurtle across the room and any equipment close at hand is seized and used as a weapon.

Fights are difficult to deal with because the children quickly get out of control, have more than usual strength and 'There is hate in their eyes and they kick to kill' (a junior teacher). They can do a great deal of damage to each other and to the furnishings and equipment. The wear and tear on the adults is considerable, particularly in junior groups where aggressive behaviour is more likely to erupt and the children are bigger and stronger.

Fights are not acceptable and have to stop

Fortunately, children who have reached the level of purposeful fights have some concept of themselves in relation to others, and to some extent can follow an explanation and grasp a simple sequence of events. So from the beginning, when the children are in the home area or at the table having their milk and biscuits, there is firm talk about fights, and the things that upset them, and the teacher makes clear that fights are not acceptable and have to stop. She puts their feelings into words. This draws their attention to unacknowledged feelings, and identifies them, and they become more aware of their feelings and are better able to control them. Positive suggestions are given that are alternatives to hitting out or fighting, in the hope that a constructive response will eventually be built in. It is useful to ritualize fighting, and some schools have formal play fights with special gear, rituals and rules. If there is a flare-up in the group, and indications that a fight might break out, the children are encouraged to turn the incident into a game. The aggression is controlled because it is formalized by the introduction of rules, as when they are required to stop at the end of each round and start again only when a signal is given, or they are expected to keep inside a chalk square. The children pay attention to the imposed conditions, and accept them. The rules and ritual interest the children who are watching and they concentrate on the rules rather than the fight, and exercise control by seeing that the rules are kept, and insist that they are kept. The 'gear' involved is simple, perhaps no more than coloured games bands to serve as a uniform and kept in a special place. Turning a primitive fight into a contest with rules puts a controlling brake on the children, slows them down and helps to contain their aggression which now has a legitimate outlet and is not immediately discharged in unacceptable action. It also provides limits, and accepting and remembering the limits helps them to keep their feelings under control. When other children are fighting, they will be the ones to impose and maintain the limits, and this reinforces their own limits because of the satisfaction of providing limits for others. Experience of the double process of imposing and accepting limits helps them to internalize controls, and to internalize a notion of authority that is more subtle than one of unilateral power. This way of managing fights demonstrates a fundamental process in the functioning of nurture groups. The teacher and assistant accept the child's level of development but build in tolerable constraints.

If possible, fights are prevented

The teacher and the assistant are constantly alert to any incident that could escalate and whenever possible they prevent fights by their rapid intervention. But fights do break out and, as with tantrums, the other children ignore them, move away and carry on with their activities. Some of these children are liable to get into fights themselves at other times, but they are greatly affronted when their activities are disturbed by fights, and they complain. This is a useful learning experience, for they see what a fight is like, and the aftermath, and get some understanding of the implications for others, and the reason for the teacher's 'no fighting' rule. What happens next depends on the potential violence of the fight. If the teacher and assistant feel, from their experience of the children concerned, that they are likely to do little more than punch each other and cry, and will cause little destruction in the room, they are left. They give their attention and interest to the children who are playing and working. Minor injuries, complaints and appeals to the adults for retribution are ignored or rejected. If it is necessary to tend an injury, no tenderness or sympathy is expressed, and any feeling shown is of displeasure. An exception is made where the fight is clearly unfair, either because one child is being attacked without cause, or he is at a severe disadvantage because of size and strength. If the fight continues at an infantile passionate level but is not completely out of hand, the teacher might try to influence the situation indirectly by collecting the other children together for a story, and in some groups sweets might be handed round. The aim is to create a close-knit family situation in which security and satisfaction are at a high level, with the hope that this peacefulness and the strength of the attachment of these children to the adult will influence the behaviour of those who are fighting. Later the fighters get the interest and attention of the teacher when they are doing something constructive.

Management of fights

If the fight seems to be potentially dangerous, the teacher or assistant or both, sometimes with the help of the other children, move out of the way anything dangerous that could be used as a weapon. Most fights, particularly among older children, become violent. There is risk of injury, and if the adults know that the children concerned will 'fight to the death' (a teacher), it will be necessary to try to separate them and hold them, usually by each one standing behind a child, arms clasped round his elbows, thus pinning his arms back. As with temper tantrums, the adults avoid the full force of a kick. The children, however, remain face to face and get relief for their feelings by snarling and spitting at each other. Each adult speaks quietly to the child, close to his ear, giving simple, positive calming instructions. It is important that teachers and assistants learn the knack of physically disengaging and holding the children, if possible removing their shoes while remaining emotionally uninvolved and calm; and they try to look calm, for if they betray anxiety, distress or anger the situation is likely to worsen. Once the fighters have been separated, either by both adults restraining the children, or one holding the aggressor while the other removes his shoes, one of them may feel satisfied and ready to give up, but the other might still be angry. He no longer has an outlet for his feelings and is liable to flare up into a temper tantrum. For about 15 minutes after the children are released he needs undivided attention. The adult concerned is alert to his feelings and at an appropriate moment when he seems more responsive might offer to read him a story. Gradually he is left and would probably go about with a scowl, but the mood slowly dissipates. Typically the children concerned avoid each other for a time but are soon together again, the upset forgotten. Sometimes, after a bad fight, a child who is still enraged is sent outside to 'cool off.' This is done in a neutral, matter-of-fact way. The usual practice is to keep the door open so that he still has contact with the group, though physically distanced from it.

Afterwards they talk about the incident

Afterwards the teacher asks: 'Why did it happen?' She brings the children involved into the discussion and she and the assistant help them to see how it happened and what went wrong. They look at the problem from everyone's perspective and put it into words for them. They give everyone a chance to talk. This has to be strictly controlled because they are all likely to talk at once. It is always everyone else's fault and they sit and fume as they hear the lies all the others tell. They protest and are outraged, and when their turn comes the others protest and are outraged. They are not allowed to interrupt. Each child is heard out and his version is pieced together no matter how long it takes. The teacher marshals the evidence and pulls it together, and remains with the children until it is sorted out and feelings have simmered down. The issue is usually very simple. One child might have been jumped on in friendly exuberance but thought he was being attacked. For the discussion it is preferable for the children to sit on hard chairs to emphasize the serious nature of the occasion, otherwise they are likely to loll about and fidget. Sometimes the situation is made more formal by taking the children into the library. The teacher gets out paper and pencil, writes down everything they say, and reads it back to them in order to gain their full attention and make the situation more important and more real.

With patience and time they can be helped to understand what happened and seem to accept comments such as, 'We won't let that happen again, will we?' They might be fighting again a few days later but the problem does not worsen. Later on, and this might be as long as two terms for some of the more difficult junior children, they are left with the problem after a disturbance, and with minimal direction are able to sort it out for themselves. When the teacher feels they have begun to accept her reasoning, and they complain to her, she tells them she is tired of sorting out their squabbles and that they have to work it out for themselves. Later, as the disputes became more reasonable and involve more complex and subtle issues, they are encouraged to turn to the adult for help.

Fighting does not stop immediately, and might even get worse for a while, and some groups reach a crescendo of bad behaviour, fights and tantrums before suddenly calming down and consolidating. Even when a group appears to have calmed, there may be occasional less serious outbreaks of fighting.

The task for the teacher and assistant in sorting out the disputes that lead to fighting is made easier because the children have a keen sense of fairness. When they understand the point the adult is making, and begin to see that she is impartial and everyone is treated the same way, they accept the sanctions. Nevertheless, for a long time they conform only because of the sanctions and are slow to acknowledge and accept responsibility for their actions.

Satisfying outlets must be provided

Although the fighting has to be controlled because it goes well beyond normal and acceptable limits, satisfying physical outlets must be provided, because opportunities for active play are so limited at home for many of the children. They also sometimes come into school in a highly charged state, often very resentful and angry, and need some means of expressing their feelings. Indoors a trampoline used under controlled conditions, and a punch bag, are helpful for older children. Ideally, however, the nurture group room should open onto a playground, preferably a relatively small and enclosed area where the children can have a run-around when they are irritable and restless. Heavy outdoor nursery-type equipment is useful for the younger children, and footballs for the older ones. Competitive games are not helpful.

Disruptive behaviour is not always extreme

Serious behaviour problems of the kind outlined were a major consideration when the first groups were established, largely because of the nature of the stresses on the local population at that time, and because a substantial proportion of the children were juniors. Not all teachers and assistants will experience problems of this order, particularly those working with younger children.

5

Earliest Learning Experiences

The developing child is shaped by experiences from the moment of birth, and even before. At the earliest stage they come through his close physical and emotional attachment to the mother, and the satisfactions of warmth and food, and with this a sense of well-being. As he begins to explore within the security of a close, holding and sustaining relationship with a supportive, caring, responsive adult his experiences widen and become more complex and organized. The early nurturing relationship the adults provide, and the experiences they make available and support, have essential and fundamental content for the development of a sense of self, interpersonal relationships and cognitive competence.

Earliest needs and interests

The starting point of autonomy is attachment, but it is unusual for children coming into the nurture group to make a normal attachment relationship with the teacher and assistant. Some attach themselves to any adult indiscriminately in seeking affection and attention, or make a strong attachment with one adult and seek reassurance all the time. Typically, however, the children mistrust adults, have profound difficulty in relating to them and no natural desire to please them. Frequently they are indifferent to their presence or may totally ignore them. They rarely make normal eye contact, but glance around indiscriminately, or defensively look away from the teacher or fixedly through her. Many of them dislike physical contact and avoid it, or they actively resist touch and shrug off the teacher's arm. Others accept physical contact, but never show a need for it. Others again tentatively put an arm round the teacher and touch her hand and face, but are self-conscious and uncomfortable, particularly the older infants and juniors, if the other children see them doing this, and withdraw quickly if the teacher gives any sign that she has noticed.

For a small number of children attempts to encourage eye contact and touch are an intolerable intrusion, but for the others this contact is built in purposefully but tentatively and is one of the adults' first aims.

Eye contact

Although few of the children at first make normal eye contact this is usually established fairly quickly, largely because the adults address and look at each child directly and individually, and meticulously respond to any eye contact made by them. Frequently the adult reminds the child, when either is speaking to the other, to look at her and the response is acknowledged with a slight nod or a smile. Fun games involving eye contact are introduced later, to reinforce the requirement. And always, when they are brought together in the home area, eye contact is required as they settle and wait.

Physical contact

Physical contact, too, is avoided at first, but is acceptable to most of the children if initiated in play. The approach on both sides may need to be very tentative initially, perhaps a foot-touching game with shoes on before skin contact is made. In a junior group, where all forms of physical contact had been rejected, foot-shaking when they left at the end of the day was treated as a fun game by the children, and led on to normal skin contact. Contact by touch can often be established very gently during the course of hand games, but for some children reasons may have to be contrived at other times for spontaneous physical contact. Eventually, virtually all the children whatever the level of attachment formed, are drawn into body contact games, and enjoy being lifted up and down and dropped, tickled, swung around, carried piggyback, and thrown. The children who respond quickly to the teacher and assistant are a help to the others, who see that this contact is satisfying and safe. Nevertheless, it may be a long time before some of them can be drawn in.

When the children are able to acknowledge the teacher and assistant with their eyes and to make and accept contact through touch, both juniors and infants readily come to sit on the adult's lap, making an affectionate physical relationship. Many of them spontaneously kiss the teacher and assistant, and some insist on a kiss and a hug when they leave them, even if only going out at playtime.

The need for physical contact

The need for physical contact with the teacher and assistant is a general one in the infant groups and is seen with equal intensity in some of the junior children. This is a fleeting and transient need in some, but in others is more continuing and demanding. The nature of the need and the level of the contact varies. In some children it seems primarily a need for reassurance and affection, and the pleasure of showing affection, while others seem to need to attach themselves passively, to saturate themselves in comfort, peace and well-being. Some children physically cling to the adult. Sometimes, when the teacher reads to a child on her lap, the others draw close and put their hands round her neck and snuggle up, or lean towards her and slip onto her lap. There might be three or four draped over her, while others sit on the floor by her feet and feel her toes, or run their fingers round and round her shoes. They often stroke the teacher or assistant and murmur their pleasure. Some of the children at times seem totally absorbed in the adult's appearance. They brush her hair and all the time they are brushing it they are feeling it. They pull it back and look at her, or arrange it with loving care. They remark on the colour of her eyes, notice her earrings and are aware of her perfume and like to put it on. The child lying on the adult's lap while she is telling a story seems even closer. He touches her earrings and feels them, and plays with her necklace. He follows her fingers with his as they move, strokes her hair and pulls it, lifts it up and allows it to fall, holds it up and looks through it, smoothes it back behind her ears or ruffles it into a fringe. Or he examines the hairs on her skin or runs his nails under hers and might suck the ends of her hair. Sometimes the children feel her and squeeze her flesh. They tug her hair, open and close her eyes, pull and twist her nose, and like her to blow on their faces. Some of them at times seem to lose themselves in the adult, and physical boundaries merge. A 7-year-old girl sat on the assistant's knee, sucking her thumb and twiddling her hair, and when this was pinned back she continued to suck her thumb and twiddled the assistant's hair.

Others sit on the floor, and look up at her devotedly, drinking in her appearance. They need to be close to her, and to hold her hands or sit on her knee. They seem physically one with her and when she moves, they move. Other children sit at her feet absorbed in a toy, and although not attending to the adult or to the story, they are aware that she is there and they need her to be there.

Recapturing the baby state

Other children from time to time and perhaps only fleetingly seem to need to attach themselves as a baby would, and are like babies or young toddlers in the way they behave. These features are particularly marked in some of the children described as aggressive and disruptive. Descriptions of these children, whether juniors or infants, are remarkably similar. As they lie in the grown-up's arms being cradled and rocked, they stretch out their hands and push into them with movements that are baby-like and undirected. They seem without conscious awareness of what they are doing, but intense concentration is quite common. They are rough at first, but as they take in the experience they become more gentle. Teachers and assistants have commented that this is not exploration, and 'they seem to be taking in the warmth, taking in what a living person is, and with their touching movements discovering life in the mother' (an assistant). Both teachers and assistants describe some of the children as clinging and moulding to their bodies as young babies do. They try to reach out, and when they touch, they hang on, 'They seem like six-week-old babies' (an assistant). A baby-like suckling posture is occasionally described, and a rhythmic curling of the feet. Sometimes the children slip into baby babbling sounds and gurgle and coo, and the adult slips into baby sounds too. Many of the children suck their fingers or thumbs, or they put everything into their mouths. Occasionally a child's behaviour is more purposeful and he uses a towel as a nappy, or asks to have one put on saying he is the teacher's baby and that he has wet himself, and he lies back in satisfaction when a towel is pinned on. Or he climbs onto the teacher's lap with the doll's bottle and behaves as though a baby and sucks from the bottle and wants to be wrapped in the doll's shawl. Sometimes they try to put on the baby clothes, and in one group, where plastic rompers were kept in the dressing-up box, they put these on over the nappies, climbed onto the bed and sucked from the bottle. The other children seem unconcerned by behaviour of this kind; they accept it and treat them as babies in their family play.

Many of the children like to be picked up, and carried around for long periods by the adult, straddle fashion or on her hip, and might go into school assembly like this. Some of them climb into the pram, even in junior groups, and might adopt a curled up baby-like posture and show great satisfaction when pushed around by the teacher. Sometimes they reach out of the pram, or they throw things out repeatedly and the teacher picks them up each time. Some of them when playing on the floor sit in one place with their legs sprawled apart, and stretch out for a toy, and pull it towards themselves without moving their bodies in relation to the toy. And they crawl around on their hands and knees, babbling and jabbering, pulling themselves along, or they walk in an uncoordinated way, fingers in mouth, and they pick things up and give them to the teacher, or bang noisily and happily on the table. Children like this need to be 'fed' with things that occupy them. They enjoy playing with the rattle, and sit there and shake it and they enjoy squashing the squeaky toys. At other times they hide in the dressing-up box, or they find a hidey-hole and curl up in it.

A developmental progression from the baby stage is seen to a striking extent in children who seem out of contact when admitted to the group, are stiff in their movements and make very little response, and in those who are more involved but interfere with the others and readily erupt into temper tantrums. The children 'egress' through these stages very quickly. The 'baby' stage is truly a baby stage. The children are not being babyish, nor are they role-playing babies. They *are* babies, in the behavioural characteristics they show. Features of this kind have been seen most clearly in children who, from the evidence available, have been markedly restricted at home when they were beginning to be physically mobile.

More usually, baby behaviour takes longer to appear and lasts intermittently for a longer time. These children are developmentally more advanced, and are more accurately described as regressing to an earlier stage rather than egressing to a later one.

Immature mannerisms are sometimes seen, even in a junior child. When he has learned not to shout in the adult's face and interrupt he prods her wrist and tugs at her sleeve, or he seizes her face in his hands and vigorously turns it to meet his gaze. But when she holds out her hand without speaking, he holds it and waits.

Baby and toddler behaviour is usually short-lived

Baby and toddler features rarely dominate a child's behaviour. Usually baby features are relatively short-lived, and a child might be at this level for 20 minutes or so in the group, and be throwing stones and swearing in the playground later on. Typically this stage is fairly quickly outgrown, and a child showing this behaviour to a marked extent goes from baby attachment to moving along on his bottom, in less than a month. Such children are usually ready to go into a mainstream class within a year, by which time they will have learned to tolerate interference and upsets, often after a period of tantrums. The following description, of a child who went rapidly through these early stages, was provided by his teacher.

> From the first or second day in the nurture group Ricky behaved like a baby of nine months. He sat like a baby, his face expressive and animated, with the toys around him, and enjoyed throwing them onto the floor for the teacher or assistant to pick up. He babbled and gurgled, crawled about making baby noises, used single exclamations by way of comment, and enjoyed simple games like peek-a-boo. He liked to be near the adults, pulled at them to attract their attention and enjoyed physical contact. He didn't involve himself with the other children but watched them, fascinated. Otherwise he played by himself, repetitively and unimaginatively, with simple toys and objects, sometimes throwing or dropping them, talking to himself a great deal. The baby phase lasted only one or two weeks. After that he was more active, and played in the home-play area conversing and role-playing. He painted, and played with the cars and Lego, sand, water and Play-Doh, interacting to some extent with the other children, and was friendly and likeable. He was affectionate with the teacher and assistant and tried hard to please, but always seemed on the verge of a tantrum or explosion.

It has been remarked by teachers and assistants that a 'fantastic' relationship develops with children who go through these early stages: 'We seem to sense each other's feelings' (a teacher).

Different levels of relationships

Most of the children make a close relationship with both adults but in the physical attachments they make appear to be expressing different levels of need. In some infant groups virtually all the children make a close baby or toddler level of attachment, and this is seen also in junior children, but less often. In other groups a close warm relationship, as with a child in the nursery, is more usual. The age of the adult might be a factor, for some of the children seem to form a closer relationship with the older one, but a settled personal life or the maturity to bear with an unsettled one, is probably more important. It may also be that baby and toddler behaviour is more often shown with women than with men, though the expectations these children have of men may be a relevant factor.

They have to learn to share the teacher

This close contact, at whatever level, means a great deal to the children, and their need for this can be met remarkably well in a group, though they often look glum when another child is on the teacher's lap and might even have a tantrum. If a child becomes more insistent in his demands, as when his situation at home breaks down, some of the others get jealous, and even junior children have complained that they never get a chance to sit on her lap. The teacher is alert to their feelings and puts into words what they feel at these times. This makes evident that her feelings are close to theirs and that she recognizes their needs. And in making explicit the need to share, the children become more aware of their feelings and the needs of others, and this helps them to accept that the others need affection and attention, too.

Sensory experiences

An important aspect of the baby and toddler behaviour shown by the children is their need to touch, feel and experience at a sensory level. Textures, colours, sound, movement, all these things attract them often more than the object itself, and juniors as well as infants have spent long periods of time absorbing these simple experiences. The feel of materials generally is important, whether a blanket, a towel, the mop in the sink, piles of fabric of different kinds – or hair. They seem to need to lose themselves in these basic perceptual experiences. They become totally absorbed in them and need unlimited time to assimilate fully their sensory content without any pressure to use them more constructively. And they need to enjoy these experiences over and over again. To some children their basic qualities seem a discovery. At first they stroke the materials, feel them, put their faces into them and sometimes smell them, though some of the children scrunch them up at first, or throw them about. All these things they need to experience and share with the adult, as a young toddler would with his mother. 'Mother' enjoys these experiences with the child, 'mother' and child share and express their feelings and 'This is the real pleasure' (the first infant nurture teacher). Any use of language to name and analyse is incidental.

They also seem to need the experience of the feel of clay, not with the specific aim of shaping it, but for the pleasure of squashing their hands in its formless softness. They enjoy, too, the slippery feel of paint on their hands and the squelchy sound it makes, and they watch as the paint drops from their hands onto the paper and then splodge it around with joy. Many of the children give the impression of not having had sufficient opportunity to 'mess' in this way and they need this experience. They need also the pleasure of simple powerful action, thus being the agent of noise and change, for example by tearing up newspapers or banging on a drum, and they look up expectantly as though hoping the teacher will appreciate the daring and will share the fun.

Sand, too, is important for both juniors and infants. They need to feel the cold roughness of wet sand; and those who are advanced enough to use dry sand need the freedom to scoop and pour it, and feel it running through their fingers, before they explore its properties by using beakers, funnels and sieves. They spend long periods of time engaged in these simple repetitive activities. And they make castles and moats, and run their cars around and around, experiencing the same simple pleasure over and over again. Water, also, is important, and they have been totally absorbed at the sink or water trough, splashing it onto their faces, endlessly pouring it, dunking the small toys and watching them surface, shaking a bottle of water and holding it up to the sunshine, sometimes exclaiming with joy. Others experiment with blowing bubbles, and finding out which things will float. Sand and water nevertheless afford too little constraint for many of the children; they fling the sand about, put it in each other's hair, and scoop the water onto the floor. Strict supervision is necessary with clear rules and limits. For some of the children more basic experiences come first: pounding the clay, squeezing wet sand, crashing the cars, pushing and pulling heavy toys in the playground, or tugging and pushing games with the adult. The children are able to lose themselves in these simple activities if an adult is with them, or is nearby while they play. Many of the children use materials in an undifferentiated way and this is a major factor in their indiscriminate and destructive use of materials and equipment in the classroom. They need the opportunity for legitimate experiences of this kind, and to share their pleasure with the adult.

Junior children, on the whole, appear to have less need to saturate themselves in basic early experiences. More often they plunge into experiences and grab.

Other-person physical interest

This need is seen in their interest in hair. They are unusually interested in the feel of hair, particularly the adults' hair. Boys and girls like to stroke it and feel it. They comb it, and all the time they are combing it they are feeling it, and arranging it in place. Some of them fleetingly stroke each others' hair and occasionally they comb it, and later, when they are able to play together, they play hairdressers with each other. Some children have shown an intense and uninhibited interest in the physical appearance of the teacher and assistant. The first infant teacher was from India. Her sari revealed a mole in the middle of her back which the children felt and examined with care. Children in another infant group remarked, with objective loving interest, on the fine hair on the teacher's face. She reacted with rueful affection.

Body-centred interests

An intensely absorbing and often excited interest in their bodies and its functions is shown by some of the children, and they express their interest and recount their observations and experiences in vivid, uninhibited detail. This interest is largely self-involved, but they readily identify with each other at this basic level and live each others' experiences, sometimes with avid pleasure. The children in the first nurture groups established were almost all at an overall pre-nursery level and this interest in bodies was very striking, and with the older children was particularly powerful. It was more than the substance of a monologue that was of interest to the others. It was the stuff of their conversation, and at the beginning of the year they talked together about 'willies' and 'titties', 'doo-doos' and 'shit-bottoms' and 'how shit comes out' and they giggled and laughed, sometimes with excitement. Everything was 'smelly' and 'pooh-pooh', there was bawdy talk of 'rip-a-bottom' and they made rude noises and held their noses and walked round imaginary 'plops' on the floor with exaggerated distaste. This awareness of bodies and the functions of bodies was close to the surface in some of the children. For the more aggressive ones it was a way of expressing their destructive feelings: 'I will squeeze your titties.' In the same junior group they made plasticine 'willies' to wee over the others, and 'doo-doos' to put on another child's book, and they crouched low and pointed to their bottoms and made noises. Much of this talk and behaviour, although primitive and aggressive in intent, was naive, but some of the children were destructively vicious in their comments, and this was readily translated into vicious acts. There was naive and uninhibited interest, too, in both infant and junior groups, in the shapes that show beneath clothes, and the children talked together about their mothers' 'boobs' and vied with each other for size, and pulled out their sweaters to show. These interests were largely ephemeral and soon passed away, and lively involvement one week had disappeared without trace by the next. With few exceptions their talk had an open quality. It was naughty talk and they looked for a reaction.

Sexual interest

Some children showed more direct sexual interest. They undressed the dolls, inspected them and sometimes put them in bed together, one on top of the other, and they rocked them and laughed and giggled. Some of them acted this together, openly, with gales of laughter from others nearby. Although much of their talk and play seemed no more than child-ish interest and excitement, this was not always so. The sexual interests of some of the children were more sophisticated, and seemed to derive from the realities of home, and television, porn magazines and videos. They were knowledgeable and matter-of-fact in their role-play in the home-play area and in the observations they made. Uninhibited basic earthy personal questions, disconcerting in the attitudes and life experience they revealed, have been crudely put to the adult: 'Did he have it up you last night, Miss?' But their talk on the whole was not personalized and only rarely were their observations and questions directed to the teacher and assistant, and hardly at all as time went on. The extent to which their developing regard for the teacher and assistant influenced the crude attitudes sometimes expressed was illustrated by their reaction to a 9-year-old boy. He had cut out pictures of young women in swimsuits from an assortment of maga-zines in the classroom, making crude comments as he did so. They all gig-gled. One of the other boys suddenly said: 'Don't be silly. Miss wears a bather like that.' The giggling ceased instantly.

In a few children, boys and girls, the sexual interest shown is of a dif-ferent order. There is a marked component of more overt and intense sex-ualized involvement, occasionally shown in histrionic posturing or overt sexual display and invitation, and sometimes sexualized excitement is an element in their aggressive physical attacks on each other. These children are usually from markedly disturbed backgrounds and have widespread and severe problems, and in some cases there is known to be a history of sexual abuse. In the safe and secure environment of the nurture group, some children will disclose and even exhibit sexual behaviour. Established procedures for child protection must be followed.

Kim, aged 5, was timid, insecure, anxious and lacking in interest and self-con-fidence; she was very dependent on adults, desperately needed affection and reassurance and quickly sought physical contact. Sexual behaviour, which had been occasional and covert in her mainstream class was soon openly expressed. She would get on top of one of the other children, girls or boys, and kiss them passionately. Sometimes she drew a boy's hand under her skirt and would egg him on, and then hit him, saying, 'no, not now'. She made excellent and rapid progress, socially and with her formal school work, but continued to be overtly sexual in the way she walked and she often looked at herself in the mirror in a seductive way.

Gerry, rising 8, showed baby behaviour as well as sexual excitement. In his mainstream class he was disruptive, aggressive and out of control. In the nur-ture group he was at first aimless and uninhibited, overexcited at times, immature and disruptive in a 'niggly, childish way'. In his second term his baby needs were very marked. He needed to be rocked and cuddled and enjoyed finger play on the adult's lap, was shy and coy when praised and pulled at the teacher's hair. He was also sexually excited from time to time. On one occasion he had an erection and charged about the room, simulating sex with a doll. On another occasion he mounted one of the boys in the group (both slept with their mothers and were thought to have witnessed sex). And in the playground he put his hand up the skirt of one of the girls, yelling 'smell my hand', and he burst into screaming excitement as he shouted 'push it up'. This child, when seen later by the writer after he had moved from his infant school to his new junior school some distance away, seemed markedly depressed, and his only comment was, 'Miss T. (his nurture teacher) was kind to me'. This school, too, had a nurture group but the head-teacher said he didn't need to be in it.

The attitude of the teacher and assistant to these issues varies with the nature of the behaviour and is essentially that of the parent with a much younger child. Immature naive sexual interest is treated with tolerance, but a watching eye is kept for 'play' that it too intense and protracted, or is deliberately out of sight. The teacher and assistant then distract or divert, or change the situation or the combination of children that encourages this behaviour, while avoiding disapproval. The overtly sexualized behaviour that occurs exceptionally in particular children is of a different order, not only for the child but for the adults too. They react with anxiety, confusion and embarrassment and sometimes alarm, uncertain of what to do, but instinctively deflect, skirt round or deflate the event, and in their different ways convey to the child that this is not appropriate behaviour. Close affectionate physical contact is a problem in these cases because it may become sexualized. The assistant in a junior school, seeing a 9-year-old boy on the teacher's lap, commented: 'That's not baby stuff; that's sex.' Where the child is exposed at home to sexually stimulating experiences that are overt, and in some cases sadistically provocative, it is usually in the context of severe and general stress, and the resources of the short-term neighbourhood nurture group are unlikely to effect lasting change.

Whatever the nature of the difficulties, the aim in the nurture group is to channel the child's interest and attention into relationships and activities that are developmentally relevant and so will give satisfaction. In all but a few cases the children's behaviour very soon gives the adults no cause for concern.

Physical self-care

Some of the children lack basic skills and have difficulty with simple tasks such as washing and drying their hands. As with every new learning experience the adult breaks the task down into stages and verbalizes in specific detail, with encouraging comments at every step taken. 'Push up your sleeves.' 'Put the plug in the bowl.' 'Turn on the warm water tap.' 'Put your hands in the water to make them wet.' 'Take the soap.' 'Rub it between your hands, like this.' 'Put the soap back.' 'Rub the soap into your hands all over. Don't forget the backs and round the nails'. 'Make a good lather', and so on. Some children also need help in managing themselves when they go to the toilet. Table equipment presents difficulties for many of them. Some need to be shown how to manage the food, whether eating a piece of toast or getting a spoonful of jelly into their mouths without losing it on the way.

'Transitional objects', a term coined by Winnicott

The children's close relationship with the teacher and assistant is given spontaneous expression in the use some of them make of their personal things, which seem to be a source of security, comfort and control. Young children at home, and sometimes very much older ones, commonly take an old battered doll or even a special piece of cloth to bed with them, and we learn that in the case of Indian children this is sometimes an old sari of their mother's. For the children these objects are invested with feeling over and above their intrinsic value as well loved playthings. In a very real sense they represent the child's emotional roots, in particular his attachment to his mother, and the security and strength that derives from this. Their importance as reassuring 'comfort' objects in the nurture group is illustrated by the child who 'adopted' a shawl. She not only asked frequently for the teacher to wrap her in it, but insisted that it must not be washed. Such things serve the same function as the 'transitional objects' described by Winnicott (1971) and are particularly important to nurture children when they are beginning to manage on their own without the immediate support of the adults. They take personal things from the adult to wear, often jewellery and detachable garments such as shawls or scarves, and they use them as though they feel them to be part of the adult. They have special meaning because they are invested with the idea and feeling of 'teacher' or 'assistant'. Normally the child would actively seek them. Two examples arising in the first term of the first infant group demonstrate their importance.

Victor was lying on his teacher's lap. He touched her earrings and felt them, asked if could wear them and went into Assembly with them on. All the children had been interested in their teacher's earrings, and had lovingly commented that they were nice. One by one they wore the earrings, taking turns and sharing them all day long. This was the first instance of sharing in this group. In a very real sense they were sharing the teacher because the earrings represented her presence and her support.

Lucy, the most difficult girl in the group, ran out from the play centre when she saw her teacher leaving at the end of the day, and asked for a kiss. The teacher kissed her lightly, not wanting to leave lipstick on her face. 'No', said Lucy, 'kiss me properly. I want your lipstick.' This anecdote vividly illustrates the importance to the children of something they can take with them that is an intimate part of the teacher.

Junior children too sometimes show this need. Tom, at playtime pulled off his teacher's scarf which he wore round his neck, and he put the scarf ring on his finger.

These naturally arising links with the adult are of great value, for they not only provide satisfaction, well-being and security but carry also the teacher's expectations and standards. They are thus objects of control as well as comfort. They are enabling objects, for they help the child to function by himself at a higher and more organized level than might otherwise be possible. Because of their importance in these ways they are often deliberately introduced by the teacher, and are accompanied by a verbal message. These verbal messages are, by association with the object, a more sophisticated form of transitional object, and their function is a more explicit monitoring of the child's behaviour. At the simplest level the teacher would make a comment about being tidy when she tied on the child's painting apron. Comment and apron would, in effect, be tied on together. Other situations have more complex content, as the following three anecdotes illustrate:

Billy was 9. His behaviour shows how transitional objects at different levels helped him to become less dependent on the teacher. As is so often the case, he was one of the more 'aggressive' children, and during his first few weeks in the group made no attachments and was markedly antisocial. At the time concerned, however, he had become extremely dependent on his teacher, would follow her around, cling to her, and lie for long periods on her lap. The teacher initiated the process of loosening him from this close emotional dependency by cuddling on her knee during storytime a large gonk she had brought into school, and Billy cuddled up on her knee, too. He became attached to the gonk, and after a few days if it wasn't there he looked for it, sat with it, plaited its hair, and wound its arms together or around his wrist. The gonk became important to him, perhaps because it was closely associated with the teacher. It satisfied his need for her affection and he no longer needed constantly to sit on her lap. His teacher further helped him to separate by giving him her scarf to wear. At first he followed her around, wearing her scarf, and then joined in with the others still wearing her scarf; and he sat quietly on her chair while she attended to the others, wearing her scarf. Later on she deliberately left the classroom for a few minutes to see how the children would manage without her, and to help Billy she indicated her chair, and said: 'Keep my place warm. I won't be long.' Her words created a feeling of attachment, support and control, and physical warmth, and Billy also had a sense of caring for the teacher by keeping her place warm. She reacted with startled surprise to the writer's comment: 'beautiful'. She had not been aware of the import of what she had said. This is another example of the spontaneity and unselfconscious quality of the work. At about this time Billy and another boy began to show interest in the dolls. They bathed one of them, washed her hair, dried her with the towels, and the teacher helped them to comb her hair. They wrapped a blanket round her to keep her warm, and when it was milk and biscuits time Billy cuddled her and gave her food. With the teacher's help he had moved from having baby needs to satisfying baby needs.

A remarkable example of the significance to the child of a transitional object provided to help him manage on his own was described by the teacher of an infant group. The anecdote concerned Stuart, a 6-years-old boy, again one of the most aggressive children in the group. He was being 'weaned' into his mainstream class and from time to time was there for half a day. On the occasion concerned his teacher, as was customary, gave him one of her bracelets to provide support. Instead of going off to his class he lingered, and said: 'Please can I have two bracelets today. There are two difficult things to do.' There were two difficult things to do because it was a rainy day, and he was not only going into his mainstream class but would be there during a wet playtime. This anecdote vividly illustrates the remarkable insight Stuart had into his awareness of stress and his need for extra help, and the significance to him of the transitional object provided by the teacher.

'Transitional objects' are proffered to provide comfort, support and control

Because of the support provided by an object of this kind, teachers have found it useful to provide something for all the children when a big new class experience is planned. The incident now described is from the first year of the first junior group established, and occurred early in the first term. It illustrates the children's lack of control at that time, and the elemental feelings that surge through them when exposed to new, exciting and stimulating experiences. It highlights the need to plan and control events to ensure they are manageable, and demonstrates the importance of describing in detail beforehand the anticipated happenings and the feelings they are likely to have. When prepared in this way the children are less likely to lose control, and something given personally by the teacher to take with them not only provides support but reinforces and keeps in mind the teacher's expectation for controlled behaviour.

The swimming trip

Soon after the beginning of the term the headteacher arranged to take a group of 12 children from the mainstream classes to a neighbouring school for swimming. The occasion was pleasant and orderly, and everyone had an enjoyable afternoon. The children followed instructions, behaved well, and in the changing rooms no one was distracted by anyone else, or interfered. The following week the headteacher included eight extra children from the nurture group. They were extremely excited, seemed overstimulated by the experience and were uninhibited in the comments they made and the language they used. Two of the boys put up their fingers and repeatedly shouted 'fuck off' to the children from the host school when they passed by. After changing, the boys on one side of the screen and the girls on the other, the children from the nurture group shoved and pushed to get into the pool first. The lesson was noisy, but they quickly gained tremendous confidence. Afterwards, when changing, they showed keen interest in each others' bodies. Boys and girls openly looked at each other and giggled, and one of the boys repeatedly called out: 'Miss is changing; look at her feet.' The changing room had half-doors revealing only head and feet, and the children were very interested in the sight of legs showing beneath the door. The following week they went swimming again, and the occasion this time was described as disastrous. The children rushed off the bus and fought to get through the doors first. One of the boys ate an apple belonging to one of the girls and left the core in her bag; another child took a trinket from someone else's purse and gave it away. There was bad language all the time. The nurture teacher was told about this and the next day there were no toys and no biscuits. She was very displeased, and they were extremely subdued. The nurture group that day was eerily quiet.

In preparation for the following week we discussed the feasibility of the teacher talking-through the swimming trip beforehand with the children: what would happen, how they would feel, and how she wanted them to behave even though they had these feelings. They were to get off the bus without jostling, change behind the screens without getting excited when they saw legs showing under the cubicle doors, and so on. We felt that antic-ipating and verbalizing the situation might help the children maintain the self-control the teacher had already established in the routine of the school setting. It might also be helpful if the children wore something that was asso-ciated with the teacher, something that could be kept on in the water, per-haps a band to go on their wrists. So the next swimming day, just before the children left, the nurture teacher talked about their behaviour last week and how upset she had been. They talked about being polite and not pushing and the consequences if things didn't improve. If things didn't improve there would be no more swimming. She then asked if they would like to wear a piece of wool to remind them, and said: 'When you think you are going to be silly, look at the wool on your wrist.' As she tied on their wool she spoke to each child by name and had a relevant message for each: one was not to push, another must try to speak quietly, and so on. To a more controlled child she simply commented: 'I expect you can remember.' He didn't want any wool and was not given any. As the children were crossing the playground two of them lost their wool and came back and asked for more. Their teacher later commented: 'It seemed more important for them to have their wool than to have their swimming trunks.' The swimming session was a success. When they returned, they said, 'I still have my wool on', and one child kept his on for two days and another for a week. This was not indifference or over-sight, 'They knew it was there' (the teacher). The following week the children behaved very well the whole afternoon, though seemed unnaturally subdued. Several were heard to say such things as, 'There's no point in pushing; we'll all get through in time'. They took their turns, sat out as required and were well controlled on the way home. There was no serious trouble again.

'Transitional objects', whether arising spontaneously or deliberately intro-duced by the teacher, have been important for both junior and infant chil-dren, particularly those described as 'aggressive'. It seems to express their need for a tangible expression of attachment, and the comfort, support and control inherent in this carries them through experiences they face on their own, or with someone they do not know well, and helps them in their growth towards greater autonomy.

The child's personal possessions as a vehicle for communication

Of importance to many of the children are the scraps of material that are available to them for keeping, and inconsequential things found during the course of the day. These, and personal possessions to which they have an idiosyncratic attachment, are intimately part of the child and are sometimes used as a communication between child and adult, and in so far as they represent the child are a giving and a taking of his feelings and needs. Thus it is common when the children are taken into the group for them to entrust nothing to the teacher, but soon they are secure enough to give her their precious things for safe-keeping. This is sometimes the first indication of a relationship, and even when a child has been in trouble one day he will give his watch or a trivial personal treasure to the teacher the following morning. The importance of this safe-keeping was seen in a junior group where it was customary for the children to leave their small belongings such as cards, sweets and pieces of string in the pocket of the teacher's yellow canvas bag, to be collected at the end of the day. Whenever the children were restless and excited the teacher put these in a row on the low table in front of her while she read them a story, and this always settled them down. The safe-keeping of their little treasures was in a very real way a safe-keeping of themselves, and when put on the table were a visible demonstration of trust and attachment.

Moods and feelings are sometimes expressed through objects that have 'attachment' significance for the child. A 6-year-old brought into school a trinket ring belonging to the aunt who was looking after him and said to his teacher: 'You wear it today. I brought it for you.' Later he was cross and asked for it back. Five minutes later he said: 'You have it back. I will be good.' This anecdote illustrates the use of the ring to express his attachment to his aunt and teacher, and his awareness of its value in helping him to control his feelings.

Presents

A present is sometimes invested with feeling in the full and fundamental sense described for transitional objects. This is so when the relationship is one of the closest attachment and the present fully represents the person and is a symbol of that person. Presents of this kind are inappropriate and unnecessary in the nurture group. Apart from professional considerations and practical complications the children need the reality of the attachment relationship, not a symbol of it. Transitional objects, which arise spontaneously, have the basic developmental content the children need.

Present-giving, in its more usual and less fundamentally weighted sense, is not a feature of nurture group practice. Although many teachers from time to time have paid for such things as class photographs, and treats on outings, they are seen neither by the children nor the teachers as presents. From time to time the teacher or assistant bring personal things from their homes, perhaps a cake, or toys belonging to their children. These, too, are not seen as presents. They are particularly valued by the children because they are a direct and tangible link with the families of the teacher and assistant. They are part of the fabric of emotional support and personal and social learning that is being woven into the group, and help to reinforce a sense of group. Special occasions, such as birthdays, are celebrated, but any presents given then are more often made than bought. Although in material terms trivial, they are important because they acknowledge the child, and are experienced and valued as an expression of affection and caring. A very special pencil the teacher gives the child when he goes back to his mainstream class *is* a present. It is primarily an object of pride, and a symbol to the child of his progress and the teacher's recognition of this, though in so far as it carries the comfort, caring and strength of the nurture teacher, it serves the function of a transitional object.

The bed as a comfort and solace

A bed was standard furnishing in all the ILEA nurture groups, but because of child protection concerns a divan may be deemed more appropriate. In the words of teachers: 'They need to get away from it all, and the bed in the classroom may be the only place in their lives where it is possible' and 'Some children may never have stretched out by themselves in bed, and they should have the opportunity for this, and if possible the experience of sheets.' It is comforting to lie on the bed covered by a blanket, and instances of crying there have been described, in some cases after an upsetting incident in school, in others after a stressful incident at home. Lucy, described earlier, cried in bed for an hour after a disturbance in the playground. Often children cuddle up in bed with a soft toy. They like to be tucked in by the teacher or assistant, and they ask them to sit with them and read a story. One boy took a doll to bed and fed it there, apparently role playing his mother with the baby.

Play

A striking feature of many of the children who show early developmental needs is their initial lack of interest in dolls and small cuddly toys, in spite of strenuous efforts by the teacher and assistant to interest them. They have brought in all kinds of dolls and have bathed them, washed and combed their hair, have dressed them and played with them. Although some of these children have shown interest when the teacher has nursed the doll, on the whole they have shown no interest in nursing it themselves, and families of small animals have been ignored. Instead they wield the dolls as weapons, kick them about or ignore them. They seem to move on to doll play and caring for the dolls only after their own need for affection has been met. In the early days of the group it is they who wear the doll's shawl as a nappy and suck from the doll's bottle. Big soft toy animals seem far more important to them at this stage, and for many of the other children, too.

Making physical contact and expressing feelings through a large soft toy

Many of the children find physical contact difficult at first, but a large soft toy is unthreatening. Ideally this is soft but firm, the size of a young schoolchild and friendly looking. Soft toy dolls, monkeys, rabbits, teddy bears, clowns and Humpty Dumptys are comfortable and comforting, but are also the object and vehicle of fierce raw feelings of love and hate. They are hugged, cuddled and put to bed, and with a rapid switch of mood have been stamped on, beaten and punched, put in prison, or tied in a bag and thrown away, or forgotten as the child switches to playing with something else. Often they are fought over.

The large soft toy animal becomes personalized

After a time the child's relationship with the big soft toy animal becomes more personal. It is a member of the group, and is hugged and fought, sometimes in front of the mirror. Often at this stage the soft toy animals are given personal names. They sit with the children at storytime, are put to bed, eat with them and are fed by them, sometimes before they take food for themselves. They seem particularly important in junior groups when the children are doing curriculum-related work. In one junior school a monkey sat at the table wearing an anorak and doing his sums, while in another junior school a bear was given a book to read. In some cases the animal seems to represent the child, and he expresses through it an awareness of his own behaviour, for example by smacking the animal for something he himself has done wrong.

The large soft toy animal as a support for 'good' behaviour

On occasion the teacher uses the soft toy animals to support the child in a difficult situation. The comment that 'teddy eats well at the table' encourages the child to eat, and the request to 'look after teddy and see that he behaves well' helps him to contain himself during Assembly. The soft toy is sometimes used by the teacher to express approval or disapproval: he sits at the breakfast table with the children but leaves them if they are rowdy and comes back only when they are quiet again.

The large soft toy animal as an outlet of aggression

A large soft toy animal is sometimes used by the teacher to rid the child of aggressive feelings. She personalizes the toy and encourages him to use it as a punch bag, and a child of his own accord might attack it, sometimes in front of the mirror.

Stimulating talk through a soft child-size toy

Some children admitted to nurture groups have never been heard to speak. There have been several examples of teachers stimulating them to speak by animating a soft toy animal.

> Sid didn't speak and barely participated in group activities. His teacher used a soft toy rabbit to 'steal' his bricks, talking through the rabbit as she did so: 'Give them to me. I want them.' He giggled and defended himself verbally. The teacher egged him on, using the rabbit's voice. She suggested different ways of telling the rabbit off, and he took these up spontaneously. Since then he has been giving the teacher and assistant scraps of news. The teacher used more baby- and toddler-level games and interactions and he continued to make progress. He was now speaking more in his base class, and was even putting up his hand to answer questions, and his mother reported progress at home.

Development of caring through play

Interest in the dolls comes later. The children treat them as babies, though usually are rough with them at first, bash them when they cry, and turn them face down or throw them away. When they are making food 'the baby' is sometimes fed, and the baby is the doll, or a passive child in the group. Gradually this area of play develops. Each child is helped along by the needs of the others, and by the new ideas and associations and feelings evoked by the teacher and assistant in the comments they make, and by the deepening security of the children as they move on from needing care to giving care. This kind of transition was seen vividly in a junior group, where one boy who had repeatedly climbed into the pram was, within two terms, pushing a hamster around in the pram.

Development of caring through a doll 'baby'

A doll 'baby' was found to be a valuable agent in the development of caring. In the group where this was originally introduced all the children treated it as a baby. One of the girls was jealous, and sat on the teacher's knee, cuddling in and sucking her fingers, but even she loved the baby and cared for her. All the children tiptoed about not wanting to wake her up, and they tenderly cleaned her eyes, ears and nose with wisps of cotton wool. They were all very gentle with her, there was a remarkably close family feeling, and the boys for the first time were involved with a doll. Interestingly, all these children had been through a baby stage. Learning to care for plants and animals comes later.

They need help in developing their play

Most of the children initially need help in using the toys and equipment and in developing their play, for when left on their own their activity usually remains limited and repetitive. They also exhaust the possibilities of each situation very quickly, and need to be constantly supplied with something to do, and with ideas. The teacher and assistant therefore involve themselves in the children's play whenever this is possible and appropriate, giving help and demonstrating what went wrong, introducing ideas and giving guidance and direction, identifying with the activity as a parent would, sharing and enjoying the experience with them. They give a running commentary, raise queries and answer them, express their thoughts aloud as they think through the problem, and they verbalize their feelings when something goes wrong: 'but never mind, we'll try again'. In this way they provide a model of how they think and feel, and behave.

Play, with toys or other people, and games developed for the purpose, foster concept development and reasoning skills.

Solitary and repetitive play

Children of very limited development and with little awareness of others do not spontaneously adjust their position in relation to another child playing nearby, and are liable to erupt if accidentally touched. They are therefore given their own protected play space. This is usually on the carpet in the home area, and here many of them engage in solitary repetitive play day after day, sometimes at the level of the posting boxes, or they spend a lot of time fitting things together for the satisfaction, it seems, of seeing them fit. Some of the junior children spend long periods each day with the same simple repetitive activity, perhaps a simple jigsaw, at times done with the plain side uppermost, or upside down. Many of them, particularly the younger ones, push cars round and round the room, or bigger wheeled toys, sometimes running into or over the others, who are no more than objects that get in the way. In the playground, too, they often play on their own with the big heavy toys. Sometimes the same simple activity goes on continuously during play periods for the first few days. The children are absorbed in these solitary activities, and need time and space for them. The adults do not intrude, but maintain a watching brief, ready when appropriate to offer suggestions or another toy. In a few children, the solitary and repetitive play in which they engage is not a needed developmental stage. It seems a defence, a retreat from the world when it is all too much.

Their play becomes more elaborate

The play of children who use the toys and materials more flexibly is at first usually solitary and the content meagre. It may remain static for the first few days, or for as long as a month, but gradually develops and becomes more constructive and elaborate. This happens because the children get used to playing alongside each other, sometimes with the same type of toy or materials. Each child independently pursues his own theme, but very gradually to a limited extent they become involved in each others' play. When left to play at their own level alongside children playing at a similar level, with material that is familiar and gives them the satisfaction of success, they notice and comment, and begin to offer suggestions, and to copy. Each gains from the other. Soon co-operative play develops. One child becomes interested in the others' play, watches for a moment, appreciates what is happening and joins in, and the play gradually becomes more complex and increasingly elaborate as the children incorporate each others' ideas, and many of them begin to take on roles and act out their feelings. The transition to more imaginative play comes about with relatively little guidance from the teacher and assistant, though they make frequent observations.

A free choice of play is soon possible

Although the teacher chooses play materials and toys individually for the children at first, she gives some of them a limited free choice within a few days, and usually all have a free choice by the end of the first half-term. They often choose building bricks, cars and trains, and sometimes farms and occupational hats. A few children are not able to exercise more than a limited choice for as long as two terms, but this is exceptional.

Make-believe play

For many children make-believe play at first centres on food. They spend a lot of time making and serving food, and this theme is particularly persistent with the more dependent children. They roll and flatten the plasticine or the Play-Doh, and make biscuits, sweets and cakes for the other children, the teacher, assistant, and any visitors who happen to appear, and serve them with endless cups of 'coffee' and 'tea'. Although two or three of them might be busy with this activity they are frequently not involved with each other, except in so far as they are giving or receiving food. Children who play at a more complex and imaginative level might be involved to some extent with each other in their play, but rarely sustain this because they quarrel and turn on each other. Very quickly, however, they begin to play quietly and constructively together, but this only happens because of the alert vigilance of the teacher and assistant and their careful choice of activities and children. Often the themes developed are domestic ones. They dress up and play at being mum, dad and the baby, sweep the carpet and wash and feed the dolls. Other typical themes are hospitals, schools, the disco and the hairdressers, and they drive make-believe buses, police cars and fire engines, and pretend to be any current figures of interest to them. Although their play is often that of the nursery or infant class the most important aspect may be its nurture content. Hair-dressing and hospitals, for example, involve physical contact, caring and being cared for, and provide sensory experience, extend self-image, and increase self-regard and awareness of others, as well as requiring sustained attention and fine motor control. They also lend themselves to language and mainstream curriculum-related concepts.

Hiding and finding play

A sturdy cardboard box is needed for the children to curl up inside, hidden away all alone, with every chink of light blocked out, in total containment and seclusion. At other times they use it for jack-in-the-box play. A child lies inside the box, still and quiet, containing his excitement, and then suddenly jumps out to surprise the teacher and assistant. Bigger cardboard boxes, to get into and out of, and to hide in with another child, and roll over in, also are well used, and sometimes the children curl up as though in a cot, while at other times they use them as boats or cars. Both infants and juniors like to build tiny enclosed spaces, with walls, covered with blankets to make camps; or they hide away under the blanket all alone in the dark chattering to themselves; and they crawl under tables and into hidey-holes. Often they draw the teacher and assistant directly into their play, for example by hiding away and asking to be 'found', and the teacher and assistant express astonishment when they are 'found'. Sometimes the teacher and assistant repeatedly pull away the blanket covering the box, unexpectedly when the children are huddled excitedly inside, to increase and release the excitement. At other times they provide ideas and create images, and in their comments on feelings and relationships they increase the children's awareness of themselves and each other.

The adult as a facilitator of play

A major contribution of the teacher and assistant to the children's play lies in their observations and comments. When a child takes up a role and develops the theme on his own, their observations can make him aware of interesting possibilities that extend his play and draw another child in; and a comment on what they are doing makes them more aware of them-selves and each other. Rhetorical questions heighten an awareness of their feelings and the needs of others, open up insights and awaken in the child a new train of ideas. Often, if the children are playing imaginatively, the adult adopts the role allotted by the child, or they take on a role of their own accord. They join in if it seems appropriate and helpful in the devel-opment of the children's play, by introducing a new role, or developing the action. They adapt to his world, and extend and enrich it. At other times they would not involve themselves, sensing that this would be an intrusion.

When the children are constructively and imaginatively involved with each other a minimal contribution from the adult can enable them to support and further each others' play. It is therefore important to group the children carefully. A child's play can also be facilitated by others who are more advanced, and sometimes it is helpful to bring in at planned and defined times children from the mainstream class who need extra opportunities for play.

Creative play

Creative play develops in the nurture group because of the availability of toys and equipment the children can use according to their need, and because the teacher and assistant constantly feed in suggestions. As time goes on the children assimilate ideas from stories, outings and conversation, and their play develops as they become aware of the possibilities of the materials and are more secure and satisfied. They begin to interact constructively and imaginatively with each other, and at this stage it is more usual to leave them to play on their own. But many of them occasionally revert to an earlier level. In the first junior group, simple basic water play was a recurring need, and the same 9- and 10-year-olds, after a period of more advanced play, made pull-along toys by tying string to tiny model cars and charged about the room with them. Teachers stress that it is not enough to give the children time to develop their play and learn to play together successfully 'they need time to experience the joy of successful play' (a teacher).

Play as an outlet for stress

Although much of the children's play is through investigation and exploration of the materials and toys or is an enactment of everyday prosaic events, it also provides for some of the children a way of working through their turbulent feelings. This is at all levels. At its most basic, as already described, any toy might be attacked or treated with hate and thrown away, though more often a soft toy animal represents the child or another person, and conveys his feelings about himself, or in relation to another person. The feelings expressed are not always negative. Sometimes he seems to be caring for himself, or is consolidating his social behaviour through the animal. A stressful event in the child's life, or an amorphous fear of frightening things, is sometimes spontaneously acted out, sometimes to an unusual extent. Occasionally a child suddenly initiates a play theme of a more vividly personal nature and, with no involvement of any kind on the part of the teacher and assistant, plays through a situation of severe stress or the feelings associated with it with dramatic improvement in attitude and well-being. Presumably this happens because in the more controlled but relaxed atmosphere of the nurture group his play is protected from the intrusion of others, and he is secure enough to demonstrate his difficulties and fears in his play.

Activities that become a stereotyped routine

The child's activity may become a repetitive stereotyped routine. Lego is an example. The more advanced children enjoy it and most of them settle well to it. It is something they can do with their hands without prior experience, and they can control the material and gain success at different levels. It gives security, but is restricted and does not progress but with the adult's help can be extended. She might, for example, show the child how to use the Lego pieces to form a track and run a car along it, or she makes a copy of his Lego model with junk. Teachers have suggested that for a more developed child an agreement could be made. The child makes his Lego model because this is something he needs and wants to do, but is then encouraged to attempt something more creative because this is what the teacher wants him to do. The teacher introduces the activity by doing it herself, and then shows him what to do and does it with him. They then both go back to the Lego, to the child's more stereotyped routine.

Self-imposed restrictive routines

The routines that delineate the day are imposed by the adults. They provide a structure and are facilitating. Others come from the child and are restrictive. They are activities to which the child compulsively returns, and are not play. Some of the children are from homes where the domestic routine is repressive and they have an excessive and inappropriate need for order, tidiness and perfection and may fear doing something wrong or making a mistake. Direct help and support may be needed to lead the child into a more flexible pattern, for example, by the teacher or assistant taking part in the activity. They show him that they find it safe, permissible and satisfying to experience and experiment. If they make a mistake or a mess they acknowledge it and demonstrate that it can be put right, and if it cannot be put right they verbalize their feelings and reassuringly put the difficulty into perspective.

The self-imposed over-routinized behaviour of other children seems a defence. It protects their limited or precarious organization against the impact of an overwhelming and demanding world, but the security of the routine may remain a restricting need. The children are reassured because the adults acknowledge and protect their preoccupations and provide organization from without. They respond to the adults' help in loosening and extending their self-limiting personal routines, and find security within a broader classroom routine.

Protective rituals

The routines of some children are protective rituals that have a more obsessional and compulsive quality. They are intense preoccupations with a restricted, ritualized and sometimes bizarre routine. The child's involvement in the world about him is limited and he seems barely aware of the broader routine of the group. He seems lost in the content of his routine, rather than supported by its structure and sequence within the broader structure and sequence of the class routine, and if disturbed shows great distress. Some of these children are at a nurture level of functioning, and their preoccupations seem to be non-productive symptoms rooted at the stage where purposeful growth had failed. The teacher and assistant protect their preoccupations from the intrusion of other children, but take opportunities as they arise to extend and develop this obsessional activity in a more reality-directed way. They make a suggestion and introduce the necessary piece of equipment, or they involve themselves in the child's play as passive objects. In this way they increasingly direct the energy that is locked up in these preoccupations into more normal forward-moving interests.

Rituals of symbolic significance

The obsessional preoccupations of other children are within more complex experience and organization, and seem to have a more specific symbolic significance. Restorative nurture has only indirect relevance for problems of this kind. The fabric of nurture has become knotted, and nurturing experiences, which will strengthen a weak or loosely woven fabric, will not remove a tight knot. The children are nevertheless helped by the support that flows from a nurturing attitude and the attentive ear available for what are sometimes quite well articulated stresses and anxieties. The structure and tempo of the group gives them 'space' to express unresolved problems, and constructive interests and relationships can be fostered at a more age-appropriate level.

Food

The intrinsic interest of food and its importance in helping the children to give attention and to control their own behaviour, has already been considered. It is the only thing to which some of them at first spontaneously give attention, and through which they acknowledge the teacher and are enabled to wait and sustain their attention, make choices, tolerate frustration, delay gratification and learn about themselves and each other. Although the controls built in may be at first the overriding consideration for the teacher and assistant, for all the children either from the beginning or later food is of enduring importance as a comforting demonstration of the adults' caring, and their membership of the group.

Food is a central feature of the mother–baby relationship, and the satisfaction and security inherent in early feeding become part of the child and supports all later being and learning. It is important in the nurture groups because it demonstrates caring, satisfies needs and provides basic learning experiences in many different ways. For some children it affirms the attachment for which they crave. For those who disregard the adult it leads to an attachment because of the implicit control, and this control is the precursor of an attachment. Virtually all the children respond to food, for it satisfies a common underlying need. The teacher therefore uses food to the full to gain and sustain the children's attention, whether or not they have a problem of grabbing. The nature and extent of the children's needs otherwise, and the difficulties that are a reflection of these needs, determine the way food is provided and used in the groups.

Food is experienced as caring

Some nurture groups are made up mainly of dependent, unhappy, inexperienced and poorly organized children who are fearful, fractious or angry. Their main need is for affection, reassurance and encouragement, orderliness and organization, and support and help with controlled and directed nursery-level experiences. They quickly respond to affection and attention, and form an attachment. They are essentially biddable children, though may not seem so at first, and when they have the security and satisfaction of the close proximity and attention of the teacher and assistant in a situation appropriate for their needs, they are to some extent able to give attention, wait and share. Behaviour problems are usually manageable and teachers and assistants experience them as normal developmental difficulties, or an expression of distress. Food for these children could be milk and biscuits as they sit with the teacher and assistant in the home area. More usually it is 'breakfast' at the table. This is a reassuring routine with a simple formality, and the demands on the children are clearly defined and minimal. It is not delayed so any frustration is tolerable, and the experience of well-being and approval is enhanced and extended by being shared with the others. It is a time of peace and relaxed, quiet satisfaction in a busy day full of new experiences 'with mother'. Food, for many of the children, seems to express the affection and attention they crave, and some respond with feelings that seem almost of gratitude. It provides not only a basic personal satisfaction but is a group occasion, and helps the children to relate to each other. It is usual for them to play on their own or alongside each other initially, with little interaction. Having food together may at first be the only thing they are able to participate in and enjoy as a group. They are all doing and enjoying the same thing, and it is something they can all do even though some of them may need help. Food also provides a valuable link between home and school. It is particularly important if the cultural gap between the two is considerable, and may enable children who have a sufficiently supportive relationship at home to transfer this to school. It seems that very few of the children sit down for their food at home, and 'family' food in school may be their first experience of this, and their first successful social interaction.

Virtually from the beginning some groups seem like warm, intimate families where gentle and quiet insistence on controlled behaviour seems natural and normal. The children learn quickly and seem thankful that they know how to behave, and are proud of themselves. They take in that the adults are caring, and when they have internalized this caring they begin to give, and to do things for them and for each other. Food is then mainly an affirmation of a relationship that is being developed on a wider front and other satisfactions with the teacher and assistant, in school and adventures out and about in the neighbourhood, usually become more important to them.

First, their attention must be gained

In most nurture groups the children are less immediately open to attachment. Typically they do not at first spontaneously make eye contact or they avoid doing so. They are poorly organized and restless, their attention is poorly directed and sustained, and they rarely engage in purposeful and constructive activities. Others equally without direction, do very little. The immediate objective for these children is to learn to pay attention to the teacher. This has been described in Chapter 2, in the section titled 'Attachment and support'.

Little games are introduced: waiting is enjoyable

Very soon all the children are secure in the knowledge that the milk and biscuits will come, and of their own accord sit as required, and seem relaxed but attentive as they wait. The teacher now introduces little games of short duration. They centre on body image and personal identity, and become suffused with a sense of well-being, engendered by the expectation of food. These little games also delay the food in a way and to an extent that is tolerable, and so consolidate the experience of waiting.

The requirements are those of a normal family

In the simple situation of milk and biscuits the children are helped to wait and take turns, and to choose and share. This may be the preferred method when all the children are to some extent biddable, have some self-control and can use a 'mother's day' level of experience. 'Breakfast' includes washing up, and putting everything away in the proper place, and can take well over an hour. This is valuable time that for these children could more usefully be devoted to other things. The constraints imposed in these relatively informal settings slow down the proceedings in a way which seems unnatural, but they are no more than the gentle but insistent requirements and reminders within a normal family, and the atmosphere is quickly that of a normal family.

'Breakfast'

The routine provision of food is essential for children who are at a 'nurture' level. In most groups at the beginning of the year, irrespective of the nature of the children's difficulties, this takes the form of 'breakfast' early in the day. Breakfast offers more learning opportunities than does milk and biscuits in the home area and is essential if the group includes children who actively resist forming an attachment and may have severe behaviour problems. It is a routinized occasion and typically beforehand the children wash their hands and tidy up. This slows them down, as well as contributing to a sense of personal worth. In a school where scented soap was used the children came to their teacher in turn and she took their hands in hers, lifted them to her face, and said: 'Oh, what a lovely smell. You do smell nice. Now you smell.' This was an intimate communication through which the child's niceness was acknowledged, appreciated and shared, and the experience was heightened because it was associated with food.

An important aspect of the nurture group breakfast is the formality of the procedures and the organization and ritual that is built into it. The food itself may be no more than half a slice of toast and a little jam, or even milk and biscuits, and typically is produced at about ten o'clock. For the children it is part of the routine. It is an important and satisfying event and helps to stabilize them early in the day when they are particularly unsettled. Most of them live at home under severe stress and the tension built up shows itself in school and may be released in school. The first part of the morning is often difficult, and the problems are particularly acute on Mondays.

Before breakfast they assemble in the home area

When breakfast time comes it is usual for the children to be collected in the home area. Meanwhile, the assistant puts the cloth or mats on the table, and arranges the plates and mugs. Later the children take it in turns to help. Until the experience is secured they are told what is to happen, what they have to do and what they are going to have. At this early stage the food and the occasion itself is kept simple, perhaps biscuits with their milk, or cereal and milk, but it is presented formally and is at the table. As the children become more settled and secure, the procedure becomes more flexible and complex. When the teacher tells them what they are going to have for breakfast she might hold up line drawings showing different items of equipment, and they discuss what they will need and not need. If they are having rice pops the teacher draws from them why they need a bowl and a spoon, and why a plate and a fork will not do.

While the preparations for breakfast are being made the children not helping remain as a group with the teacher, preferably in a position where the breakfast preparations are not in direct view. She engages them in simple group activities such as rhymes, songs or hand games, or limited conversation if they can manage this. When everything is ready the teacher brings the activity to a close, and the children settle and wait.

The children are sent off one by one: everything is specified

The teacher tells them that they are going to have their milk and biscuits and explains step by step what they have to do. She speaks slowly, in simple language that conveys one piece of information at a time, because they attend only to the first two or three words of a long complex sentence. The more impulsive children are likely to rush in before she is finished, and so she builds in verbal restraints, as she does before launching them into any activity: 'Sit quite still'; 'Wait until I say your name'. The most unrestrained child is likely to have been placed by her feet and if necessary she holds his hands if he is about to get up. Every step is described and specified in detail, and finally: 'Wait. I'm going to tell you to go and sit at the table. Wait until I say your name.'

The children are inexperienced and poorly organized. Some have never sat down to eat at a table; some have never used a knife and fork, nor even drunk from a cup or a beaker. Few of them have mastered the complexities of what to most children would be a simple situation. They are not able to anticipate what is required and are not able to organize themselves in relation to what is required, nor to each other. The teacher, therefore, specifies everyone and everything, and maps out and organizes the situation for each child in turn. One by one she sends them off to the table in a considered order, each identified and acknowledged by name, and each in turn is directed to where he is to sit. It is usual for the most competent children to be sent off first. The others need the close proximity of the teacher for as long as possible, and it is a useful learning experience for them to see what the others do. Less secure or competent children might need extra support and help, a word of encouragement or a personal comment, given individually as they go off.

They are given individual help as needed

The assistant is at the table to receive each child, and shows him where to sit by going to the chair and drawing it out. Care is taken to see that the children are seated comfortably. If necessary they are helped to sit in the best position in relation to the table, for some of them are not only poorly co-ordinated but are poorly orientated to their surroundings, and have a poor sense of their own bodies in space. At this early stage the teacher and assistant decide where the children are to sit, for the situation is new to them. Even the more competent children may be uncertain of what is expected and may not know what to do, and without direction might choose one chair and then go to another, or would fight over them. They are therefore not allowed to choose where to sit. Later, when the teacher knows them better she chooses where they are to sit on the basis of likely compatibility. Later still a free choice is given. The teacher draws to herself any child needing this extra help and explains to him exactly what he is to do, and to make sure that he understands he might be asked to tell her what he is to do. A child who barely functions is reassured, and is told that there is milk and a biscuit for him too. Another, who plunges unrestrainedly into everything, is told again what is expected, that he is to sit quietly waiting while the biscuits are handed round, and can take his biscuit only when it is offered. Children in need of this extra support and guidance are likely be taken by the teacher to the table, hand in hand, and placed by her side.

Controls are built in

Breakfast is very carefully controlled, and it is usual when a group is new for the biscuits to be kept out of sight until the children are sitting down and are still. They sit at the table expectantly, but no food appears if they are digging their elbows into each other, playing with the knives if they have reached the stage of having them, or wriggling about. The teacher and assistant make positive requests, gently but with quiet insistence, if necessary to each child individually. At this stage they control even minor fidgeting or posture which suggests that the child is not fully involved and attending, by asking him to put his hands in his lap, or to turn round and sit properly on his chair. Many of the children are restless and their attention is poorly directed and ill-sustained, but most of them quickly become biddable and are able to sit still if given something simple and specific to do. When incidental undirected activity is controlled the children are more likely to concentrate their attention fully on the teacher and assistant, on the expected food and on the social requirements, and this is the immediate aim. Later, when the children's behaviour is more constructive and purposeful these requirements can be relaxed, and in practice this happens very soon.

Waiting is made tolerable

When the children are still, the assistant goes around the table with the milk, filling each child's mug in turn. If funds allow it, it is preferable at this stage to have plain mugs, all the same colour so the children are not distracted by having to make a choice. A range of mugs can be made available later. Children who are least able to wait are the first to get their milk, served individually, and are allowed to drink it straightaway provided they are sitting as required. Waiting is in this way made tolerable. More usually the children are expected to wait until every child's mug has been filled. They watch as they wait. They drink their milk only when everyone is ready, and the teacher or assistant has told them they can begin. In a newly formed group the biscuits would be offered only when all the children had finished their milk. This is partly because the biscuits might excite them too much, but also because most of them cannot concentrate fully on more than one thing at a time. Delaying the biscuit is, furthermore, a way of building in more waiting time. Gratification is delayed, expectation is heightened, and the motivation for controlled behaviour is increased. Grabbing is strictly controlled. If there is any indication, albeit momentarily, that a child is about to grab, the plate is drawn back slightly though still kept within his grasp, and he is reminded to wait until the plate is close at hand before taking a biscuit. He is praised when he holds back. At first the biscuits are all the same, and the children take the nearest one and are not allowed to grab. Those least able to wait get their biscuit first. They are allowed to eat it straightaway, and holding back and waiting is gradually built up from there. A child who can do little more than sit on the teacher's lap and trail around behind her, and for whom the situation means nothing, is given 'privileged' treatment. No demands are made of him at first, and delays and constraints are gradually introduced in a close baby-type relationship 'on mother's lap'. In most groups, however, the children are able with reminders to wait until all of them have taken a biscuit, and then they are told they can begin. In some groups the children from the beginning are able to wait without touching their milk and biscuit until everyone is ready, and imposed constraints are unnecessary.

The way food is managed is thus related to the social competence of the children and their tolerance for frustration, and the extent to which they can take in more than one thing at a time. But always the requirements are manageable and tolerable, and the satisfactions match the requirement and at every stage are considerable. Food is rarely withdrawn, though it might be held back, for example by returning the biscuits to the tin until the children have settled again. Occasionally a second biscuit might be withheld.

Virtually all the children need this basic training

In most groups almost all the children need this basic training. They are inexperienced and without the self-control required, or are used to fending and fighting for themselves at home. Purposeful and controlled behaviour is the teacher's immediate aim and usually this is soon established. The children quickly grasp that there is enough to go round and that they are included, and when they see what is required and realize that these requirements have to be met, they readily accept the constraints. In a few children, however, usually older ones, there is an aggressive and more deliberately purposeful aspect to their grabbing. They flaunt the constraints, size up the situation and see what is in it for them, and manipulate to get what they want, or they take what they want. Exceptionally a child scorns the food and treats it and the teacher with contempt.

The procedure becomes more complex

When the children are used to having food as a 'family' in school and can take in turn what is offered, verbal reminders to hold back are dropped. If any child still finds it difficult to wait, it is sometimes helpful to ask him to hand round the plate. He is pleased to be asked, and offering the food gives him pleasure. Socially desirable behaviour giving satisfaction has replaced the more immediately gratifying but undesirable grabbing, and his self-control has been strengthened. Handing round the food has become a special treat and is sought after. The children no longer have problems of holding back, waiting and taking turns and so the child he chooses is the one who is the first to be ready. He then offers the plate to the next child who is ready. When the situation is fully in the children's hands they are keenly aware of those who are behaving well, and when in charge are very strict and insist on 'please' and 'thank you'. As basic behavioural achievements become consolidated it is usual to introduce simple activities that have inherent personal interest. These prolong the waiting, increase the expectation, and delay gratification in a pleasurable way, for example: 'The boy who is wearing a ... (pause) ... red jersey can take his biscuit first'; or 'The girl whose name begins with ... b ... (given phonically) ...'.

Their behaviour is now controlled and they can savour the food

When basic patterns of behaviour have been established, the children's attention is directed to eating properly and savouring the food. At this stage externally imposed detailed requirements become unimportant and unnecessary restrictions can be relaxed. The children by now have some personal organization and self-control. Their behaviour is no longer at the whim of immediate impulse and they are free within themselves to eat in a more relaxed way. They notice and enjoy what they are eating and take part in conversation. Initially inhibited children respond well to this approach. They need to be shown what to do and to be given a clear indication of what is permissible, and in this controlled situation they can be encouraged to participate and to take. They get acknowledgement, appreciation and approval for making eye contact, and for taking the food. They become more confident when they see that some of the other children are able to take and may even grab, and are reassured that the teacher controls this grabbing, but wants them to take. The children who at first uninhibitedly grab also learn from the others. They become aware of the needs of these children because in this slow-moving and controlled situation there is time to take in what is happening.

Basic language is fostered

In the early stages of a group it is usual for the teacher to make a running commentary on the food they are eating, for the children are not attuned to noticing and attending to their experiences, and their basic vocabulary is extremely limited. If they are particularly unaware of themselves and their surroundings she might comment on the shape of the biscuit: 'It's round, and the plate is round', and the children take this up: 'I've got a round biscuit, I've got a round plate.' She remarks with enjoyment on the taste of the biscuit and the crunchy sound as she eats it, and they all stop eating and listen to her crunchy sound, and then their own crunchy sound. A very simple level of conversation develops.

They learn to make choices

A general problem for the children is difficulty in making choices. Often this is related to a paucity of earlier experiences, and limited internalization of the experiences and the memory of the feelings that went with them. It is a common observation that some of the children seem dead to experiences and have no spontaneous impulse for doing or having anything. Some are fragmented by anxiety and have too little identity to bring to the task of making a choice, while others fear to commit themselves, or to demonstrate that they exist by committing themselves. These children are confused and distressed when expected to make a purposeful choice. Others have a zest for experiences and have the agony of knowing that when they make a choice they must forgo the things they have not chosen. Whatever the nature of the children's indecision, in this slow-moving, quiet, orderly and controlled situation the problems are verbalized, and they can be helped to choose. The choice arranged for them is at first very simple, perhaps between two kinds of familiar equally attractive biscuits that look different. Each kind is on a separate plate because the children have become accustomed to taking the nearest, and this principle would interfere with making a choice. The children have had both kinds of biscuits on separate occasions, eaten slowly and with enjoyment. They remember each in imagery, and so are able to make a real choice. If a child dithers an uncomfortably long time the adult relieves his distress by commenting on the alternatives. If necessary she chooses for the child, by saying: 'I think you would like this one.' Making a choice is a considerable achievement for some of the children, and even though progress is carefully built up from simple to complex, immediate satisfaction to delayed satisfaction, they may have difficulty in accepting the consequences of their choice. A girl who was offered the choice of a banana or raspberry milk shake chose the banana milk shake, but cried when it came because it was not pink. She was helped to cope with her distress and frustration because the teacher and assistant shared the experience with her. They know how overwhelmingly disappointing and frustrating it is when a banana shake is not pink, and because they were emotionally close to her they could put it all into words and help her through her feelings of distress. Soon the children learn to accept these disappointments. One teacher provided chocolate biscuits of different shapes. All the children had the major satisfaction of chocolate, but had to take the nearest biscuit and thus sacrifice the relatively minor satisfaction of the preferred shape.

They learn more about each other

Watching a child as he learns to choose helps the others. They wait and watch with interest and savour the experience in imagery, knowing that their turn will come. A sense of identity and personal value is enhanced, the experience is heightened, and a spin-off is consolidation of self-control. In imagery, too, they share the choice and the struggle of the choice. In doing this they begin to remember the foods the other children like, and do not like. They get a picture of them as individuals, and begin to feel empathy as they identify with them in their struggle to make a choice. Support is inherent in this experience. A child watching in this way has a sense of providing support and so feels supported when he makes a choice. He thus becomes more aware of himself as a person who makes choices, has legitimate wants, and is able to control them. The teacher's comments indicate that she, too, remembers what he likes, respects his tastes and treats them as valid, with the implicit acknowledgement that he is truly a person, is valued for himself, and has wants that are legitimately satisfied by others. All these things contribute to a developing identity and maturity. Situations like this are helpful also for the unforthcoming child. He begins to take part with more confidence when he sees that everything is orderly and everyone has a turn, and can be helped to acknowledge and express his preferences. He may suddenly refuse, often with passionate feeling, a jam he has accepted daily without complaint, either not daring to say he does not like it, or not being sufficiently aware of himself or the experience to know that he does not like it. He learns to establish an identity by realizing and saying that he does not like a particular jam. He learns to make decisions and becomes, in the words of a teacher, 'a proper person, not just a wishy-washy nothing'. The pleasure the teacher and assistant feel when a child takes the first step in self-realization is tremendous, and there is often a sense of exhilaration in the child.

They learn to share

Sharing, too, is important, and later the requirement to share is deliberately introduced. There may be too few cakes to go round, or one of the cakes is bigger and nicer than the others, and it is a tremendous step for some of the children when they offer to share. These expectations are built up very gradually so the children are able to tolerate them, and learn from them. They are helped by knowing that the teacher and assistant are absolutely fair, and often give up nice things for them or go without.

Food occasions vary from school to school

As with families, food occasions are idiosyncratic and have their own routine and ritual. Some groups have tablecloths; others have place mats, usually made by the children. As well as adding to the preparation time and increasing expectation, they are in the collective ownership of the group, are personal to it and usually distinctive, and contribute to a group identity. Knives and forks are useful even if the food is simple, not only because they add to the ritual and the importance of the occasion, but because some of the children need help in using them. Cups and saucers are usual, though some groups have a range of beakers. They are essential equipment because without help some of the children are liable to pour the contents of a cup or mug over their clothes. A few have drunk only from cups with feeding lips before coming to school, or from a feeding bottle, while others have had experience of cups or mugs but are clumsy. Straws of fine bore are frustratingly difficult to suck from and are not recommended by teachers and assistants. Many of the children have very limited experience of different foods and so it is useful to introduce basic foods that are handled in different ways.

The children help as soon as they are able to

Although the assistant prepares the food and the table on her own at the beginning of the year and clears away, very soon when everything is nearly ready she invites one or two children to help her. She involves them as soon as they understand what is expected, and are sufficiently well organized and orderly to set out the mugs or cups, spread out the tablecloth or arrange the mats. Later they clear up and take their things to the sink. By the time the children have grasped the whole operation the food is usually more varied and interesting, and in some groups they have a spoonful of beans or fried bread and a tomato, but this is not usual. They are now capable of assisting in the preparation of food and do so in turn, while others help to clear away, wash up and put away. The assistant is always there, showing them what to do, chatting with them and doing things with and for them, and is available to help when they want to do a job on their own and cannot quite manage. Everything is now more complex but a high

level of organization is maintained, and although there is still a clear routine this is more flexible in detail.

They enjoy helping to prepare the food

Helping to prepare the nurture group 'breakfast' is a very special experience for all the children, for it is a shared and satisfying enjoyment in the
context of a warm and friendly supportive family relationship. For some of
them it is a totally new experience. Others have heavy responsibilities at
home. They carry these alone, often under stress and with considerable
anxiety. In school it is different. They enjoy watching the toast go brown
with the assistant, and talk without anxiety about the hazards of burning
it, and they learn what she feels and does when she burns it. Afterwards
they spread butter on the toast. All these are manageable responsibilities
and are positive and happy experiences. When the food is ready the children sit round the table with eagerness and enjoyment, and conduct themselves well. They have usually been shopping beforehand for the things
they will need, and this makes the experience even more positive.

Soon they help with the washing up

It is fun to help with the washing up because the assistant is there and they
chat together and laugh, and there is the special joy of immersing their
hands in the bubbles in the sink and experiencing the feel of the bubbles.
They blow them away and watch with the assistant as they float away,
break and disappear, exclaiming, enjoying, participating, making more
and blowing harder . . . gone! But this fun is under the control of the assistant, and she sees that the washing up is done properly, from collecting
and stacking to putting everything away in the right place. This, too, is an
enjoyable experience. They all want to do the washing up and get pleasure
from doing it all in an orderly way. Gradually the children are able to do
the washing up on their own, and this and other tasks like folding the
tablecloth quickly become a treat, and are sought after.

The situation fosters conversation

The family table also provides an opportunity for fostering conversation.
During the controlled introductory period when the children are learning
what to do, there is likely to be hardly a sound other than the quiet voice
of the teacher as she makes simple observations, and the slow and deliberate champing of jaws, and the occasional nervous giggle. Very soon
everyone is more relaxed. The children know that breakfast is part of the
routine, and they know how they are expected to behave. They manage
the food more naturally, talk about funny things that have happened in
the group, and laugh together. They become interested in the others, and

their opinions, and begin to influence each other. The teacher and assistant follow up and develop the comments the children make by referring to their own experiences. They make a point of talking about their homes and domestic things generally whenever an opportunity arises, but the breakfast table affords a particularly good opportunity for developing these personal themes. In this situation the children are responsive and are stimulated to talk, and remarkable conversational exchange develops. And because throughout the day their experiences are being extended, they gradually become interested in a wider range of things and have more to talk about at these family times.

They learn to listen, and consider each other

Food within a family setting is also a means of fostering concentration, for the children listen better to a story or an anecdote that is told, and in this context they get into the habit of listening. It is the best situation of all in which to develop responsive and responsible attitudes. They learn to say 'please' and 'thank you'. These courtesies are a genuine acknowledgement of the person providing the food, and everyone in the group becomes associated with food and the good feelings that go with food.

Food carries a wide range of learning experiences

The food provided is trivial in relation to the experiences that are built in. As one assistant put it: 'We have a tremendous palaver for a tiny piece of toast.' In some groups the 'palaver' begins in the period immediately before the food. The children tidy away their things and wash their hands. This is done in the expectation of food. Tidying up and personal appearance is therefore suffused with the good feeling and positive attitude associated with food and with the teacher's caring, and is experienced as pleasurable. In these circumstances, more than in most others, a positive attitude is likely to become internalized and self-motivating. This is important because nurture group children typically have a poor self-image and poor personal organization. A positive attitude, deriving from the expectation of food, is perhaps later attached to the more formal attention-demanding tasks that in an established group immediately precede the food. Lastly, the formality, routine and control established at the breakfast table provide a structuring which persists for a considerable part of the morning, even in a newly formed group.

Breakfast is highly regarded by the schools

Breakfast is so highly regarded that one headteacher, in a school where the nurture group continued, introduced breakfast for a group of children who were not in the nurture group, but who needed an extra boost at the beginning of the day. Breakfast was in an alcove in the school and was run by two learning support assistants along nurture group lines. Another headteacher routinely invited children from the nurture group to have 'breakfast' with her.

Many headteachers have said that if they lost their nurture group they would retain a formal breakfast for children who needed these learning experiences. In a school where this happened the nurture assistant and another school assistant ran a formal breakfast for children who would have been in the nurture group had they still had one.

The way food is provided changes as time goes on

Breakfast in many groups is crucial at the beginning of the year in order to affirm or establish a relationship and as a vehicle for building in constraints and controls, but it does not necessarily continue throughout the year. When their basic emotional and social needs have been met the children usually find it more impelling to explore the possibilities of the activities and toys available, and may of their own accord choose to work or play. At this stage it is customary to provide food only exceptionally, as a stabilizing comfort for children who are being tried in their mainstream class and are finding it difficult; or more routinely on Monday mornings if there are children whose home circumstances are particularly unstable and disturbing. At another time the teacher or assistant might spontaneously suggest breakfast, to re-evoke the experience they used to have and consolidate the feelings that went with it. Many teachers and assistants at this stage in the life of the group provide a little daily 'tea' at the end of the afternoon. This rounds off each school day with a sense of satisfaction and approval and is an acknowledgement of the effort that has gone before. It is an incentive to maintain high standards and gives a good start to the evening ahead.

When the children are more organized and can cope with a more complex and demanding exercise, a formal class lunch is introduced by many teachers, either as a special occasion with invited guests or as a weekly group event. The children help to plan and buy the food and prepare it, arrange the table, serve the food and wash up. Some groups have flowers on the table, and name cards. It is exciting for the child to find his name, and the particular place is easier to accept without protest because his name is there, and the name itself acknowledges the child's identity and presence and enhances his self-esteem. These formal occasions are a stimulus and provide interest, and reinforce a sense of personal well-being and of group. They require of the children considerable organization and control, and affirm their developing competence.

Birthday parties are always a very special occasion, but are introduced only when the children can cope with milk and biscuits. In most groups special food is prepared for birthdays, and all of it is put away until the time of the party. Some of the children do not know what birthdays are, 'She never told me', but they are always recognized in school and provide an opportunity for acknowledging the particular child, and for having a party in which everyone shares. The birthday child chooses the menu, goes shopping with the assistant and a friend, and the other children buy or make him a card or a small present. On occasions of these kinds it is usual for children from other classes to be invited in. The nurture children experience the pleasure of giving, and are proud to offer food and share their toys.

Some children are hungry

Some children, not necessarily those in the nurture group, come to school physically hungry. Some schools have simple food available, but this is unusual. More commonly, breakfast in the nurture group continues on an optional basis, and other needy children from the mainstream of the school come in to make a specially formed family group.

Some children have feeding difficulties

Some of the children have eating difficulties. These are of many different kinds and include picking at food, food fads, fearing to eat, gobbling and choking, failure to chew and swallow, indiscriminate eating of anything at hand, and squeezing the food with their hands or crumbling it. Some refuse to eat unless fed. A small number are still on a bottle at home and cannot feed themselves. In this relaxed slow-moving setting they can be given small amounts of food selected for them at first, and can be helped step by step to eat more normally. Occasionally a child is hungry and feeding him comes before learning to wait and not grab. Others may need to be shown how to manage the food, spread butter on a slice of bread, hold a piece of toast and eat it, hold a mug and drink from it, and use a knife and fork.

Baking

Baking is an important activity in the nurture groups. It is far too complex and demanding a task for most of the children at first but is introduced as soon as they are sufficiently well organized and co-ordinated to cope. It is kept very simple, and at first the children might do no more than stir the mix, and watch the assistant as she eases the little cakes from the tin onto the cooling rack. As they progress they begin to help at every stage, and in time are able to manage a sequence of steps on their own. In most schools the oven is in the classroom and the smell of the cakes pervades the room. Later in the day they have the cakes. There is no need to put them in a tin meanwhile because the children know they will have them at a specified time quite soon, and are able to work or play with them in sight. When the children have fully experienced the pleasure of cake in the nurture group, they are satisfied with a little taste on the day they bake and are able to put the rest away 'for later'. In some groups the children whose turn it is to bake take some of the cakes home for their families. This is usually a good experience, for even those parents who initially feel critical of the activities in the nurture group recognize that this is an achievement, and value the child for this. His self-esteem is enhanced and because he is giving something of himself to his parents, they feel proud too. Very rarely parents see the cake as a free handout and put in an order for more.

More imaginative baking is possible later and in a broader social context, for example at Easter the children in a junior group provided for every class in the school a chocolate egg Humpty Dumpty on a cake wall. Later still it is sometimes possible to invite the children from a neighbouring nurture group to their class for a party, but this requires detailed preparation in both schools. Festivals give scope for food from other countries to be baked, and is a happy tribute to children from ethnic minorities. In some schools these festivals are a whole-school event held in the evening, and all the parents and siblings are invited. Some groups have parents' parties and the children are helped to write the invitations and prepare the food.

Another special occasion is a picnic. They shop for the food and prepare it, and think through what they need to take with them, and the best way of packing and carrying the food.

6

Developing Autonomy

In infancy the central strand running through normal development is the child's attachment to the mother, and his trusting 'oneness' with her. Their relationship is one of mutual absorption and intimate interaction, given forward-looking and constructive direction by the mother. It is a unitary learning experience of intermeshing emotional, social and cognitive developmental strands that in infancy are so tightly intermeshing that they cannot be separated out. This earliest and crucial first stage of learning carries emotional and cognitive experiences that with continuing support lead to self-awareness, self-regard, a positive self-image and empathy with others. These are essential determinants of a positive attitude to others and an enthusiasm to experience and explore, and to latch onto problems and try to solve them. These dispositions, and the sense that someone has faith in them, motivates the young child to achieve and is intimately a part of early cognitive growth.

Nurture group children are not like this. Typically they lack trust in people and events, have a poor self-image and are without constructive purpose. They fear failure and may even fear to function, and for some children the response of the adults to their achievements means as much, or even more than the achievement itself, so great is their need to be valued. The limited cognitive competence of the nurture child is thus bound into a general impairment of early developmental learning opportunities. It follows that in meeting the child's emotional and social needs at the earliest level the teacher and assistant concomitantly build in the foundations of cognitive growth.

The nurture curriculum

The immediate objective of the nurture teacher and assistant is to provide manageable earliest years' experiences that will contribute to a more positive emotional and social development. The context is a close, intimately supportive relationship, within a structured environment. Early individual and interactive play with the adult, domestic activities and simple body-centred group games provide a much needed emotional/attachment experience. They also have cognitive content. They familiarize the child with himself and the world of things and people immediately about him. He becomes better organized, gains mastery of simple skills and has some understanding of process in the world.

Perceptual and motor experiences are essential precursors of the National Curriculum

There is a high incidence of perceptual and motor co-ordination difficulties in children in the nurture groups. Attention to these is a priority and takes the form of structured games centring round listening and looking, discriminating and remembering, finger games, fun activities and romps.

Learning to think is part of the 'nurture curriculum'

Purposeful attention-giving and an interest in experiencing underpin the skills, language and concepts normally gained in the first three years and are an essential part of the nurture curriculum. They come through the close relationship of adult and child and lead into the 'stepping stones' set out in 'Curriculum guidance for the foundation stage' and the language, mathematics and science of Key Stage 1 of the National Curriculum. They are its essential precursors, and elements of the nurture group curriculum are of value in the mainstream class.

It does not follow that the teacher and assistant foster the child's cognitive development only by extending his awareness, as a parent would, through spontaneous ad hoc involvement in earliest years individual play, and through general pre-nursery and nursery experiences. Although this is their immediate concern, formal activities related to the National Curriculum are not delayed until this pre-foundation stage of learning has been established and consolidated. Few of the children are so grossly retarded in all areas of development that no mainstream work of any kind is possible. Most of them are able, if only briefly in some cases, to sit at a table holding a pencil and make meaningful marks on the paper. Formal work, for reasons that are touched on later, is therefore introduced for nearly all the children from the beginning.

The learning content of the structure of the nurture group day

The detailed organization and structuring that goes into a nurture group day is an attempt to re-create the conditions of the pre-nursery years, and within this to provide a saturation of developmentally relevant pre-nursery and nursery experiences. The teacher and assistant help the child to give attention by verbalizing in detail objects, events and expectations. They maintain routine, clear time intervals, sequence and order, stress looking and listening and recall, and provide the repetition needed to establish and consolidate the experience. All this contributes to the ordered fostering of skills and concepts, enriched by the adults in language, and strengthened because they are personally involved with the child, share his experiences and give support and purposeful direction. He gains a sense of relationships in space and time and events in relation to each other, and in the course of this a sense of himself, of himself in relation to the world and of himself as an agent of change. And in experimenting with change he begins to grasp cause-and-effect relationships.

Some of the learning inherent in the child's experiences in the nurture group derives directly from the organization and conduct of the day, some from the experiences within this structure. The observations which follow are reminders only of the structure and content intrinsic to the child's day that is of immediate and direct relevance to cognitive growth.

The organization, conduct and content of the day: its relevance to cognitive growth

In lining up, the children gain a sense of discrete units and order, and from the moment they come into the nurture group room the routines that provide security and identity also delineate the day and contribute to a sense of time. In some groups the child's first experience each day is to select the card that has his name and photograph on it, though he may need prior experience of identifying himself in a mirror before this can be attempted. For some children this ritualized task is their first meaningful introduction to symbolic representation. The process of finding the right pocket on the wall to put the card in provides the experience of one-to-one (1:1) correspondence, left to right order and a notion of categories. The class ritual of establishing the day and the month gives an experience of number, sequence and category, and contributes to a sense of time. The action songs and finger and hand games that begin the day provide organization, rhythm and pattern; and giving news and talking about yesterday's class events requires recall, verbalization and the ordering of ideas. These things, and the activities at carpet time, extend their vocabulary and help them to build up basic concepts, and gain a sense of periods of time. And underlying everything is the fostering of attention-giving which is the primary precondition of learning.

The children are sent off to their activities. The room is well organized, and the materials and equipment needed are stored in trays and boxes on a clearly defined basis. The children take out the contents and put them away, with the help of the adult in the early stages. She talks about the ways in which things are the same or are different; of properties of colour and shape, relative size and ordering by size, function, and the concepts underlying the classification of equipment into logical groups. The choice of activities is at first restricted, or the teacher chooses. They are manageable in content and in the attention required, and the children are able to pursue them with a sense of purpose and direction. They are cognitively and emotionally relevant experiences in which the children are agents of simple, direct and visible cause-and-effect relationships. The experiences themselves are dwelled on, and are shared in enjoyment with the adult. She registers them in language that is simple and direct, and her exclamations and gestures carry a high level of pleasure, expectation and wonderment. The teacher and assistant also provide organization and direction, and reinforce the memory of the experience by recalling and describing, and they verbalize what they expect will happen and the effect of their actions. As with parents, they pick out key features and provide context and meaning. They analyse and extend the experience, review, elaborate and reorganize, and map out the way ahead. They monitor the process in language, make personal links with past experiences, and by introducing new observations kindle awareness in the child of a broader concept. In simple activities a very great deal of structured and controlled experience is provided, and there is support and encouragement, and anticipation of simple hazards and mistakes. The situation is optimal for internalization of the experience. All this is within a day designed to provide clear demarcation of experiences, thus developing in the child a sense of sequence and time, and the teacher reinforces this by regular recall of events at the end of the day.

There is formal pre-foundation stage 'work' also

Whether incidental or more contrived, the teacher builds in directed, constrained and focused work from the beginning, by purposefully developing the learning possibilities of experiences and situations as they arise, at the level the child has reached. This explicit teaching is in some cases at a very early level, perhaps no more than finger play deliberately introduced. Even junior children may not manage a 1:1 correspondence when they count, or even know that they have five fingers on each hand, and some have difficulty with nursery and infant hand games. They need help with these simple activities, and are not being resistive when they do not engage with them. This pre-nursery teaching follows that of the parent with a normally developing younger child. The objectives are the same but the circumstances are not, and the process is more complex than in the pre-nursery years.

Earliest learning experiences

The interests and experiences of the baby and toddler are intrinsically bound into his physical growth, and in particular his mobility and physiological rhythm. His parents intuitively provide an appropriate environment and relate to him in a developmentally relevant way, and without special planning on their part his growth follows a hierarchically developing pattern of increasingly complex organization. The older nurture child has the same early developmental needs but he is physically more advanced, and many of the experiences that are normally gained 'in mother's lap' are more likely to come to him 'at teacher's knee' or during the course of the nurture group day. And because the process for the nurture group child has lost impetus and constructive purposeful direction, the nurture teacher tries to assess his developmental needs in a more considered way, and formulates explicitly the end towards which she is working, and the ways in which this can be achieved. The learning experiences involved have developmental content equivalent to that of the pre-nursery years. They may be different in form, and an activity or situation may have different developmental content for different children and satisfy needs at different levels for any one child, as is apparent in the project work described later.

Teacher-extended learning during 'mother's day'

The nurture group provides developmentally appropriate experiences equivalent to those normally gained on mother's lap, at mother's knee or during the course of mother's day. Some, 'in mother's lap', may recapture not only an awareness of warmth, softness, comfort and movement in cradling, but also a passive experience of simple sequencing as the adult plays 'this little piggy . . .'. The cognitive content hinges on the close involvement in action and language of adult and child and is intuitively structured, as with a parent, in accordance with his developmental needs. 'At mother's knee' or during 'mother's day' a child who needs to be shown how to hold a doll the right way up and to put its clothes on the right way round, learns to manipulate and match objects in space. He experiences movement of his hands as he manages a pair of scissors and learns to use them to cut. He learns the feel of his body in romping games or when swung, and the different feeling when he clings piggyback, and his different perspective of the room from on high. All these activities involve action and shared feeling. The adult supports these experiences in language and develops them incidentally but purposefully. Choosing the right clothes for the doll involves concepts of relative size, and the fun of wearing a shawl in dressing-up play can lead into verbal concepts of length and size, and then measurement and area. These different activities are part of the nurture group day. They satisfy an emotional need and engage and hold the children's attention, are fun and further their personal and social development. And because they engage and hold the children's attention and are fun, and satisfy an emotional need, they are an important vehicle for cognitive development.

Basic concepts in everyday experiences

'Mother's day' offers such things as incidental counting as they jump up the steps of the school as though with mother, or they put spoons alongside bowls of cereal with an adult nearby. Other experiences are more complex and elaborate. When preparing breakfast the children learn where the necessary things are kept, and that certain things are stored together because they are linked by function or by size, and are classified in that way. Line drawings on the cupboard doors are an indication of the things inside the cupboard and are another experience of symbolic representation.

The knives, forks, spoons and other equipment in use when this stage is reached provide widening learning opportunities. The cutlery is in a box that can be carried around. The child whose turn it is counts the others and remembers to add one for himself. He checks the number reached with the wall attendance chart. The knives, forks and spoons needed are then counted out, and he sets them out, properly spaced and in the right place, counting as he goes round the table. An extension of this is for the child to go round again, turning the plates upside down one by one, and then round again, turning them the right way up, counting each time to check that the number is correct. An important task for one of the children is to put the mugs, or the cups and saucers, on the table in the proper place. He takes them from the cupboard and carries them to the table, on a tray if this is manageable. These operations require skill in co-ordinating movements, visuo-spatial judgement, and experience of orderliness and 1:1 correspondence. Helping with these tasks is particularly satisfying because they are associated with food and enhance esteem, and any anxiety is manageable because the assistant is there to support them and share the problems and the pleasure. The situation is therefore one in which learning is at a high level. Later on a more difficult task is to fill the mugs, and detailed instruction and supervision may be necessary. Breakfast itself provides opportunities to develop concepts of volume and size, subtraction and division, addition and multiplication. After breakfast they wash up, stacking according to size, and they recall where the different things go and put them away in an orderly fashion. In the course of this there are many opportunities for matching, ordering, sequencing and categorizing, and basic practical mathematics.

Baking provides learning experiences of many kinds

Baking is difficult, but the children enjoy it and it is rich in learning experiences. It is usual to have a weekly bake, and the children work with the assistant in groups of two, three or four, listening and watching, and giving practical help when appropriate. She tells them what the end result will be, and reminds them that the oven must be put on before they begin as it takes time to heat up. The names of the ingredients they need are on cards which the assistant holds up, and the children check the cupboard to make sure that everything required is there. She takes them through the whole process verbally, step by step. They set out the equipment in an orderly way and plan the sequence of actions. The assistant might do much of this, but they follow the process. 'What do we need?' 'What do we do first?' 'What do we do next?' The assistant at first provides the answer and helps the children to set out the ingredients accordingly. They give attention as they manipulate the ingredients, and experience not only their sensory qualities and the language that describes them, but learn that liquids and solids have different properties and can be measured and weighed, and they implicitly estimate volume and space when pouring the ingredients onto the scales. They get an impression of the way the ingredients change when put together and when heated, and the time it takes for cakes to bake in the oven. They begin to recognize cause and effect and the consequences of error. The assistant tells them about oven settings and differences in temperature and how to use the timer. They see how carefully she pours the mix into the cake tins. The recipe is simple but the operation is a complex one, and is carefully controlled at every stage. Some assistants have found it helpful to make the same biscuits repeatedly, as the operation is difficult enough already, and to vary the procedure by using different cutters each time. It is so difficult that even a junior child may be able to do no more than lick the spoon at the end.

The opportunities for the development of skills, concepts and language are considerable, whatever the level of the child, and learning is maximized because of the fundamental importance and interest of food and baking in purely personal terms, and the anticipation of something nice to eat at the end.

'Work' with real things and three-dimensional models of real things is particularly important because the basic life experience of many of the children is inadequate, imperfect and often distorted, and their concepts are vague and poorly developed, or are false.

The adult shapes the child's language

The adults share all basic experiences with the children and in a running commentary describe qualities, draw out similarities and comment on differences; and they invent games that reinforce these 'lessons'. Together they recall what has happened in the group and in the stories they have heard, and they have games of 'What does this do?' and 'What is this for?'. The past experience of the children is so limited that the adults rarely attempt to draw observations from them at this stage but instead provide a great deal of information. For a long time, too, they avoid direct questions, but indirectly ask a question of themselves, and answer it: 'Let's do this . . . I wonder what will happen? Oh, look, it's . . .' or they accept a fragment from the child and develop it into an idea on his behalf, as a parent would with a younger child. 'Why?' questions are rarely appropriate. They presuppose an advanced level of understanding and the maturity to reflect on an experience or process and analyse it, and are often experienced as a threat or taken as an attack, especially by the older children. A parent in a developmentally comparable situation would not distance the child in this way and leave him exposed to failure, but would verbally re-create the situation, bring it to life and share the problem. Concrete examples and demonstration make meanings absolutely clear and just as the normally developing pre-nursery child spontaneously echoes what is said, the teacher often asks the child to repeat back what she has said. This focuses the attention of a less experienced child on the sounds, and directs the attention of others to the content. This is important, because the attention of many of the children is poorly sustained, and they sometimes pick up a fragment only and incorporate this into an existing imperfect or distorted concept, often by association rather than logical connection. And all the time there is reinforcement of simple experiences through repetition and explanation.

The importance of language

The nature and structure of the language spontaneously used by the teacher and assistant is evoked by their close identification and involvement with the child and is an integral part of the nurturing relationship. In emotional content and cognitive style it is relevant to the stage the child has reached and so consolidates his development. At the same time it leads him forward and so provides direction and a sense of purpose. At an early level it helps to foster a sense of well-being and positive self-image, and later as it progresses and changes it engenders in the child a sense of himself as an achieving self and a moral self. In all these ways it is of profound importance, and in the nurture group the teacher and assistant verbalize everything throughout the day. Language is also of great importance in shaping the development of concepts and thinking skills through description and comment on situations and behaviour. It also extends the child's experience beyond the immediate situation thus creating a wider conceptual context in which awareness and understanding can be developed, and generalizations made.

The children are encouraged to listen and talk coherently

Not surprisingly, most of the children when they come into the group have very poor language. Some say little that is coherent, or may comment in single words or say nothing at all, and their articulation is in many cases poor. Some of them have no wish to speak. Others have nothing to say, but talk nevertheless and shout each other down. Encouraging them to talk coherently, and to listen to each other and develop conversation, is an important part of the work of the group. Valuable opportunities arise in the home area around the family table, or in incidental talk with the teacher or assistant as she irons or when they bake. Some of the most productive conversations develop on their visits to the local shops or the park, or on their journeys further afield. Later on, the teacher and assistant frequently remind them of the things they have done together at these times: 'Do you remember . . . ?' At first most of the children have little or nothing to talk about, but as their interest is engaged and their experience widens they become more aware of and interested in each other and talk together about the things they have heard in stories, and begin to ask interested questions. Photographs taken in class or on their outings evoke lively observations, reinforce personal and group identity and provide material for their personal and class storybooks, written with the teacher's help.

Their intense interest in the teacher and assistant facilitates language

Many of the children love more than anything else to listen as the teacher and assistant talk together about their homes and their domestic lives. They eagerly ask what their children have done and whether they have been naughty, what they have had to eat, and how many pairs of shoes they have. The teacher and assistant make a point of referring to their own homes. They enquire about each other's families and show interest and concern. They chat together about things that have happened, decisions they have to make, and problems that have cropped up. They talk about the food they cook at home, and draw from the children comments about *their* food at home. The children become absorbed in these personal stories. They learn a great deal from them and ask for the same anecdote over and over again with all the details. Some of the younger children at first assume that the teacher and assistant live in school, and at night sleep in the home area in the nurture classroom, or in the stock cupboard. As they listen to their domestic talk they begin to build up a picture of the teacher and assistant. They become real people to them, with real families, living in real houses and flats, and they feel closer to them. Not all these conversations are of immediate interest to the children, but they help to fill in vast empty areas in their experience. They also provide links with their own lives, and sometimes the children take these up and little conversations develop. When the teacher and assistant sit together and talk, some children listen avidly, while others play quietly at their feet with a simple toy, perhaps running cars up and down their legs or feeling their toes, hearing the sounds of the words but not taking in the content. The children are happy at these times, at peace within themselves and secure in their worlds because the adults are there.

Individual storytime

Storytime, too, is important. All the children have individual storytime, sitting beside the adult, or on her lap, either in bed or sprawled on it with the teacher or assistant alongside. It is natural at these times for the adult to put an arm round the child and for them to be physically close together. The more immature children seem to be taking in the warmth of the adult and the music of her voice rather than the story itself, as they stroke her leg or suck her hair. Individual storytime has a very special closeness, but children nearby become absorbed in the magic too, and several might draw near. The most dependent children sit closest to the adult, by her feet or against her legs or snuggling alongside, while others listen from a distance while doing something else. All at some time like to be very close, and to be read to, and might look glum when it's another child's turn. For all of them, their own special time with the teacher or assistant is very important.

Reading

The adult introduces the children to reading individually or in twos or threes. The context is relaxed, and affection and approval are evident. All are absorbed in the story and there is a pleasurable feeling of closeness with the adult. The children spontaneously comment and ask questions, and those who otherwise show no interest in books snuggle in and twist their faces to look at the page, and they get some idea of turning the page and the right way up for the book.

Group storytime

There is group storytime as well. This is more formal, and the children sit on the carpet in front of the teacher and look at her, and listen. Most of them quickly give their full attention to the story and become totally absorbed. The stories have to be very simple with clear uncluttered pictures held up by the teacher to illustrate the story. The same story is read to them many times because the children typically have a poor attention span and are likely to fasten on to one element of the story and remember only this, or may be muddled about events and sequences of events. Simple stories and fairy tales are very popular with juniors as well as infants, and the children *demand* repetition.

The importance of the attachment relationship

The experiences that arise during the course of the nurture group day are thus at many different levels. Some directly reflect the attachment relationship and the child is 'lost' in the closeness, peace and security. Other experiences and the language that is part of them have more cognitive content, but they too are bound into an attachment relationship. Their cognitive content is part of the nurturing experience. It is fostered and developed largely intuitively and so derives as much from the assistant as from the teacher. It does not stem from professional training but nevertheless has direct implications for cognitive growth.

Formal educational input

At a later stage the teacher provides a more consciously purposeful input and makes specific demands of the child in order to develop visuo-spatial and motor skills, basic language, and mathematical and scientific concepts.

Teacher directed activities

The basic skills and concepts normally gained in the first three years are the essential underpinnings of the foundation stage of the National Curriculum. Their acquisition is of great importance in several other ways:

- Lack of basic competence causes frustration, and this may lead to outbursts of temper, inconsequential behaviour, avoidance or listlessness, as well as being damaging to the child's self-esteem.
- When an integrated skill is built up the child gains a sense of organization, orderliness and sequence, and the pleasure of achievement.
- He internalizes these complex activities, experiences them in imagery, and can therefore anticipate the effects of his actions and so modify his intentions. He thus learns to think before he acts, and is able to inhibit action.
- Mastery of these skills meets a developmental need and so the child is motivated to give considerable attention to the task. This creates a disposition to concentrate, and cumulatively developing interests are opened up to him.
- His experiences with the adult have a feeling content of closeness and shared satisfaction. He feels secure and contained, and is responsive. His motivation and involvement in the task increases and his attachment to the adult is strengthened.
- Acquiring a basic competence increases the possibility of constructive interaction with the other children. Without it he might directly or indirectly disturb or disrupt their activities.

The task of the adults in developing the children's competence is threefold. They engage and sustain their interest and attention by providing relevant experiences at an appropriate level, they help them differentiate and organize these experiences, and they build on this competence in the hierarchical development of skills and concepts. A great deal of individual work is necessary, because few of the children are initially able to manage for any length of time on their own. Unlike normally developing younger children, many show little interest and spontaneous involvement in the things about them, and even when engaged at an appropriate level their attention is rarely sustained. Others are greedy for experiences but cannot use them. It is therefore important, no matter what the age of the children, to build up a treasury of games and activities that carry the learning experiences normally gained in the years before school. Some of these activities also provide an outlet for energy. They become familiar to the children, capture their interest and attention, and through them they learn to look, listen and give attention, and as they experiment and explore they begin to connect up different aspects of their experience.

These early experiences, often involving basic domestic equipment, are the early precursors of the concepts and thinking skills required for the National Curriculum. They are essential prerequisites of the ability to reconstruct in imagery and language, and so lead on to problem-solving. Many of the games introduced in the home area serve this function. They are typical of those found in the mainstream class, though the immediate aim of the nurture teacher may be to capture the children's attention, and provide an enjoyable activity through which they are made more aware of themselves, and more motivated to use experiences constructively.

Their sensory and motor experience is limited

The teacher often picks up basic deficits in early-level competencies during the course of directed group activities, or when a child is being introduced individually to a new toy or task. He may have difficulty in indicating body parts, have poor directional hand control or fine motor co-ordination and so time is given to developing his body image, perception of spatial relationships and hand–eye co-ordination on an individual basis, in some cases on the adult's knee. Many of the games played in the home area draw on basic experience that school-age children are assumed to have, but quite often reveal unexpected difficulties. Thus when required to guess by feel what is hidden in the 'feely bag', a child may fail to identify the object by touch because he has not had adequate prior experience of seeing and feeling each object on its own. Even when he has had this experience, the objects in the 'feely bag' may have to be very dissimilar at first if he is to make the discrimination required. In one school, a modification of this activity was more successful. Objects of different size, texture and resistance to touch were spread out on a large plain coloured square cloth, and the teacher described their qualities. The children looked at them, touched them, felt and explored them, shook and banged them, and the teacher made a running commentary. Specially designed felt masks that were acceptable to the children were used as blindfolds. One by one they felt and tried to describe and identify the object placed in their hands. At first the others called out, but very soon they learned to contain their eagerness, and to wait for their turn.

Visuo-motor co-ordination difficulties

Many nurture group children are clumsy and poorly co-ordinated in their gross movements, and have a poor sense of their bodies in space. They bump into things and people, and knock them over. Teachers comment on their poor judgement of distance, and often an additional factor is the excessive attention they give to one aspect of the situation. In many cases these difficulties seem related to restricted opportunities for movement and exploration at home. Motor co-ordination difficulties are apparent when the children try to dress themselves, or are taking part in a simple game in the school hall. They need to develop a more valid body image and to manage their bodies in space through simple activities such as cushion-throwing games, hand-clapping with the teacher, or holding hands with her and hopping together on one foot. Lifting the right leg or the left leg on request is a very popular game as are swinging games and romps with the teacher and assistant. There are many enjoyable activities that help them to experience and manage their bodies in space. They bounce on the bed or on a PE mat or trampoline. They make themselves very small and stretch out to be very big and take giant or pixie steps to reach a goal; and in wriggling through hoops of different sizes they learn that they must make themselves smaller to get through a small hoop. Passing a bean bag round the circle requires practice because it involves watching, taking, holding and passing on, all difficult operations for inexperienced children. A school that worked hard on activities of these kinds found that when two bean bags were passed round, the children continued to watch the progress of the first bag instead of turning to wait for the second one. Passing a ball between their legs or over their heads to another child also presented problems because they did not let go until they could see the other child. Co-ordinating two simultaneous tasks, for example walking upstairs holding a plate, is often difficult for them. They need help with balance, movement and directed action, and verbal instructions of up, down, forwards, backwards, which are directly linked with the actions, lead to an internalized sense of spatial relationships. Much can be learned from work done in special schools and from physiotherapists.

Many of the children who have poor control of their own movements and of themselves in relation to the objects around them also have a poor sense of volume and quantity, and little idea of what is practicable. They have difficulty in carrying a full jug, and need an adult to be there to watch them, and to tell them to go slowly and carefully. Even junior children may have difficulty with simple tasks of this kind and need monitoring help at every stage. In school a 9-year-old boy was asked to put orange squash in the jug 'up to here', and the teacher indicated. She then asked him to fill it with water 'up to here', and she indicated and 'carry it across the room, like this', and she demonstrated. Finally: 'Watch very carefully how you hold the jug, and watch very carefully where you go'. Children like this need to be shown, and told, that if a mug or jug is filled nearly to the brim it is difficult to carry it across the room without spilling some of the contents. They also need a warning to watch where they are walking, because often they attend to one thing only, and have difficulty in co-ordinating what they are doing with what they see.

Some children have difficulty with fine visuo-motor co-ordination evident when they try to button their clothes, or their hands are limp and movements poorly directed. Finger movement practice with a stickle ball, and digging their hands into Play-Doh to make patterns is helpful.

Learning to listen, pay attention and remember

The children have difficulty listening, paying attention and remembering, and a lot of the fun games in the home area centre round learning to listen and pay attention to sounds. They identify, locate and imitate sounds of differing kinds, and they make a game of discriminating between sounds, starting with very easy ones. Concepts of same, different, loud, soft, first, last and in the middle are later introduced. Rhythmic patterns, tapped out, similarly lend themselves to games of remembering, copying and discriminating. These games become more elaborate, for example the child whose name is clapped out as a rhythm is asked to get the biscuits. Verbal memory games, which also foster listening and remembering, are often very simple, for example the children pick out items specified by name from a collection of small objects presented afterwards, or they 'play' at following simple instructions. Functions of objects can be built into these games. Action songs and singing games are an important feature of the day, as they are in the mainstream infant class, and junior children as well as infants love them. They attend to the sounds and become more aware of sounds and rhythms. They learn the names of parts of the body, and the use of prepositions, and in linking words with actions gain a better sense of body image. Many of the children have speech problems of varied kinds and origin, including poor production and enunciation of words, and these games are helpful both directly and indirectly. They also contribute to a sense of self because of their direct focus on the person of the child, and because they often involve taking turns the children begin to listen to each other as they wait for their turn, and a personal interest develops. Tape recorders are useful; the teacher records what they say and plays it back to them.

Looking and remembering

Other games in the home area centre round paying attention to the things they see, and remembering them. The teacher puts a lot of familiar objects on a tray and they identify these by name, distinguish them and describe them, and they recall what is missing when she takes one away. They guess what she is describing when she starts off, 'I am thinking of . . .'. They match the doll's house furniture or the animals to pictures on cards, and when they are put into the 'feely bag' they find by touch the one represented on the card the teacher holds up.

Many of these activities are features of the mainstream infant class too, but the need in the nurture group is much greater. They are basic learning experiences for many of the children, even juniors, and they need to be taken purposefully through them. They enjoy these games and activities, and do not reject them as babyish.

Informal and more formal work on basic concepts

A great deal of work on basic concepts develops from experiences within the nurturing relationship. Everyday domestic items are a natural vehicle for early concept development but other equipment is typically that of the infant class and is developed more formally. Thus there is a range of items for grouping and ordering according to size, shape, colour, function, families, pairs and so on. There are picture cards for sequencing, action cards, pictures of objects that make familiar noises, card games involving listening and looking and then formulating an answer or making a decision, as well as dolls' houses, villages, railway sets and so on. Multi-purpose equipment is useful. Coloured shapes can be used for matching and grouping and sequencing by shape and colour, and later for copying patterns or following instructions to work in a particular way. Children gain through these activities much needed experience of fine motor control and co-ordination, and persistence as the pieces are put together. And for all of them, they are the basis of verbally formulated mathematical concepts, developed individually.

Supported pre-foundation stage learning

Activities otherwise in nurture groups are very similar to those in the mainstream infant class, but are weighted to an earlier level of experience and learning. Music, for example, is for some children the exuberant pleasure of being the agent of a great big noise. For others it involves taking turns with another child to make a great big noise. For others again the learning experience may lie in stopping and starting, making loud noises and soft noises as required, and so on. Making a collage may be less of a creative effort – though the end result might *appear* to be creative – than an experience of choosing colours, cutting round an outline shape provided by the teacher, and waiting while another child sticks his piece on. In all these activities the adult's involvement is important. She gives direct support, shares the experience, and participates in the activity as an equal partner to a greater extent than in the mainstream class. Appreciation of the child's efforts is also directed more to the growing edge of the child's developing skills, for example for holding the scissors well or showing initiative, than to the end product though this, too, would elicit pleasure. Work on a full-scale outline of himself, or his hands or feet, direct records of height and mirror work are features of the mainstream class, too. They carry the same learning experiences, but for the experienced child they are a way of consolidating and developing existing concepts, while for some nurture children they contribute to the first awakenings of physical self-awareness. A child in a junior group saw himself for the first time when he looked in the classroom mirror, and another junior child who was painting-in an outline of himself, coloured brown only the parts he could see, gradually extending this as he pushed up his sleeves to see more.

Play activities have important learning content

Many of the play activities in the nurture group are similar to those in the mainstream class, but there is more licence to enjoy the sensory properties of the materials. Finger-painting and hand and foot printing are fun; they contribute to body image and self-awareness, but they require control and this is gradually built up. Similarly crayons come before paints, and wet sand comes before dry sand. Co-operative play is also similar to that in the mainstream class. The teacher and assistant become involved in these activities and provide ideas, create images, highlight feelings, and by their interjections lead the children into new understandings and awareness. A great deal of purposeful learning is achieved in this ad hoc way.

Topics

The teacher introduces and structures work on topics, for example hospitals, hairdressing or the chemist's shop. The children draw on stories read to them, or from direct experience on their outings. All involve thinking through what is required, planning in discussion, and finding, making and organizing the necessary equipment; co-operation and sharing; and giving and accepting roles, active and passive. Hospitals and hairdressing involve making and accepting physical contact, which many of them find difficult, caring for each other and physical awareness. When playing hospitals they find and name body parts, also difficult for many of the children. At the hairdressers they cut out pictures of hairstyles and make magazines for the customer to read. They become aware of their appearance as they discuss styles and care of the hair, and with this is self-esteem, and indirect eye contact as the customer and stylist look at each other in the mirror. The learning opportunities are at different levels and are immense, and the role-play can develop imaginatively and sometimes has therapeutic content.

Teacher-directed and formally presented 'work'

Every nurture teacher stresses the importance of formal work. Many of the children are potentially able and want to succeed in school, and their frustration and profound sense of failure when they cannot understand or do what is required is sometimes a factor in their behaviour difficulties. Formal work, furthermore, can be a respite. It provides organization and direction rather than requiring it, and for inexperienced children who have little organization and direction it is less demanding than free play. It is also a support to a teacher who is bewildered when starting work of this kind, but is reassured to fall back on proven skills, albeit greatly modified. Formal work, therefore, is stabilizing, provided it is within the child's competence, and is likely to fit into his expectations of school, and those of his parents. Lastly, the teacher's aim is to get the child to the stage when he can use constructively the wide range of experiences and relationships of the mainstream class, and can engage with the National Curriculum. To achieve this he needs formal attainments and the personal resources for adequate participation in age-appropriate activities. Stress is therefore placed from the beginning on basic skills work and the widening of experiences, and through this the development of concepts, for the longer this is delayed the wider will be the gap between the child's achievements and the expectations of his mainstream class teacher.

Formal work is not relevant for some children

For some of the children formal work in any conventional sense is not relevant. For them, reading is at first being read to on the teacher's lap. Mathematics may be no more than the teacher or assistant counting the child's fingers or toes, a formal supplement to the incidental counting that is important for many of the children, including juniors. Writing may be no more than a scrawl on a piece of paper, and the child's first need in relation to formal work may be to learn to sit at a table and hold a pencil. Nevertheless, except in the case of the most undeveloped or out-of-touch children, conventional formal work of some kind is possible and is required. It is patterned on that of the mainstream class and is built into the day's routine from the beginning. Most of the children, however, function constructively only within an early and close 'mother–child' relationship. Even when they seem able to manage an activity on their own they may need the pleasure, reassurance and security of doing things with the adult. Their response to the homely running commentary that accompanies this is not necessarily because they need this level of language, though some do, but because they need the more intimate relationship of which it is a part. Even older junior children accept and use a close relationship of this kind when they are secure within the group. Formal work is therefore in the context of a more intimately supportive relationship than is usual in the mainstream class.

Formal work may be very basic at first

For many of the children the formal work attempted is at first very simple, for most of them have only limited competence. Every aspect of the situation is therefore carefully monitored to ensure that the task and the social requirements are manageable. Launching the children into their activities has already been described. They are sent off one by one, with individual support, a word or a touch, and are handed over to the assistant, or are taken by the teacher's hand. The adults physically help each child, whether infant or junior, into his place, because they do not assume that he will sit at the table in the best position in relation to his work. They ensure that he has sufficient space because the close proximity of another child might disturb him. The work itself is done on paper, or in a large book with very few pages, and the teacher waits until everyone is attending before putting this and other necessary materials on the table. Many of the children are initially not able to share and choose, and so a pencil or crayon each, or an individual carton of crayons, is more appropriate at first than a wide selection of colours stacked in a communal jar. They are each given a pencil or a crayon, and are shown how to hold it, how to position the page, where on the page to write or draw, and how to turn the page. Many of them have difficulty in understanding simple instructions involving spatial concepts, and so the teacher indicates or demonstrates what she requires. She gives instructions to each child individually in short simple sentences, clearly expressed. She may then, as at other times, ask the children to tell her what she has said, sometimes more than once, or she repeats it and asks the child to listen again, or she rephrases what she has said.

She chooses an activity that is well within the child's capacity and concentration span, perhaps no more than a colouring-in or copying activity that is as simple as it can be made and can be finished very quickly. It has to be done, though her expectations may be minimal at first because the pressure, initially, is on trying and taking care, and not interfering with the other child. The children respond to the controls and formality, and appear to get great pleasure from knowing what to do and how to manage these simple manoeuvres.

Basic activities are carefully monitored

The level of development catered for in different groups and within a group varies considerably. The less experienced children might begin by copying a simple line drawing, the teacher doing it first to show them what is required. Some teachers prefer this to be done in pencil initially, and as each child finishes his drawing and is ready to colour-in she gives him a crayon, or a carton of crayons according to his ability to manage. The rationale for this procedure is that the child does not draw initially in colour because this is exciting and might distract him from his first task, which is to copy or draw, and a number of crayons might present him with a choice he is not capable of making. Once the pencil drawing is done, time can be given to making a choice, if necessary with the adult's help, and this would be a shared pleasure. Here, again, the acceptance of constraints, the forgoing of a pleasure, is followed by the satisfaction of the shared pleasure. Most teachers, however, provide a single colour at first and a choice of colours later. It is also usual to restrain scribbling at formal work time. The children need this level of expression, as they need the joy of using colours, but they are satisfactions in their own right, and so are left till another time, usually later in the day during a period of play when they can give themselves fully to enjoying the fun. And no matter what the level of competence of the children, the teacher and assistant watch over them and intervene and give active help to any child who seems confused. They anticipate anything that might go wrong, because most of the children have a low tolerance for frustration and might express this in destructive action.

Potential interference is controlled

A general problem in children in nurture groups is their poor tolerance for real or imagined interference by others, and so it is particularly important that they are well spaced, otherwise they might inadvertently nudge each other or interfere. Partly for this reason some teachers stagger formal work throughout the day and have only two children or three at the most at the worktable at any one time, well spaced to avoid accidental nudging or interference. Tables, around which perhaps half a dozen children sit, encourage a high level of peer group interaction but also distraction and interference. For useful work to be done in these circumstances the children must have considerable personal organization and self-control, and a high level of motivation for the task in hand. These are not characteristics of 'nurture' children but, when the situation is carefully controlled and the teacher and assistant are close by to give help, they are able to give attention and persist. The old-style classroom with individual desks and teacher-focused work on the wallboard is probably more appropriate, developmentally, for the nurture child than is a shared table; it confines him within his own area, as a playpen would, and he makes direct eye contact with the teacher. Tables are usual in nurture groups, but in two junior groups where desks were tried the teachers commented that the children settled better and were more attentive. Corrals in infant and junior groups were helpful because there was less outside stimulation and interference, and the children concentrated better on their activities.

A slow pace and much repetition and encouragement is needed

Formal work proceeds as it would in the mainstream infant class, but at a slower pace, with a big component of early skills and listening experiences, and a great deal of direct support, encouragement, reassurance and praise, and detailed verbalization. More repetition is needed, partly because the children are mastering unfamiliar tasks and are co-ordinating skills that normally would have been well practised at an earlier stage, but also because they need the pleasure of anticipated success, and the satisfaction of the reality of success. It is important that the activity gives a visually gratifying end result, but above all else it is essential that the requirements are realistic and commensurate with the child's developmental level. Pressure to achieve at this level is considerable and good standards are expected, but at the same time high expectations for the future are maintained. In practice it is not easy at first to tune in to an early enough level and to work unhurriedly at this level when there is so much ground to make up. But, although for many of the children the formal work they do is very simple at first, in time it extends to storywriting, properly set out number work, and in some cases more abstract language work including concepts of time and space.

Growth towards personal and social autonomy

A stable and predictable environment is a universal need for young people, but for nurture children it is of critical importance whatever their level of personal organization and control. Experiences within this are carefully controlled from the beginning, and supports are provided at a level commensurate with the challenge and the child's resources to meet it. But he is not confined to the nurture classroom. He is within and part of the school, and is exposed to complex and changing events and reactions of other people over which the nurture teacher has comparatively little control. These situations cannot be avoided, and have to be faced. Assembly, dinnertime and playtime are major areas of difficulty, as are outings, to varying extents, and the period during which the child is being tried in his mainstream class. Christmas time also is stressful. All these situations require of the teacher and assistant an imaginative anticipation of possible hazards, and even more planning and thought than is necessary for the familiar experiences of the nurture group.

Assembly, dinnertime and playtime demand considerable personal organization and self-control, and for the nurture child present particular difficulty. He is thrust into the close proximity of large numbers of unfamiliar children in a big space that has no immediately visible limits. There is no familiar structure and routine, the situation is bewildering and he is without the direct, immediate and personal support and control of an adult with whom he has a special relationship. Situations of these kinds are likely to exacerbate problems, and may generate them.

Assembly

Assembly presents less difficulty than dinnertime or playtime, for all the children go into the hall, class by class, in an organized and orderly way with a familiar adult, in the expectation that high standards of behaviour will be maintained by everyone. 'Last in, first out' works well for the nurture group children as they find it difficult to wait for the other classes to come in and go out. Assembly itself is a ritualized event which is repeated day after day, and has form and familiarity even if it means little to some of the children. Distraction and interference, whether accidental or deliberate, is usually minimal because most children in the school are able to sit reasonably still when required, and focus their attention on the person leading assembly, though in some schools restless, interfering and fidgety behaviour is general. Assembly presents considerable problems for children who are poorly organized and distractible, and have difficulty in listening and maintaining attention, because they are expected to keep still – itself not always easy – in a situation which, with the greatest care on the part of the headteacher, holds their attention only momentarily.

Assembly varies from school to school, not only in the time of day and the form it takes, but in the number of children collected together, and the latitude that is allowed for disturbing behaviour. Small assemblies present fewer problems, and the introduction of two assemblies, each with half the number of children, reduces stress in big schools. Whether assembly is at the beginning of the school day or later on, a reassuring peaceful time in the home area with the nurture teacher and assistant beforehand is relaxing and they are reminded to sit still and not interfere with the others.

They need preparation and support to manage in Assembly

In a small school where every member of staff understands how difficult Assembly is for nurture group children, it is usually possible for most of them, given adequate preparation and support, to participate from the beginning. A very inexperienced, unorganized child for whom the situation was meaningless would not be able to manage on his own. The teacher might carry him in on her hip and he would lie or sit on her lap. Others in need of direct support would be given a soft cuddly toy to take with them. More usually such children do not go into Assembly. They have a special time to themselves and are taken in only when they have a concept of the larger school group. Children who are developmentally a little more advanced may be able to endure Assembly if they are close to the teacher or assistant, and some may need to sit propped up against her legs, or on her lap. Otherwise they are likely to disturb the others with their poorly controlled and interfering behaviour. Children who register with their own class go from there into Assembly only if they can sit still without disturbing the others. A problem that sometimes arises is clapping to the music. This may be a familiar activity in the nurture group but is not required in Assembly.

In bigger schools the stress is greater, for there are large numbers of unfamiliar children and adults. The situation is disturbing and frightening, and some nurture teachers feel it is preferable, and may be necessary, to keep their children out of Assembly until they have sufficient self-control to manage.

They are not expected to take part in Assembly

Going into Assembly is a recognition that the children are part of the larger school group, but the extent to which they are expected to take part is sometimes a problem in schools where each class in turn presents work or gives a display. The stress is likely to be more than the children can withstand and the work involved takes time and is likely to conflict with the nurture teacher's immediate aims for the group. Participation at this level is rarely feasible at the beginning. Some children barely function at first, even in the nurture group. For others, a public display is likely to exacerbate showing off and antic-ing and could lead to uncontrolled excitement and tantrums, while for those who have serious problems of self-regard it is a situation of embarrassment and humiliation. Other children thrive when the centre of attention and gain from the experience, provided they are carefully prepared and closely monitored. In spite of the difficulties, most nurture groups are able to provide something of interest on these occasions, if the context is sympathetic. In one school a vigorous Lambeth Walk was performed by the children, made possible because the teacher and assistant took part, all appropriately dressed.

Dinnertime

School dinnertime is more difficult. It comes at the end of the morning and for all the children in the school is a time of physical release after a long period of disciplined confinement, and there is the expectation of food. Some children come into school without breakfast and will be hungry. The dining hall is crowded, noisy and full of unfamiliar people. Frequently the acoustics are bad, and noise and excitement rises. The dinners are usually served quickly and used cutlery gets slammed into metal containers to be washed for the second sitting. Many of the children have loud voices and now talk even more loudly. Standards slip, and greedy, grabbing behaviour is not confined to children in the nurture group. The situation is inherently stressful, and for nurture children is intolerable. Space is limited but they are required to wait patiently, without jostling or overreacting to interference from others. Time, too, is limited and they are expected to choose quickly from the foods provided and even junior children may have difficulty with this. Some children are too inhibited to say they do not like a particular food; others are reluctant to eat anything. Others again have a restricted choice for religious reasons and find the needed discrimination difficult, though colour coding the different foods has resolved this problem. They then have to carry their food without spilling or dropping anything across a crowded hall to a particular place, and then have to manage the cutlery. Many of them have poor manipulative skills, are clumsy and have difficulty with the sequence of complex operations required, but everything is rushed and they are expected to be quick. For these reasons many teachers take their children into the dining hall and stay with them until they have collected their food and are seated at the table. Even then there is stress, because they have to relate to children they may not know, and if anything goes wrong they expect to be blamed. The difficulties are considerably eased when the teacher has her dinner with them, particularly if they sit round a 'family' table. There is less trouble in the playground afterwards and most teachers feel that this extra time with the children is well spent. It is clearly helpful if the dinner staff know the children and are sympathetic to their difficulties.

Dinnertime is very trying for everyone

The conditions in most dining halls are very trying for staff and children alike. The situation eases in time, partly because of the attention given to food as a social occasion in the nurture group and in some schools experience of a cafeteria on outings, and partly because the children all the time are gaining increasing self-control in the face of stress. And as the group becomes established and change in the children is evident for all to see, the ancillary staff become increasingly involved in the process, and any initial scepticism or hostility usually disappears.

The playground

The playground is the worst situation of all, and many children throughout the school are unnerved by the lack of direct teacher organization and control, and dislike going out at playtime. In most playgrounds there is little opportunity for safe and constructive play, though strenuous attempts have been made in many schools to remedy this. The children have a long stretch of time ahead with nothing specific to do, and few are able to initiate and develop their own satisfying activity. Playgrounds, furthermore, are big places full of lots of other children. The situation is complex, fast moving, often chaotic and sometimes dangerous, and there is sudden movement and real or imagined attack. Excitement is at a high level and provocation, unintentional or not, is considerable. The sudden release of energy under these unstructured conditions inevitably shows itself in aggressive behaviour, and the nurture children are not the only ones who cannot cope.

Most of the children go out at playtime

In spite of the problems that were expected and the initial misgivings, virtually all the children are sent out at playtime with the other classes. The teacher and assistant need a break from the children, and the children need to feel part of the school, and must be seen by the other children to be part of the school, and to be potential friends. Out-of-touch children who cannot manage in situations of this kind sit with the school secretary, nurture teacher or assistant, or headteacher, by her feet with a toy as she has her coffee or gets on with her work. Such cases are rare. The rest go out. The timid unventuring children are likely to attach themselves to the adults who are supervising, or they cling together doing nothing very much. For the other children there are grave difficulties. They have insufficient personal resources and internalized structure and control to use the situation constructively, and cannot co-operate with others or tolerate anyone getting in their way. Dislike of physical contact also is common, and many of them see provocation where none is intended.

They need preparation for playtime every day

They need special help in anticipating what might happen at playtime and in learning what to do and what not to do. A great deal of preparation is needed and this is repeated before playtime *every* day until controlled behaviour in the playground is an established pattern. The teacher describes the sequence of events from classroom to playground and the situations that are likely to arise there. She anticipates their feelings in detail, tells them what they are to do and then asks them to tell her what they are to do. If any child is not attentive she addresses him by name and repeats the question. If he does not answer the teacher might answer the question herself, and then turn to another child and ask him to give the answer, and then reinforces this further by again reminding all of them what they are to do. Even a junior group may need to practise, on their own and during lesson time, the sensible way of going to the playground, and coming back.

The situation is eased if the nurture teacher and assistant are there

If the nurture teacher or assistant is supervising at playtime, the nurture group children often cluster round and have been described as clinging like leeches; or they take something from her to wear as they go off on their own, and then return and go off again. It is helpful for the nurture teacher and assistant to be there because they are a secure base and a visible reminder of attitudes and standards. They remind the children of their expectations, provide ideas and show the children how to organize themselves and develop the ideas. The children manage better with this help, and are able to do more when left on their own.

The situation is more difficult if an unfamiliar person is supervising at playtime

If someone else is supervising the nurture teacher goes to the playground with the children and takes them to him/her to say 'hello'. They know they are to go to that person if there are difficulties. They also know where the nurture teacher and assistant are and can go to them if they need to and are reassured to know that they really are where they said they would be.

The nurture teacher reassumes responsibility if there is trouble in the playground

If the situation goes badly wrong the children concerned are brought back into school and the nurture teacher or assistant reassumes responsibility for them. They sit at her feet with a book or small toy. They sit quietly, and although not criticized they are not given extra attention. Sitting with the teacher or assistant at playtime is preferable to the playground for most of the children, but they are not intended to experience this as a treat, for the aim is to help them to learn to manage in the playground.

The playground is inherently unsatisfactory

It is recognized that the playground is a difficult place for all children and that work has to be put into the physical surroundings, the facilities provided and the organization of the space. Structuring the time spent in the playground also is important, for at midday this can be as long as one hour or more, and appropriate activities may need to be taught and practised in the classroom beforehand. A fenced-off area with seating for quiet activities has been found to be helpful, as has the availability of indoor play in the school hall for any child who prefers this.

In some schools all the teachers are in the playground just before the end of playtime, and the children line up by them when the end-of-playtime signal is given. Lining up formally appears to be usual in schools where the level of disruptive behaviour is high.

The nurture teacher is always told about incidents in the playground

Problems in the playground nevertheless arise, and it is the nurture child who is often at the centre of trouble. There are, however, two important stabilizing factors. They know where the teacher and assistant are, and that they can go to them if in difficulties and this is a reassurance. They also know that the nurture teacher will be told about incidents in the playground, and those involved will be taken to her, or she will be brought out to deal with it. The situation may not be propitious. The person supervising may be upset and angry. The situation is beyond the child and it is not his fault that he cannot cope. Equally, the person supervising cannot cope either. It is clearly inappropriate to punish the child, though sanctions may be necessary and, if he is upset, comforting him may weaken the possibility of more mature behaviour. The only thing to do is to affirm that behaving properly in the playground is a requirement; it has to be learned but is difficult. Unfortunately, the adult concerned has already made her negative feelings and condemning attitude clear to the child, and will hand him over to the nurture teacher in the expectation that she will follow the same line. When this does not happen s/he is likely to feel even more negative, and her feeling that the nurture teacher's sympathies are with the child rather than with her leads to further estrangement from the teacher and the child, and disenchantment with the whole notion of 'being nice' to those 'awful children'. Clearly, the more everyone in the school understands the nature of the difficulties of the children who cause disruption, and the method of approach in the nurture group, and the need for a co-ordinated and consistent response, the less likely is this kind of situation to occur.

Incidents in the playground are talked through afterwards

Although all the learning that goes on in the nurture group contributes eventually to better behaviour in the playground, specific attention to this is nevertheless needed and problems arising are not only anticipated and discussed beforehand but are talked through afterwards in the classroom.

The nurture teacher asks the adult involved to tell her exactly what happened, and the children know that she knows exactly what happened. Some have no idea at all of what went wrong. Others can, with difficulty, be helped to think it through and put it into words. These are usually older children, and a great deal of time and patience is needed to obtain a reliable story. All the children concerned are in turn asked what happened, and what went wrong, and they have to sit and listen, and contain their outrage. Not surprisingly, an imperfect perception of the situation is common. Increased understanding usually comes only when the children have learned sufficient self-control to maintain some awareness of what is happening at the time, and the main value of talking-through at this stage is to focus attention on the teacher's requirement for self-control, self-awareness and personal responsibility.

Some children may need to be kept in school at playtime

When a child is persistently a problem in the playground it may be necessary to let him stay in school. An activity that keeps him occupied and busy is provided. Washing up is a sought-after privilege and is seen by the children as a reward, and if the class breakfast comes before playtime it is logical to do it then. This keeps the child out of trouble and he gets the teacher's appreciation for doing a needed job well. It is, however, a privilege; it is not a regular event and the other children must have a turn. This method of handling the problem is not usual and has serious risks, because washing up is more attractive than playtime. It may even be counterproductive because of the privileged nature of the task, and it will not help him to take part in playtime activities. The problem is difficult to resolve and it is the general view that strenuous attempts must be made to make the playtime situation more manageable and attractive, and that provision should be made in school for children who cannot manage without direct help.

Many children have no prior experience of playing in a group

In many schools, often where the level of tension is high, there is a relative absence of traditional ritualized games, presumably linked with loss of continuity from generation to generation, seen particularly in schools where the children are from different ethnic backgrounds. A contributory factor is that many of the children have no prior experience of learning to play with other children in a small-group situation that is less chaotic and confusing than that of the playground. Some are not allowed by their parents to go outside to play and appear to spend many hours watching television and videos instead. Their talk suggests that they are receptive to undifferentiated themes, of which violence is the most striking. They accept this as normal behaviour, are imitative, and any games they develop in the playground are likely to have violent content. Here again, it is helpful to provide the possibility of structured play in the playground by explicitly teaching the children traditional games as a classroom lesson, or even as a feature of assembly where perhaps once a month the children learn a new game. Active help from an adult in the playground, by providing ideas or direct leadership, is clearly of value, for even when the children are able to initiate their own game they may not be able to organize themselves and develop the game, and need an adult to lead them. But more important than anything else is the attitude of all the teachers and support staff in the school. Where they have an understanding of the special difficulties of these children, and are alerted to what might go wrong and how to deal with it, the total situation is easier, particularly if expectations and management are consistent and become anticipated by the children. And, of course, it is not only the children in the nurture group who are in difficulties at playtime. The problem concerns the entire school, and little can be done by the nurture teacher alone.

Many of the children attend after-school clubs. This is very difficult for them. They cannot cope with team games, which even when simple require many co-ordinated skills. They do not take in the full picture but tend to concentrate on one aspect only of the situation, and they are slow to draw on relevant skills and to process rapidly changing events.

Christmas

Christmas is an exciting time in schools and the preparations for it usually start shortly after half-term and build up to a climax of a publicly performed nativity play or concert, sometimes a film show or other entertainment, and parties and a Christmas dinner. It is a time of special stress for the teachers and support staff who work hard to make it a success, but it can be an overwhelming experience for some of the children and may exacerbate their difficulties.

Unexpected problems arise

The problems that arise are sometimes entirely unexpected. In a junior school, when a film was shown in the school hall as a treat, the children ignored the screen and turned excitedly to the source of the light, nudging each other and exclaiming. The film was stopped and their attention was drawn to the screen. Then there was another unanticipated hazard. One of the characters when appearing for the first time was very amusing and they laughed. When he appeared again he was not funny but they laughed uproariously, inappropriately and disruptively. The teacher was disappointed by their behaviour. The film was stopped again and they were taken back to class. The incident was talked through and the teacher and assistant now understood what had happened; 'We'll try again', and the children were able to follow the film at a second showing. In another junior school the children had been carefully prepared for a supervised and well-rehearsed musical parcel game. They all went to the Christmas party in the school hall and took part well, but in the parcel-passing game one of the boys was unable to contain his excitement. He tore off the wrapping with his teeth when he should have passed the parcel on, and stuffed the chocolate bar into his mouth. This was a child who did not know, when he came into the group, that he had five fingers on each hand.

The stress has to be controlled

All that can be done in school when Christmas approaches is to slow the pace, control the excitement and regulate the extent of participation in the school activities in accordance with the coping capacity of each child. Nevertheless, in spite of the problems and stress, most children in the nurture groups are able to make a modest contribution to the school Christmas festivities, and respond with pleasure to the especially nice happenings at this time. But success is possible only because of careful organization by the nurture teacher and assistant, and a sympathetic attitude in the school as a whole.

Christmas at home may not be a happy time

Another factor is that the children leave a situation of heightened stimulation and high expectation in school, and may go home to restricted conditions where nothing special is happening. There may be no presents there and if they take home with pleasure a present for their parents made in school it may not be well received. The gesture may intensify the parents' depression and sense of deprivation, and the feeling that they are failing their child as they feel themselves to have been failed by others. In some homes the present may be resented as an unwelcome intrusion and resisted by parents whose religion is different. For these families the time spent on Christmas is a waste of time, and the festivities an affront to their situation. Far from being a festive occasion, Christmas for many families is a time when a sense of deprivation, loneliness and alienation is at its most intense. Tempers are likely to be frayed and recriminations rife, and the exuberance of demanding children can be the last straw. Other families, equally under stress, are kept highly charged by a wild rush of noisy and overstimulating parties which keep everyone up virtually all night long.

Many of the children are kept indoors during the holidays. For much of the day there is little to occupy them and any presents provided may be unsuitable or readily broken, and cause frustration. For a long period of time they are in an unusually stressful situation, and when they return to school after Christmas have usually lost ground.

Out and about

Many children in nurture groups have an unusually confused and fragmented picture of the world beyond home and school, and this was particularly so in some of the recently arrived children of immigrant parents when the groups were first established. Some had never been on a bus, and when taken onto the top deck thought the bus was falling over, or dashed from side to side, not connecting up the views but treating each as though a separate television screen. Some had never been in a shop, not even a shoe shop, and were frightened or overwhelmed by the experience, or were intoxicated by the mysterious and exciting things they saw.

Outings are important, but preparation is needed

Outings for all the children continue to be important. They are introduced gradually and with preparation. Simple outings come first, and any kind of outing suitable for a family with pre-school children is likely to be successful. Preparation for all outings, however simple, is made with care. Detailed planning is essential, and all the children are thoroughly prepared for a new experience even if this is only a slight extension of something they have done before, and all possible deviations from the familiar pattern are anticipated. The teacher tells them in detail what to expect, what to do and how to behave and, if necessary, the situations they are likely to encounter are set up in the classroom and they enact the desired behaviour beforehand, sometimes for several days. Even junior children may need to be shown, in advance of the event, how to wait at the kerb before crossing the road. The teacher describes how excited they feel, she verbalizes their likely fears and explains that if they feel excited or frightened they must not rush about and disturb other people but must tell her about it instead. If it is a major outing, perhaps to the city farm or museum, they know they must go straight to her or the assistant if there is any trouble, or if they do not know what to do. But not all disasters can be anticipated. One assistant took four children to Woolworth's. They were used to going to small local shops and at first all went well. Then one of the children spotted the contents of a burst packet of rubber bands, scattered on the floor. All the children swooped on the rubber bands and crawled on the floor to retrieve them. Chaos followed. But not all outings go badly. Another teacher and assistant took their children to the Science Museum, and the teacher later said with pride: 'There were lots of other classes there, but *we* were the best behaved of all.'

Outings can be overwhelming

Situations which might overtax the children are as far as possible avoided, and they are not expected to do too much too quickly. Even the prospect

of an exciting trip can be overwhelming, and a successful outing is sometimes followed by fidgety, restless, overexcited and giggly behaviour, and
the next day may have to be modified if the children are still in an unsettled state. Indeed, many seem happier when back to a known and secure
routine, and may prefer this to what was intended as a treat. Anxiety,
excitement and tiredness all contribute, compounded by frustration as the
children begin to cope less well. They become fractious and tearful, disappointed and desolate.

They go to the local shops

It is usual for the children to go out with the assistant, one or two only at
first. She then gradually, with careful mixing, builds up to bigger groups.
They like to hold her hand, and quickly learn to behave well. The first visits are usually to the local shop to buy food for the group. They go regularly in turn and it becomes a routine event. Some of them pass the shop
each day on their way to school and know how to get there. They could
go alone, but need and respond to the security and warmth and the very
special pleasure of the shared enjoyment of an adventure. Many of them
talk very loudly when they first go out, and have difficulty in walking in
an orderly way. Others are overwhelmed, whisper to the adult and cling
tightly. The shop is a new and wondrous experience for some of them and
they have difficulty in controlling their excitement. For others, who know
about shops and have the anxiety of domestic responsibilities at home, it
is an opportunity to learn to choose and to count out the money in a situation which is carefree and enjoyable. For all of them it is a needed extension of experience and for many is an exciting adventure, and they ask
questions and comment eagerly. These are relaxed and enjoyable occasions. Very close relationships are built up, and many of the children talk
more freely on an outing than they ever do in school, and the teacher and
assistant feel they get to know them in a much more personal way. On
other outings they simply look in the shop windows, and many of them
seem fascinated by all the things they see. They visit the bank, the laun-
derette and the post office and learn what grown-ups do, and watch or
help. Later they might go to the supermarket with a breakfast or birthday
shopping list. They carefully take the tins from the shelf without knocking
them over, and queue without jostling the others. Occasionally they go to
the cafeteria and take pleasure in learning the procedure, in choosing what
to have and in behaving well.

They make social visits

The assistant in the ILEA groups usually lived locally, and if a visit to her
home was suggested the children anticipated this with eagerness, and it
was immediately a favourite event. They had milk and a biscuit there, or a

cup of tea and a piece of cake. They behaved well. Some of them were unduly subdued, but most chatted freely, were interested, asked questions and were thrilled when they saw where the assistant's children slept. Although initially there were misgivings about these visits, and sometimes they were not feasible or were contra-indicated, the teachers and assistants found that their relationship with the children was strengthened. Another local trip sometimes undertaken was to the nurture group in a nearby school that was within walking distance or was a short bus ride away. The visiting children took flowers or baked a cake and were received with great pleasure. The children in the host school had prepared food and handed this round with pride, and enjoyed showing their guests how to play with their toys. Invitations and thank-you letters, written individually where this was appropriate, or by the teacher in collaboration with the class, were part of the experience and added to the pleasure and interest of the occasion, as well as having social and educational content.

They go to the library

A visit to the library is also an important outing, and the children learn to cope with this surprisingly quickly. It is usual for the teacher to tell the librarian in advance that they are coming and the problems that might arise, and to choose a time when few other people are likely to be there. Some teachers prefer to hold back this experience until the children are established in their mainstream class and they then visit the library with *them*. The library books are very important to the children. They are theirs, to be looked after carefully and kept in their work trays. They give a feeling of ownership but are regularly exchanged and so are shared with the others; and there is a sense of permanence, as well as continuity and progression.

They go to the local park

Other local visits are to a nearby park and the same features are seen in many of the groups at the beginning of the year. The younger or more inhibited children are timid and overwhelmed, and cluster round the teacher and assistant, frightened to leave them and uncertain of what to do. The older and more outgoing ones seem intoxicated by the experience. They strain as though on a lead and when 'released' rush round in circles at tremendous speed. The teacher of the first junior group described how one of them tended to lead and the others would run after him, then another would go off in a different direction and they would then all follow him. They seemed intoxicated: 'They didn't look but seemed to need to touch . . . excited, but greedy. They see; they want.' They sulked and got into fights, squabbled, had tantrums and returned to school exhausted. This greedy quality was no longer apparent by the summer term, and in the park they fed the ducks, ran for the swings and played ball together.

Later they go on longer outings

The most important outings are the local out-and-about ventures two or three times a week, and a half-day in the local park every two weeks or so. Later in the year some of the groups are able to manage a whole day away. Outings in the country, or locally if there is plenty of space to run, are preferred and shopping for food and preparing a picnic lunch beforehand is an important part of the event. The children are often not interested in playing with a ball because there are too many other things to do, and plenty of oddments to collect. Some of them are frightened of animals, but by the time they make these long trips they are beginning to overcome their fears. In the nurture group they have played with furry soft toy animals and later have managed to stroke the school animals, and when out of school have watched their teacher pat an approaching dog, and while holding her hand have mustered the courage to do this themselves. Another successful outing early on is a visit to a (city) farm. Towards the end of the year, when the children are more experienced and are accustomed to going out, visits to the museum or the zoo are manageable. As they become more confident and enjoy being independent they can be left on their own for long periods, or they go off on their own returning regularly to the teacher as they have been trained to do. They feel secure because the teacher and assistant are there, and they can look back for reassurance from time to time. These more important and formal outings are treated as special occasions. The children tidy up beforehand and might even polish their shoes. Outings of this kind require of the child an adequate level of organization and experience. They are of no relevance to some of the children. One teacher described a visit to the zoo, and her dismay when one of the children determinedly stayed just within the gates, happily absorbed in making traces in the dust with his fingers.

When a visit has been carefully thought out in relation to the children's experience but nevertheless goes wrong, it is often because the unexpected has happened, or there have been too many things to do in the time available. The more elaborate outings have to be built up very carefully, in planned stages, and then taken very slowly. Bringing the children back to the adult to calm and reassure them and reinforce the attachment is as important on an outing as it is in the first few weeks of the group in school.

Outings provide important learning experiences

A great deal can be built into these outings. Apart from the shared anticipation of a pleasurable experience, the children need the experience itself, and to share the experience. But at first few of them remember, or appear to experience anything other than the basic, dramatic or personally relevant things, like seeing two dogs in a fight, being stuck in a tunnel in the train or having an iced lolly. They need a lot of help in noticing and remembering at the time, and some may need to be told beforehand to try to remember one thing to tell the others when they get back to school. As they become more experienced and controlled they notice more, and ask about the things they see about them and what they are for, and begin to remember more. The teacher and assistant elaborate and develop the situation in language, making personal links for the children that extend their experience, evoke imagery and give feeling to it. They help them to notice the warmth of the sun on their faces and the crunch of leaves beneath their feet, and although some of them say very little they begin to take in a great deal, and gain a greater awareness of themselves and their feelings. Treats, on these outings, are a shared indulgence, an affirmation of the shared satisfaction of the experience, and the relationship that supports it. Outings are also an important contribution to class identity, and provide a bank of class memories of events and feelings that can be recorded in photographs, to be recalled at leisure. They lead to observations and comparisons, and evoke links with other events. They also enhance awareness and acknowledgement of the children for each other, and encourage conversation.

There are other learning experiences. Standing in the queue in the cafeteria is an exercise in containing excitement and sometimes fatigue, and involves waiting and letting someone else go first. It also requires awareness of physical boundaries, and tolerance of the close proximity of other people as the children wait without jostling each other. Carrying their lemonade and a bun to the table is so difficult for many of the children, even at the junior stage, that the situation is enacted in the classroom beforehand.

They learn to manage the class money

These outings also require acceptance by the children that a choice has to be made, perhaps between an attractive looking red jelly with a blob of cream on top and a seductive chocolate wafer. Discussing the cost of different things, and whether or not the class money will run to an ice cream each, is also part of the occasion. The children may decide not to have the biggest and most expensive ice cream, in order to leave enough money for ice creams the following week. In situations of this kind they are helped to tolerate the disappointment of delaying or giving up a satisfaction, and in doing so become more aware of themselves as self-determined agents of choice. Frustration is sometimes deliberately built in by the teacher and assistant, in ways they feel are tolerable. Time ran out for a junior group on an out-of-school trip, and they missed a promised ice cream: 'We were having such fun, but never mind, we'll have a sweet in school instead.' The teacher and assistant could share with the children the loss of the ice cream because they had shared the enjoyment of ice cream in the past; and in offering sweets they acknowledged the disappointment, and in sharing the sweet they faced up to the disappointment together.

Suitable clothing is collected

Because outings are so important, many schools collect outdoor clothing for the children to wear – anoraks, scarves, socks, gloves, wellingtons. Splashing through puddles in their wellies is a very special pleasure, and if they get wet they enjoy having their feet dried afterwards, and being helped to put on fresh socks. The class clothes mean a great deal to them, and from time to time they are washed and hung up to dry.

Firm action is sometimes needed

The behaviour expected on an outing is solely to ensure each child's enjoyment of the occasion and the well-being of the group as a whole. But in spite of all the care that is taken, and the very reasonable restrictions imposed, not all outings go well. If a child fails to meet the requirements, and after adequate warning persistently fails to conform, he is immediately taken back to school even if this is a long way away. Considerable strength of mind is needed to go through with this, as the teacher may be left with a large group on her own and the assistant has the job of getting a resistive child back to school. The teacher and assistant try to be single-minded and show no hesitation, and if necessary everyone returns to school. The children remember occasions like this and sometimes refer to them: 'That was when I didn't go.' When a child has to be taken back to school, the assistant if possible rejoins the group at a prearranged place and the child concerned is left in school. He gets no special attention though care is taken to acknowledge him at a later time. Clearly, on a day outing where difficulties might arise it is helpful to have extra adults with the group, and in some schools this is always done.

Later they go on outings with their mainstream class

There comes a time when the children are mature enough to make up bus loads with children from the mainstream class for a special outing. They seem to realize that certain expectations have to be met and sometimes ask afterwards: 'Were we good?' On occasions like this, the teacher finds it helpful to give them special reminders, or something from herself to help them manage on their own. The children take pleasure in learning what to do on these outings, and in behaving well. They are now well on their way to being full members of their mainstream class. They will already have joined them on several occasions for planned activities in school and feel increasingly at ease and secure there. This careful induction to the mainstream class is the joint responsibility of the nurture teacher and class teacher and is described in Chapter 10 in the section titled 'Return to the mainstream class'.

PART II
SETTING UP A NURTURE GROUP

7

Fostering Communication

The aim of the nurture group is the successful return of the children to their mainstream classes. This requires everyone in the school to be positive in attitude and supportive in practice, based on some understanding of the rationale and implications of the approach, and agreement with it.

Gaining informed support

The nurture group would not have been established without the support of the school governors, and the role they have developed in the school will influence their subsequent involvement.

The nurture group is Stage 3 provision. The Special Educational Needs Co-ordinator (SENCO) is involved from Stage 2 onwards of the Code of Practice (DfEE, 1994) and in liaising with class teachers and learning support assistants will have a considerable influence on attitudes. The central people, nevertheless, in gaining informed support are the nurture teacher and assistant, but when the group is newly established and they are inexperienced they are likely to feel uncertainty and anxiety when discussing basic issues concerning nurture group practice and the results they will achieve. Without experience they cannot talk with confidence about the difficulties of the children, the rationale of the approach and the essential requirements for a well-functioning group. This is a major anxiety, particularly in the first year.

Advance preparations

Well before the group is in being, preferably the previous term, members of staff are introduced to the principles underpinning nurture-work, and the nature of the difficulties of children appropriately placed there. Time should be given to discussion of the nurturing process, from induction to the nurture group to transfer back to the mainstream class. It will make evident that, for the children to become full members of their mainstream classes, links there must be cultivated and the class teachers and learning support assistants will continue to be closely involved. This preparation is usefully done in conjunction with the educational psychologist, and this is likely to be essential if the teacher is new to this work. During this preparatory period staff should be introduced to the process of referral to the group, and the referral forms and screening and developmental assessments that are being used. It is necessary, also, to discuss with them the relevance of the content of nurture-work to the needs of the children and the National Curriculum. The best procedures for contacting the parents and putting the school's concerns to them have to be worked out, and their views sought on their child's needs and the acceptability of the nurture group. All these things go along together and cannot be hurried. This advance preparation is necessary because when the group is being formed the time available for discussion is limited. Without an adequate conceptual grasp, the class teachers cannot make valid referrals or introduce a new child to the group with the care and skill that is needed, and their support for the group is likely to be less enthusiastic. There may well be conflicting pressures at this time, but it is essential that the group does not start precipitately. Also before the group is in being, the nurture teacher and assistant must prepare their room and devise a manageable programme of initial assessment and ongoing record-keeping.

Attitudes

The personal environment for the child in school includes not only the teachers and learning support staff but also office staff, meals staff and the caretaker, and as far as is possible all should understand the purpose of the nurture group, and be positive in attitude and supportive in practice. Typically they give an immediate and deeply felt response to an outline of the contemporary pressures on family life, the vitality needed and the debilitating special stresses and disastrous events in the lives of some families. Any negative attitudes usually change and involvement with the children becomes more constructive. But this is not always so and there may be resistance to the nurture group in both teaching and non-teaching staff on either educational or more personal grounds. They see the children as abnormal, mad or bad, and insist that they should not be in a normal school. Some have been brought up, or are bringing up their own children, in circumstances of stress and feel that the parents could have done better. Or they may feel unease with problems that are close to their own. Professional pressures from other members of staff are likely to contain and modify negative attitudes expressed by teachers and learning support assistants. Others in the school are sometimes openly contemptuous of the group and the 'awful' children in it, particularly as they are more likely to be involved in difficulties with them in the playground or dining hall, and may live near them in the neighbourhood. Angry and negative rejecting attitudes may be so extreme that nurture group children are sometimes blamed for upsets on days when they were not in school. Negative attitudes unfortunately are given implicit support when national policy legitimizes a simplistic quality ranking of schools. But criticism of the children is rarely an expression of a considered objective view. Their difficulties leave the schools feeling helpless and de-skilled, and this is expressed in rejection of the children themselves. Attitudes change when they see that a lot of hard and carefully considered work has gone into the group, and that the children have worked hard too, and when the children make progress they are able to acknowledge this and revise their views. Negative feelings nevertheless remain in a few cases, a natural defence against the pressures of life in schools today. It is a stressful and demanding life, and the children's difficulties impinge on unresolved problems and stress in the teachers and assistants concerned. This being so, change is likely to come about only slowly, from the evidence of greater well-being in schools that have been able to adapt and change. At the present time, unless satisfactory value-added criteria are developed for evaluating school performance, these difficulties will remain. Other doubts are resolved when the rationale of nurture work is more fully understood.

Rationale for imposed constraints

The most pressing issue raised when the groups were first established was usually the imposed constraints on experience, which many teachers opposed. Far from restricting opportunities for the children, they would enrich them and allow greater freedom, not less. However, the rationale for the structuring and control of experiences in the nurture group rests on the difference between disadvantage and deprivation. The disadvantaged child has internalized sufficiently the trust, personal organization and self-control on which further learning is based and, with support, can use a richer experience. The deprived child is without the personal foundations on which later learning is built and needs controlled, slowly paced experiences that are simple, basic and incremental. Only in this way will he assimilate them. An analogy is the hungry child who is given food, and the starving child who needs a drip feed.

The children taken into nurture groups are undeveloped in different ways. Typically, their concepts and personal organization are limited, and they are not able to direct their own behaviour. They need planned and organized experiences and, in some cases, strict monitoring and control of their behaviour, and a great deal of direct support. The nurture teacher is therefore 'being strict' in providing a situation that is appropriate for an earlier developmental level rather than 'being strict' with the child. The mainstream classroom provides an experience that for him is both complex and overstimulating. He is immobilized, flounders or explodes into it. The class teacher would have to be strict and repressive with children like this, but in the structured, more relevant context of the nurture group they engage with experiences and have full freedom. They have no freedom in a situation they cannot use. In controlling the environment the teacher gives them more freedom, not less, and in restricting choice for children who are unable to make a choice she provides appropriate and manageable learning experiences which in time will enable them to make a choice. When teachers have experienced the response of the children when the environment is modified in this way, it no longer seems a curtailment of opportunities but is seen to lead on to a greater and more effective use of opportunities. It enables the children to function at their real level, and the adult responds in a developmentally appropriate way. The relevance and immediacy of the adult's response thus hinges on appropriate structuring. It is a close constructive involvement with the children from which the nurturing/learning process stems. Freedom of choice, self-expression and enriched opportunities come later. A carefully controlled situation is important also for children described as 'in need of nurturing'. They have adequate outer-world experiences but are disorganized by stress. The controlled situation of the nurture group contains their anxiety and enables them to function better and to achieve success.

Why food, play and outings?

An objection sometimes raised by other teachers and assistants in the school, who may be equally concerned about the children, is the provision of food, which they feel is an insult to the parents, or they interpret as a bribe. Others focus on what seems to them to be a permissive and overindulgent attitude to the children. They complain that they play a lot in the group, have toast and jam, and go on more outings than the others: 'Some of them are the worst children in the school but they get all the treats'. Clearly, a major task for the nurture teacher and assistant is to convey to other members of staff the rationale for the learning experiences of the nurture group. Life there is hard work for the children. The demands on them are considerable because they are expected to meet strict behavioural standards and to bring disciplined attention to their activities. These activities to a large extent centre initially on domestic experiences, toys and play, and are provided because they meet the child's developmental needs and carry necessary and appropriate learning experiences. They are enjoyable and give satisfaction but they are nevertheless not relaxation. They are work. The more developed and better organized children would very quickly lose interest. They have different needs, there are other things they want to do, and the mainstream class makes better provision for this.

Responsibilities and relationships within the school

The key people in fostering the nurturing process in school are the nurture teacher, the nurture assistant, the class teacher, the headteacher and the SENCO. Positive relationships are critical, and are based on awareness of the particular responsibilities and stresses the others carry, and respect for their efforts to cope. The posts of nurture teacher and assistant are advertised but appointments are ideally made from within the school if suitable people are available and are interested. They will already be known to each other and to the headteacher in a work situation, compatibility of temperament and attitude will be apparent and there will be some confidence in the quality of the relationship that is likely to evolve. Within-school appointments are also more likely to establish nurture-work as 'normal' provision in which everyone in the school can have a part, rather than being something beyond their experience and expertise, and not their concern.

The teacher

The nurture group is educational provision, and although therapeutic is not a form of psychotherapy, and the qualities of a good strong primary school class teacher with academic objectives are essential. She must be firm in setting limits and have a clear idea of social and academic standards, and the conviction to convey to the children that these expectations will be reached and maintained. She must also have the sensitivity and easy rapport to relate constructively to the assistant and to the rest of the staff and the parents.

It is her responsibility to ensure that there is a close working relationship with the assistant in an equal partnership.

Demanding work

The children's difficulties make considerable demands of the nurture teacher. Careful organization of the day, meticulous attention to group management, developmentally appropriate activities, careful assessment and detailed planning for each child, and consistency of expectations are as important as they are in the mainstream class, but more vigilance is required for the situation is complex and changing and she must be alert to make a rapid appraisal and have the flexibility to act quickly. She might swing in seconds from total mobilization of resources in the control of what is sometimes violent and even dangerous behaviour, to the gentle, quiet, more passive and relaxed absorption with an individual child in a slow-moving world of feeling and being where it is peaceful, enjoyable and rewarding, not boring, to spend a lot of time doing simple things.

To respond constructively to nurture children certain other qualities are needed in the teachers, and the nature of their work, as with adults who become parents, often brings this out. Of crucial importance is the disposition to form a close and whole-person relationship with the children, and to identify at an early level with the child's feelings and needs, and the personal resources and security to interact freely and intuitively within this. A relaxed attitude to difficult behaviour is important, as is the disposition to 'play', to be light-heartedly 'not adult'. They must also, like the parent, have the maturity and discipline to be committed to the child's ultimate well-being rather than the short-term comfortable success, and provide restraints, constraints, and direction and uncompromising opposition when necessary, as well as continuing support and affection.

The teacher should also be equable enough to take awkward and even disastrous episodes not too seriously or personally, and to have the resilience to shake off mistakes, disappointments, frustration and criticism, and the optimism to hope for better things tomorrow. The essential underlying attitude is regard for the child and acknowledgement of his value, within a perspective which enables them to maintain this attitude sometimes in spite of very negative behaviour. An easy relationship with authority figures that elicits neither anxiety nor provocative negativism is important because much of the work for many of the children is in the area of self-determination. An alert intelligence within a broad perspective is needed, but not necessarily high academic achievement, though an interest in conceptualizing their experience with the children and in discussing ideas with others doing similar work is important in developing their expertise.

Experience in the mainstream class is essential

Although recently qualified teachers have been remarkably successful with this work, it is felt by headteachers generally that at least two or three years' experience in a mainstream classroom is important, because this provides a basic expertise from which other skills can be developed. Without this background the nurture teacher is likely to lack confidence in discussing the children with the class teacher, and will be insecure in relation to the curriculum expectations of the mainstream class. In the words of a headteacher: 'They must feel like teachers and be sound as teachers, yet need to do more, to add a new dimension.' Headteachers also stress that this work must not be seen as an escape. It is not an escape, and 'no teacher should be pushed unwillingly into this work. Motives must be positive and come from the teacher, for only from the teacher can the resources needed for this work come' (a headteacher). Nurture teachers inevitably vary in the strengths they bring to their work. This does not matter, for it is their personal qualities that are important. These are not necessarily revealed at interview, but headteachers have suggested that reliable pointers are enjoyment of young children and a ready response to babies and toddlers, alert and responsive feelings, easy emotional rapport, and a natural sympathy and interest in other people and life's problems.

Insights gained

But insights gained through nurture-work sometimes stir up personal agonies that were under control. A teacher: 'You are (i.e. could be) talking about my own child. You are (i.e. could be) talking about me.' Other teach-crs under enormous domestic stress have gained strengths and insights that have helped them to weather their personal difficulties: 'The nurture group saved me when my marriage was falling apart' (a teacher).

The nurture group assistant

Current selection and training procedures for all learning support assistants ensure that they have an acknowledged place in the school and that confidentially is built into the contract. Formal interviews are required. Particular care is nevertheless needed in making this appointment, not only for the personal qualities needed but because the assistant is closely involved with the teacher in a shared task, attends meetings with her and sometimes the headteacher too, and contributes equally with the others. Integrity, personal security and objectivity are needed for constructive work with the nurture teacher and children, and with other school staff and parents.

The nurture assistants are ideally secure and sturdy people, with easy give and take in their relationships. They are energetic and competent, with natural insights, relate easily and with humour and warmth to young children, and are tolerant of their behaviour but firm in their management, and single-minded about the standards they expect and will accept. Ideally they are easy talkers who find it natural to chat with the children and give a running commentary on everyday events. They understand the pressures on the parents and their life situation. They are of vital importance in the groups and in the school generally. It is usual for them to settle to nurture-work very quickly.

The teacher and assistant relationship

Funding for a new group normally starts at the beginning of the school year, but it is counterproductive for the group to be in operation from the first day. The nurture teacher and assistant in the first few days prepare their room, observe in mainstream classes and become familiar to adults and children as members of the school. They have time to talk informally with other each other, and with the school psychologist and SENCO, and to air their difficulties and their fears. After that it might be possible to visit an established group. Early contact with others doing similar work is important because discussion reinforces the underlying basic principles and leads to ways of implementing these in different situations. It is also the basis of an ongoing support structure for the teacher and assistant, through which they adapt and extend their skills.

It takes time to establish a productive partnership

The relationship of the nurture teacher and assistant is crucial in fostering and maintaining the progress of the children, not only in the group but in the school generally, and a great deal of care and attention goes into this and into communication with others. But it takes time to establish the relationships that will support the nurturing process and to prepare appropriate physical surroundings. Two or three weeks is normally put aside for this when the group is a new venture in the school, and is possible because the children will still be in their mainstream classes. This time together is very important because a good relationship between the nurture teacher and assistant provides the support they both need, as well as the learning experiences that come through good rapport and communication. This develops rapidly during the first two or three weeks in a shared interest in preparing the nurture group room, and the pleasure of choosing and making equipment. Whether the group is newly established or is carrying on from the year before, there is always something to do, for example mending toys or putting up a fresh piece of wallpaper. The fun and intimacy of together making a home for the children is specially conductive to this, and rapidly fosters a warm and close relationship. Setting up the classroom orientates them to the nature of their relationship with the children, for in preparing domestic nursery surroundings they become children themselves. They capture the spirit of the young child's world and from this flows a great deal of caring and giving. During this period they observe the children being considered for the group and talk about them with the class teachers. They relate their behaviour to the babies and toddlers they know, and develop an interest in understanding process. Conceptualizing the problems in this way is important because they have not lived the children's lives as parents have.

An interdependent relationship

Implicit in their relationship is respect for the other's contribution and willingness to learn from each other at a human level, and the maturity to take a subsidiary role when this is appropriate. Should any friction emerge, unease is likely to be felt on both sides and it is wise to talk through the problem with as little embarrassment as possible, for it is easier to make a change at this early stage than later. Tactful intervention by the headteacher can be very helpful. But the assistant, even if the relationship with the teacher seems potentially a good one, may have initial difficulties, and the teacher must ease the way because she has overall responsibility for the group and her position is less ambiguous. For this to happen the teacher must be secure enough to be dependent on the assistant for support, to learn from her and discuss the children's problems and progress on an equal basis, to take a subsidiary role when this is appropriate and on occasion to accept criticism and advice. And the assistant must be mature enough to accept and develop the potential of her new role in relation to the teacher. Neither must hold back, not certain of what the other expects, and perhaps not even fully assured that it is 'permissible' to relate to the children at the nurture level. It takes time to reach this position, and sometimes there are initial difficulties. Provided these are recognized as problems of mutual adjustment, inherent in the situation and likely to arise in all close working partnerships and are openly discussed, it is almost always possible for the teacher and assistant to feel their way into progressing and mutually helpful and satisfying roles. These are not stereotyped, but vary with the temperament and talents of the people concerned. Inevitably they overlap considerably, because the total commitment of the two people to the children necessitates total participation of themselves.

Mutual respect

It is equally important that they are sufficiently secure in the relationships they make with the children to acknowledge, respect and foster the other person's relationships. Neither must feel threatened and be put on the defensive, or become intrusive, by being or feeling excluded. This demands the maturity and objectivity to keep intact and support a constructive situation in which the other is involved, and to avoid intruding on a communication in which they have no real part. It implies a respect for the positive contribution the other person can make, awareness of a different point of view, sensitivity to the other's feelings, and the maturity to make an objective judgement and give up a personal satisfaction when this is required.

Teachers and assistants thus work with each other's strengths. This happens because they are not circumscribed by roles. The assistant is not undermined by the nurturing relationship the teacher has with the children, nor is the teacher threatened when the assistant involves herself in curriculum-related work, or takes the initiative and becomes the central figure in the group. The expected outcome is constructive family-type relationships.

Personal characteristics are key factors

The extent to which the children respond differently to the teacher and assistant seems related to their personal characteristics rather than their perceived roles. It is a common observation that the children with poor self-control gravitate to the person who provides the firmest control. The age and gender of the adults is sometimes relevant. Another factor is the children's prior experience of relationships between men and women. Some of the boys are contemptuous of women and may also fear men. Others are tough and well-versed in survival in a harsh world, have no feelings for the adults, and expect and want nothing from them. They make a rapid assessment of the roles of the teacher and assistant and, in spite of all demonstrations to the contrary and the give and take of responsibilities, they sense that it is the teacher who has overall conduct of the group, and treat the assistant with contempt.

An important function of the assistant in the early stages of a difficult group is unobtrusively to support the teacher in gaining control. She makes it clear that she has the same expectations, and supports the children in meeting the requirements. Later, when the group is fully established the partnership becomes more balanced, and each reinforces the other's expectations. Assessment of the situation is then likely to be more crucial than standards of control, but any differences of judgement usually are resolved fairly quickly as the teacher and assistant get to know the children better and discuss them, and management becomes increasingly consistent. Where it does not, it is usually because one of them is not sufficiently receptive to the child's unspoken changing needs to make a flexible relevant response, but instead is always either passively over-permissive, or assertively over-controlling. Partnerships like these do not usually work out well.

The teacher's special responsibilities

The work done by the assistant and the teacher cannot always be distinguished. This is inevitable and necessary, and differences in their participation are likely to stem more from their temperaments and talents than from their formally defined roles. Group activities directly related to the National Curriculum are different, because this is where the teacher must lead. Nevertheless, this ambiguity in the practice of their work is sometimes a source of anxiety to the teacher at first, and she may wonder what her special responsibilities are. These responsibilities are considerable, no matter how great the overlap of the work otherwise. It falls to her, as the teacher, to formulate the overall needs and objectives of the group and of the individual children within it, and to bring disciplined thought and objectivity to the shared task of meeting these needs. This includes developing the special teaching skills that are needed at this level. It is the teacher who is responsible also for the overall organization of the group, for establishing structure and routine, for setting objectives and liaising with the SENCO in formulating IEPs. She also has to maintain purposeful direction in all aspects of the child's development, has responsibility for assessment and record-keeping, and for action involving other people in the school, and sometimes outside agencies, in consultation with the SENCO. The whole area of social development, furthermore, is an educational one, and demands the analytic thought and creative action that a good teacher brings to her work. Conceptualization of the aims and processes of the group, and the formal development of basic social and cognitive competencies in the children is thus the teacher's particular professional contribution, and is essential if the work is to be purposeful. The mother of the normally developing infant and toddler has no need to conceptualize and structure her role in this way because the child's natural growth has its own inherent patterning and structure, and evokes in her a facilitating response without conscious thought on her part. It is therefore important for the teacher to make explicit to the assistant the general organization and conduct of the day. She establishes the framework within which the assistant will work. This is her responsibility.

The assistant responds freely within the structure provided

The assistant, within the structuring provided by the teacher, can be like a mother. She is free to be absorbed in the child and does not have to consider in detail where the process is leading. It is because she is free to be herself in relation to the child that the assistant can be of value to the teacher, for she provides a model of spontaneous earliest adult–child interaction. Given this structuring the assistant is free to develop her role to the full and a relationship of interdependent support develops in which there is considerable give and take of activities and the potential for an interchange of ideas.

Support to the nurture teacher and learning support assistant

An invaluable source of help to the nurture teacher and assistant is from others doing the same work. Meetings foster friendship and shared enthusiasm, and make it easier for anxieties and difficulties to be aired and shared. At meetings they become more receptive to new ideas and ways of doing things. They hear other teachers and assistants talking uninhibitedly and in personal detail about themselves and the children, and it becomes apparent to them that the groups described, although very different on the surface, have an underlying pattern. They begin to see why this is so, and when they follow the same general principles and find that their children settle in and begin to make progress, they become more confident and get increasing satisfaction from their work. They are helped, too, by hearing about the problems other teachers encounter, how they deal with them and the despair they sometimes feel. Their own difficulties fall into perspective when they realize that most of the problems described are transient and, if not, they begin to see where the limiting factors might lie. These could be within the structure and orientation of the school or the group, or attitudes within the school, or between or within themselves, or the nature of the difficulties in the home and within the child.

The headteacher

The qualities of empathy and responsiveness that are so essential in the nurture teacher and assistant are important also in the headteacher. Effective work in the group depends on adequate and appropriate support from the rest of the school, and for this to be forthcoming everyone in the school must feel valued and supported. It is the headteacher who is the key person in this process. S/he must also be sensitive to the particular stresses carried by the nurture teacher and assistant, and be able to provide personal and practical support, and reassurance during periods of despondency. S/he has responsibilities, not only where the work of the group is concerned, but also in relation to any difficulties with particular members of staff. Another function of the headteacher is to communicate to sceptics within the school and those without some realization of the hard work and skill that goes into a well-functioning group. The relevance of their work to the objectives of the mainstream class must be conveyed because this is not always apparent and some may have the impression that a nurture group is nothing more than 'cakes and cuddles, and daisy chains in the park'. They must also ensure that all members of staff, and newcomers, are aware of the influence of the nurture group on the orientation and ethos of the school, and that they are part of this. Although the headteacher is concerned to support and protect the nurture group s/he has responsibilities to the other teachers too, for they need to feel supported and valued, and s/he has her own work targets to meet. Happily, the ethos of a nurturing school leads to positive attitudes and shared support.

They foster communication within the school

Headteachers know the children in the nurture group well and, to a greater or lesser extent, become important to them individually. Their essential function, however, is to facilitate the work of the group within the school and the eventual integration of the children within their mainstream classes, by fostering communication and giving opportunity for concerns to be voiced. Unless everyone is wholeheartedly positive about the developmental approach being followed in the group, and understands what this involves and the implications for the school generally, they will not be alert to any organizational changes that might facilitate the nurturing process.

Their more distant perspective is important

The headteacher has a broad perspective of the progress of the group and individual children within it. She might need to suggest, for example, that the group as a whole should be moving towards a school day that is more age-appropriate. This might be when a formal breakfast is kept going for longer than is needed, or when transition to the mainstream class is being delayed beyond the optimal point. The headteacher, with the SENCO, has an important function, also, in structuring discussion of the progress of the children at regular staff meetings, or by giving support and 'space' to the nurture teacher to do this. With increasing responsibilities devolving on the headteacher and the SENCO, their roles here will need to be clarified and documented accordingly in the special needs policies of the school.

The headteacher has to consider the overall needs of the school

A major concern of the headteacher is the stability of all the classes, but it is particularly important that the strict routine and continuity of experience essential to the nurture group is not avoidably disturbed. The nurture teacher should therefore not be used as a supply teacher at times of staff shortage. It is preferable for classes to be split, with the nurture group taking its share. The assistant, too, should not be expected to have general responsibilities in the school when this means being out of the nurture group at critical times of the day. She should be available for the nurture group children, especially at playtimes and dinnertime. The situation, however, is not always straightforward, and the inherent problem for the headteacher, nurture teacher and assistant is that they understand and identify not only with the needs and stresses of the children in the nurture group but with those of the school as a whole. While this is an essential aspect of their strength, at critical times it is a source of conflict and distress. It is important, also, that time should be allowed for attending meetings, whether case conferences or in-service training, and for record-keeping and liaison with colleagues. These, too, are difficult issues, as all teachers now have an explicit and formal responsibility for assessment and evaluation of progress. In the event of the nurture teacher's absence it is usual, wherever possible, for the children to go to their mainstream classes, and individual arrangements are made, usually with support staff, for children who would find this too demanding.

Excellent working relationships are usual

An excellent working relationship of the headteacher, nurture teacher and assistant is usual, though the relationships formed and the extent of the headteacher's personal involvement with the children vary with the personalities concerned, and the nature of the school population as a whole. Where nurture needs are widespread, and there is a nurturing orientation throughout the school, the headteacher is usually personally and actively involved in a nurturing relationship with the children, and this inevitably affects the relationship formed with the teacher and assistant. By and large the role that develops in these circumstances is often that of the grandparent or aunt or uncle who is available for help when needed but leaves the 'parents' to do things their own way at other times. This is not always easy.

Maintaining supportive relationships within the school

Although all members of staff may have supported the establishment of the nurture group and are constructive in attitude, initial concern and goodwill is not enough. A great deal of continuing work is usually necessary if they are to become sufficiently interested and well informed to involve themselves directly and constructively in the progress of the children. An obstacle in developing good and ongoing communication is the children themselves. They are very demanding, particularly at the beginning of the year, and during this critical period the nurture teacher may have little time and energy to spare for other members of staff, and may even find it difficult to be physically about the school. The other teachers, too, have their own preoccupations and problems, and an increasing workload.

Optimism and involvement are usual

In most schools interest and support is usually gained during the preliminary discussions, and any continuing resistance typically disappears when the group is established and is seen to be functioning well. Optimism and involvement is usual but depends on a great deal of discussion with every teacher in the school. The nature of the children's difficulties and the approach followed in the group is conveyed, interest is built up and the children remain in the teacher's mind. Regular discussion of their progress helps the teacher to feel involved in their well-being. These discussions also lead to a sense of shared responsibility, and to a more considered and uniform management of any difficulties the children have at playtime and dinnertime. The children then experience consistently positive attitudes from a wide range of people, and when the time comes to be tried in their mainstream classes will be actively welcomed there. They will have controlled opportunities to make constructive relationships with a wider range of children, and will not be irretrievably rejected if they fail to meet the teacher's expectations.

Responsibilities and relationships beyond the school

Involving the parents

Schools will have a policy regarding their work with parents and this needs to take into account any special home circumstances. Opportunities are always made for parents of nurture group children to discuss their child's progress with the teacher, either ad hoc at an appropriate moment or by special arrangement, and with the headteacher and SENCO should they have any special concerns. Open evenings are also available each term and younger siblings are welcome to come with their parents. Parents' parties in the ILEA, to which all the family members were invited, were run initially by local psychiatric social workers on an experimental basis. They proved to be an invaluable setting for meaningful communication; an Educational Welfare Officer (EWO) commented: 'I achieved more this evening than in a week working from my office.' The food for the party was made in the nurture group and the children, with help, wrote the invitations. The ambience was welcoming and relaxed, and conversation was more lively and feelings expressed more freely than in the more formal setting of a clinic or the headteacher's office. They were invited to use the materials available to the children and it was salutary to see how limited their products were. But it was more usual for the nurture teacher to be available for the parents at the beginning and end of each day. A few parents, mother or father, have spent part of the day or the entire day in the nurture group, and it was not uncommon for parents to go on outings with the children. One school, in an exceptional initiative, prepared a wedding reception in school for the hard-up newly married parents of one of the children. The experience of the schools suggests that criticism of the groups on the grounds that they undermine, threaten or are an affront to the parents, is misplaced. Indeed, it is apparent from the nature and quality of the relationship with some of the parents, essentially one of nurturance and friendship, that they themselves are being helped, both directly by their contact with the group and indirectly by the progress of their children. Some parents have maintained contact with the group after their child is back in his mainstream class, or even after he has left school. One teacher put it to a parent: 'We are in it together.' Another commented: 'Most of the parents don't understand what has gone wrong and what we are doing. Those who do understand mind deeply, and are grateful.' Close involvement of some of the parents in school increases the isolation of those children whose parents never come, particularly as they are often the most deprived, but involving the parents is so important that school staff prefer to work with these difficulties.

Inter-professional collaboration

Many children in nurture groups have subsidiary specific difficulties, most commonly motor co-ordination and limited or disordered speech and language. Nurture group teachers have found it beneficial to involve physiotherapists, occupational therapists and speech and language teachers and therapists, either with specific children or for suggestions for activities that would be useful for the nurture group as a whole. Their more circumscribed but intensive work is very relevant to that of the nurture group because they too 'begin at the beginning', but along separate developmental strands that come together in nurture-work. It is helpful to make contact with them because they will be involved in the assessment of any children whose specific difficulties are extreme. When the teacher and assistant feel sufficiently secure they could invite them to see the nurture group in action to get an impression of the extent of the more specific difficulties of the children and to suggest activities that would be helpful. All this is done through and with the SENCO.

A potential difficulty arises if a child is having some form of off-site psychotherapy. This is an undesirable situation because psychotherapy is not appropriate for the nurture-level child, though there is scope for a partnership and co-ordinated work for 'children who need nurturing'. Situations like this can be negotiated only when they arise, and productive discussion depends on the nurture teacher's grasp of the principles underpinning nurture work.

An inclusive training is needed

Although it is useful to distinguish 'early developmental learning needs' and 'special educational needs' to demonstrate the relationship between the two, they are not separate. Both provide experiences at an early developmental level, the one general the other more intensively specific, and training for everyone concerned with special needs should include something of both. This is essential, because integrated concepts and practice lead to a better service for the child, and equip the teacher to meet a wide range of needs. The special contribution of nurture-work to an integrated course of this kind is its stress on the intermeshing nature of the different developmental strands at the earliest level. The implication is that all special needs work should be in a nurture context, and the gain for nurture-work would be an enhancement of the nurture group curriculum.

The rationale of the nurture group thus provides a useful conceptual basis for a wide range of in-school and off-site provision for children with special educational needs. It is fundamental to the learning process and generates practice that is of relevance to all children with special educational needs.

Positive attitudes and ethos: a rewarding experience

Although initially there may be unexpected problems, and occasionally these persist and seem intractable, it is usual for the nurture group quickly to become, in the words of infant school headteachers, the 'heart and hub' of the school. It increasingly influences its way of working and approach to the difficulties of the children. This comes about only slowly through ad hoc day-by-day interchange about specific children with all the other members of staff. They gain some idea of the rationale of the work, the way the group functions, and the nature of the progress of the children. They become more aware of themselves and others, and draw unreservedly on this experience. The process is cumulative, irrespective of any formal training input.

Hard but rewarding work

It will be apparent, from the ground covered so far, that the nurture teacher and assistant have a mature and demanding role in relation to other teachers, the parents and, in some cases, other agencies. The considerable personal reorganization and learning involved is particularly acute for the teachers. They have to conceptualize their work within a broader educational context, and they also carry a professional responsibility for the overall functioning of the group and the progress of the children. When times are difficult there is a professional as well as a personal obligation to think things through, realign views and try again. Under stress and provocation they might doubt their motivation and self-control, but they have found this to be a good learning experience, nevertheless, and in responding to the children as whole people the nurture teacher and assistant have become more aware of their own needs and the roots of their own behaviour. Many have commented on the greater self-knowledge and self-realization this brings, and the sense of well-being: 'I'm a whole person for the first time with the children and I feel terrific.' 'I'm giving my whole self to the children, not just the teacher bit.' 'Being the teacher gets in the way.' 'The best years of my teaching life.' And: 'It all sounds so complex, but it's easy, really. All you have to do is be yourself.'

But 'being yourself' is not easy for everyone, but nurture-work is a way into being oneself, and the process is circular and the gains are cumulative. Adults and children grow together and, although the work is exceptionally demanding and the task a daunting one, it is at the same time an exhilarating and energizing adventure.

The difficulties, the stress, the hard work and the doubts and fears, are very much like those of parents with young children. As with parents, the best way of bearing with these is to have the support of each other and the readily available friendship of others in the same situation. And as with parents, the rewards for the nurture teacher and assistant are very great, as they have been for the writer, watching from the sidelines.

8

Preparing the Classroom

The nurture teacher and assistant need about two weeks to prepare their room, and to help class teachers with any difficulties arising in the assessment procedures and information needed on children referred to the group. A useful pattern, until the group is in being, is for the nurture teacher and assistant to spend the morning organizing their classroom and sharing views and ideas. In the afternoon they help in the mainstream classes where they pick up observations of the children causing anxiety, become familiar to them, and get an overall impression of the class, the behavioural expectations and the extent to which these are met. This close involvement is not always possible, but most class teachers welcome it.

The account which follows incorporates the observations of many teachers, assistants and headteachers working in widely differing settings. It is a prototype, not a model, and modifications of organization and equipment will be needed in different situations, and as circumstances change from year to year within the same school. But whatever the differences in the children being catered for, and in the personalities and talents of the adults, it is very important to plan and provide for the full range of pre-nursery needs, from the baby stage to Key Stage 1 related activities.

Type of classroom and location

There is rarely much choice of accommodation and considerable ingenuity may be needed to devise a physical environment appropriate for a nurture group day.

The type of room

An enclosed area with visible physical boundaries is essential because the children must feel secure and contained. With 10 to 12 children on roll, two adults in charge and extra visitors from time to time, the room ideally should be big enough for about 16 people. A traditional classroom of generous size is satisfactory. It can be made to feel containing, and yet is big enough for free movement and play, and a wide range of domestic and school activities.

The location of the room

The typical infant school child quickly acquires a concept of the school as a whole, and the headteacher fits spatially and functionally into a complex meaningful pattern of events and relationships. But the world of school for many nurture children ends at the classroom door, or even at the teacher's hand. For them the headteacher is essentially an extension of the group, and is their main reference point in the largely unknown world beyond and a symbol of the wider experiences that lie ahead. She has a warm relationship with the children and they associate her with well-being and security. This eases their transition into mainstream school life. Her relationship with the teacher and assistant is close and supportive, and she reinforces their authority. This gives the children the extra security of knowing that the person who looks after them is looked after by someone else, and is a model of the supportive/dependency nature of relationships. The Early Years Co-ordinator, or the SENCO also will become a familiar and trusted figure, and part of a wider world. For these reasons a readily accessible room is preferred. This makes possible an easy flow of children and adults, in and out, and ensures that the group is seen to be fully part of the school. It is likely to become the pivot of the school when nurture needs are widespread and the group is used flexibly, and a central position facilitates this.

Close proximity to an outdoor play space is desirable. The whole group can be taken there with their toys without difficulty and effort, and individual children who need a physical outlet or to be away from the group for a short time can be on their own there but close to the others and readily supervised. Lastly, the toilets should be within easy reach.

All these are points to be borne in mind when classrooms are being allocated.

Organizing and equipping the classroom

Nurture teachers and assistants are school based and school orientated, and when organizing their room and buying and making equipment tend to look back to the earliest years from this position, and prepare what is in effect a small school nursery. Expectant parents, however, are preparing and choosing for a vulnerable and totally dependent baby, and it is important for nurture teachers and assistants to take up this from-birth perspective. This draws them immediately into a highly motivated and personal interest in the behaviour of the young baby, and the learning content of the things that engage his attention. They identify with him, and their 'oneness' with him heightens their awareness and sensitizes them to the nature of the work. It is an invaluable learning experience, as it is for parents.

Health and safety, and child protection

It is important that all equipment in the room and anything done to make it 'homely' conforms to health and safety requirements. Child protection guidelines must be followed, for example, a comfortable sofa or divan may have to take the place of a bed with full-size sheets and blankets that was standard furnishing in the 1970s and 1980s.

Creating a nurturing ambience

Most nurture group children have internalized very little coherent experience and have little or no sense of well-being and purpose. They need to feel sufficiently relaxed and calm to fully absorb baby and toddler satisfactions, some gained through close physical contact with the adults. As indicated previously, their room must therefore be comfortable, containing, protecting and unthreatening, and yet provide space and opportunity for free movement and play, and a wide range of domestic and school activities. The environment is thus both home and school for children with a wide range of developmental needs. But the teacher and assistant are sometimes faced with a very unpromising room and have to make the best of it.

The following observations may seem to be given in tedious detail but they derive from direct experience of teachers' queries and concerns in a wide range of situations. It is a composite account of many different groups, and even when money is available it takes a long time to build up the equipment needed and to create a classroom that 'works'. Many parents in the school generally are pleased to give toys and other things their own children no longer need, and occasionally major domestic items.

Please note that the home area is not the 'home-play' area. It is the comfortable carpeted area where the children are collected together many times during the day for hand games and stories, and chat.

The windows

Most 'nurture' children give their attention only to the meaningful world within the walls of their classroom. Events beyond this are of only occasional and limited interest. For others the window provides lively experiences which they share excitedly with the adults. Some are interested but need an adult to point things out, to comment and explain, and inject feeling and meaning as a mother would with a child in her arms. These experiences are for the most part incidental, but it is nevertheless an advantage for an infant group to have an interesting view, and for the windows to be just low enough for the children to look out.

The size of the windows is important. An extensive area of glass does not provide needed visual boundaries and a sense of physical containment, so it is helpful to partially obscure a big window with curtains. If the window is from floor to ceiling, and other children playing outside can look in or jump up to look in, hardboard or a painted scene covering the lower panes provides effective screening. Some nurture group children overreact to adverse physical conditions, others under-respond or appear not to notice at all, so the teacher and assistant are particularly alert to conditions likely to cause irritability and tension, as they would be with much younger children. If strong sunlight beats in the windows are canopied, or blinds or net curtains are fitted inside. It is generally felt that all windows should have curtains, but certainly in the home area. Sometimes they are made in school, or plain old curtains are brightened up with patchwork. The children enjoy watching and some are able to help. In this purposeful, pleasurable activity opinions are expressed and choices made.

Small rooms with tiny windows are gloomy and claustrophobic. Little can be done to improve this and a part-time group is preferred.

Lighting

The lighting in the room is important, but particularly so in the home area. In classrooms it is often strip neon on the ceiling which is usually high, but wherever possible lights in the nurture room are at a lower level. Table lamps and standard lamps give a welcoming light but are liable to get knocked over, particularly by a child in a temper or tantrum. If a limited amount of re-wiring is possible, wall lights above the children's reach are a good compromise, but these must be firmly fixed. All lights of this kind are shaded, to give a softer light, and because some children see only naked bulbs at home.

Power points

Power points are needed, at least one but preferably two in the kitchen area, and one in the home area for a lamp. A sewing machine was a valued item in the schools concerned, but these are not standard equipment and it is very unusual to have them. Provision is needed for a computer in the work area.

The arrangement of the room

Most nurture classrooms have four areas of roughly equal size: a home area, a kitchen area, a work area and a play area. It is usual for the work area to be nearest the door, so that the first impression is of an ordinary classroom. The home area is in the corner of the room that can be made the most inviting and comfortable, and is often by the window, diagonally across the room from the work area.

The home area usually connects with the play area on one side and the kitchen area on the other. These areas are flexible, and with judicious arrangement of the furniture the space given over to each at any one time can be varied. Thus a divan can be extra seating in the home area or is the basis of a camp in the play area, as needed, as well as providing the comfort of a bed. However, clearly defined areas and functions are maintained when the group is newly formed, and always when the children are poorly organized.

Although each area is roughly one-quarter of the floor space, staggered boundaries are useful and give a less formal overall impression. It is sometimes helpful to stack the furniture, for example by putting a cupboard or bookcase on a chest of drawers. This provides increased storage without encroaching on valuable floor space, is often visually interesting and makes the room seem more spacious. *But all furniture, however arranged, has to be completely stable, and remain so even when assaulted by a child in a tantrum. Anything with projecting metal is unsuitable.*

The home area

Ideally, the entrance to the home area is wide and the enclosing furniture low enough for an adult to look over. It is the focal point of the room and the gathering place many times during the day; the children play there a great deal and some are there virtually all the time at first. It is carpeted. Dark colours are not a good choice; medium tones show the dirt and fluff least of all.

Mobiles

Classroom ceilings are often high, but some effort is made to reduce the apparent height of the ceiling in the home area, for example by stringing mobiles across the room, most conveniently across the home and play areas together. Big mobiles are preferred when the room is large. Anything the children have made is put up: aeroplanes, animals, faces, etc. and shapes that are colourful or shiny. If the children are very inexperienced and unskilled, it is sometimes more appropriate for the adults to buy or make them. The children enjoy watching the mobiles move and making them move, and it is worth having them even if the ceiling is of domestic height, but in this case the mobiles are smaller. The mobiles are strung, at the lowest, 6 feet from the floor to allow head clearance for adults.

Wallpaper

The home corner is usually papered up to domestic ceiling height and wallpaper is stuck or stapled onto the backs of outward-facing cupboards, giving a feeling of wholeness and containment. Wallpapers with large patterns are avoided. They are sometimes powerful and dominant, and a dazzling background when out of focus. Red is unsuitable because it appears to advance from the paper. Warm colours, yellow and orange, are popular. Subdued colours and patterns are less stimulating and distracting, and are preferred by some teachers and assistants.

Furniture

Inward-facing cupboards with shelves above are needed. They display storybooks, ornaments, photographs, games, toys, and things made or cherished by the children, and have storage space below for toys and equipment. A chest of drawers is useful for any spare clothes specially collected for the children's use, such as socks, pants, T-shirts, trousers; and scarves, gloves, sweaters, coats and wellingtons for outdoor play and walks. The home area usually has a big sofa, and sometimes two or three armchairs, all preferably with padded arms, and sometimes a divan. A rocking chair in one school was a valued acquisition, and in a big room a domestic sideboard is useful. Second-hand furniture must be fumigated. Stretch covers are not recommended because shoe buckles snag them.

A divan in the home area provides valuable seating space and with blankets is a place to snuggle into. The children enjoy the feel of the satin borders, but car rugs are multipurpose, show the dirt less, and can be used for tents. In the 1970s and 1980s most infant groups had a small bed or a playpen with a mattress, usually with sheets, in addition to the sofa. It was usual to make a cover for the mattress that was easy to take off, for washing, and to have a waterproof undercover. Whatever was used for a bed wherever possible was set up permanently, and preferably it had the appearance of a divan rather than a proper bed. The aim was to provide homely comfort and the opportunity 'to get away from it all' (a teacher).

A shallow padded basket that is large enough for a child to curl up in is an important item. A dog basket is ideal, made comfortable with cushions. For both infant and junior groups there should also be a large container, such as a cardboard packing box for a refrigerator. This can be made sturdy with cloth reinforcement, and with cushions serves as a cradle, though more often is a boat or a hideaway. A synthetic sheepskin rug is greatly valued. The children like to lie on it and stroke and cuddle it, and it is useful for lining a box to make a cot or snug hideaway. A patchwork rug made of materials of different textures, colours and patterns is valued.

A small table is useful in the home area if there is room for this, and a low coffee table in a junior group was found to be very pleasant for milk and biscuits, and for talking around. It is rarely possible to have a dining table in the room, but school worktables covered with a tablecloth are satisfactory for a simple breakfast or a more elaborate lunch later on, and it is usual for this to be in the work area.

Soft furnishings

Cushions are important. They make the home area more welcoming and interesting, add to the comfort and are useful for imaginative play and for the release of feelings. Those with appliquéd animal faces or in the shape of animals are popular. They are particularly valuable for older children who may not immediately take to soft toys. Some of the children are frightened of animals and are scared to touch fur. Animal cushions, particularly when fur is incorporated, help them to get used to animals and to gain more confidence when approaching them. Two-sided cushions, one side having a smiling face the other a sad face, are greatly valued. Cushions, like curtains, are made in school if funds are short, and are stuffed with cut-up old socks and tights collected from parents. The children help with the cutting and sorting. This is a purposeful, pleasurable activity with the adult, and mathematical language can be introduced. Older children with help have made personal cushions with their names embroidered on. Texture, contrast, pattern and colour are important when choosing the coverings. Massive bean bags or floor cushions are useful, the bigger the better, as the children like to lie on them on the floor, and sit on them during storytime. A metre square is a good size to choose, and three or four are needed for a group of 12 children. They are suitable only for medium- to large-sized rooms, or for temporary use in a small room. Old curtains are sometimes attractive enough to be used as a covering. These are preferably held together along one side by tie strings or press-studs, as they need to be washed very frequently. Offcuts of foam are easy to cover, but must meet safety regulations.

A mirror and a clock are needed

A full-length mirror or even two, screwed onto the wall, is essential here or in the play area. A shop-style mirror is ideal, or one taken from an old wardrobe. An interesting variant of this pattern in Enfield derived from a different perspective: the teacher and assistant felt that the area near the door should be welcoming and so furnished this as the home area. A full-length mirror was installed just inside the door which was left open, and they found that other children in the school regularly stepped inside to look at themselves. This arrangement is not recommended for junior groups: it would be likely to evoke unhelpful comments from other children in the school, and would be unacceptable to the parents. A clock with plain, well-defined numbers is needed, and the home or work area is the best place for this.

Photographs

As soon as possible photographs of the children are put up on the wall or on a cupboard, preferably enlarged and framed, and they should have at least one photograph of themselves to take home, if they want to. Photograph albums of class activities and outings are usually kept in the home area. They are important for recalling and describing happy occasions in the group and sequences of events, and in gaining a sense of time. They also contribute to group and personal identity. It is usual to have plants or flowers here, and the more personal things the children have made in school.

Soft toys

A wide range of soft toys is provided. Animals are popular, particularly teddy bears or a big Humpty Dumpty. Clowns with a happy face on one side and a sad face on the other, or happy/sad, asleep/awake upside-down dolls are useful. It is important to have at least one animal of roughly the size of the children, one that is soft and yielding but firm enough to sit on a chair, and is not too awkward to carry. All these are equally important for junior groups. They are dressed and undressed, put to bed in a cot, used as mascots, and incorporated into play and work sessions. They are important members of the group and are spontaneously used to express feelings, and for the enactment of anxieties and problems. Current cult figures, too, are popular.

Dolls

A well-equipped group has dolls of many different kinds and sizes and of different racial types. The eyes are preferably not detachable as the children poke them and pull them out, and it is better if the limbs are in one piece with the body. Dolls made in school are particularly valued because the children know they have been made especially for them. They are of soft material, of different textures and of rough outline, the eyes are painted on or made of sewn-on felt, and wool serves as hair. In addition every group has at least one commercially produced doll for the children to bath, preferably one that will not easily get smashed in a tantrum. Clothes for the dolls are usually made in school and the children watch with enjoyment and interest. They are made in great variety, not only to provide more scope for changing the dolls and for gaining concepts of size, shape, area, 1:1 correspondence and so on, but because they get lost so quickly. A valued possession is a realistic doll baby. The more advanced children treat it as a baby, they put it to bed, take it for walks, and treat it with tenderness and care. The equipment for the 'baby' should include a shawl, nappies and at least one baby's feeding bottle. Other children show little interest at first. In the early days it is they who wear the nappies or suck from the bottle. Junior boys also play with the dolls at times, but usually they accept rag dolls more readily.

Cradle and pram play

Also in the home area, in both infant and junior groups, are opportunities for cradle and pram play. There are objects to suck, chew and shake; squeaky toys and rattles, soft balls and small textured soft toys; and over the bed a mobile that swings and makes a noise, for example plastic cartons glued together with beans inside. Spinning tops and wobbly clowns, nesting, stacking, posting and pull-along toys, and a hand-held baby mirror and the 'Discovery Basket' are conveniently kept in the home area because the children usually play with them there. The basket (Goldschmeid and Jackson, 1994) is a container full of everyday bits and pieces such as rattles, spoons, ribbons, keys, etc. The way the child plays with these (Lucas, forthcoming) gives the teacher insight into different aspects of his development, and she uses them to further his language and concept development.

For those children who need to suck and chew the teacher provides suitable personal things as there are problems of hygiene to consider.

The kitchen area

The kitchen area usually takes up one-fifth to one-quarter of the total floor area and is useful as an overspill for academic work or for play.

A family breakfast early in the school day is important. It provides basic learning experiences and is essential for children who have difficulty in paying attention, waiting and sharing. Facilities for this may be no more than a classroom painting sink set into a standard bench, and a point for an electric kettle and toaster, but every effort should be made to set up a recognizable kitchen area. The floor covering is preferably vinyl or other material that can be cleaned easily and, if possible, the wall behind the sink is tiled or covered in formica. The balance of opinion concerning the height of tables and fitments is towards the lowest domestic height available. This is awkward for some of the children, but the experiences they need are those normally gained in mother's kitchen at home. Playing at kitchens with mini-fittings comes later.

Equipment

A cooker is standard equipment and should be of domestic size, with four hobs and an oven, but safety regulations must be met. Those few schools who have a fully equipped kitchen area have preferred a kitchen sink with a double drainer; the children can then stack, wash and dry. Cupboards are necessary for storing foods needed regularly, such as bread and biscuits, and basic ingredients for cooking. The equipment needed includes cups, saucers, mugs, plates, preferably in an unbreakable material; knives, forks and spoons; whatever cooking and baking equipment is available, if possible including balance weighing scales, a kitchen timer, measuring beakers and a funnel, and domestic pans, preferably in a graded set. All these items lend themselves to the demonstration of mathematical concepts. A self-regulating electric kettle is useful if there is no hot water supply. If a refrigerator is available the racks should be glued in place for safety.

Cupboards and drawers are needed

Pictures of the contents of the cupboards, and recipes displayed on the cupboard doors, introduce symbolic representation and are useful for language work generally. It is convenient to have somewhere to keep tablecloths or place mats, tea towels, hand towels and aprons. Hooks are needed for those in use, and for an oven cloth. The children take it in turns to set the table so there should be a drawer for class cutlery, one that is easy to pull out and carry around, or a transportable cutlery tray.

Cleaning equipment is essential and ironing equipment is a useful 'extra'

Cleaning equipment is needed, if only a brush and a dustpan, as clearing up sometimes involves simple cleaning and is done as though with mother. An ironing facility is highly valued, but safety considerations are likely to preclude this. Dolls' clothes and cushion covers, and sometimes children's clothes provided by the school need to be washed and ironed from time to time, and the children cluster round and chat.

Facilities for the preparation of food are needed

Simple food can be prepared even with very limited equipment, and essential personal and social learning experiences are built in. A well-resourced kitchen area is more enjoyable for everyone, but the main advantage is the wealth of opportunity it provides for practical activities 'with mother'. The learning outcomes are considerable: the pleasurable atmosphere and shared experience reinforce attachment; visuo-motor-spatial skills, language and logical sequencing of activities are inherent in the process; and mathematical and scientific concepts can be developed. Money and space dictate what is possible, but groups in cramped surroundings have managed happily with an electric kettle and a toaster, or even nothing closer than the facilities of a distant staff room, used only for baking.

The play area

This is usually at least one-quarter of the room, but the space available for play is effectively far bigger than this because a lot of quiet play takes place in the home area, and in many groups the only place for wet and messy activities is the kitchen area. The clean and dry play area is often carpeted, but if not should have a vinyl-type floor covering. It is stocked with nursery and infant equipment, and has a furnished home-play area, adaptable frame for use as a shop, large building bricks, pull-along toys, dolls and feeding bottles, telephones, etc. Large pieces of material of different size, shape, pattern and texture are highly valued. The children get intense pleasure from feeling, burrowing into and swirling in them, draping and dressing up, and the adults, as appropriate, introduce basic language and mathematical concepts. It is important to have a baby-buggy or preferably an old pram that is strong enough to sit in and be pushed around in, and toddlers' reins are a useful item. A simple woodwork bench, even in junior groups, is rarely appropriate.

Big storage boxes are necessary for materials and junk. Ideally there should be a rack or a cupboard for dressing-up clothes, and a shelf for shoes, hats and handbags. A large toy cupboard is needed, and this makes a useful room divider.

Sand and water are important for both infant and junior children, and the equipment includes bath toys as well as funnels, sieves, etc. Most groups have a table for clay and paints. Hooks are needed for waterproof aprons, and a high shelf for the storage of paint, etc. All these materials are used under strictly defined conditions, and in some cases under supervision as some children need help in using them constructively, while others need to mess and slosh.

A large fibreglass sand tray, preferably with a lid, is best placed in the corner so that only two children can use it at a time, and should have gravel and pebbles as well as sand. Ideally the water tray should be like the sand tray, but with tap and drain, and fixed in the corner at kneeling height. A large plastic washing-up bowl is useful for water play for one child. Sand and water are covered when not in authorized use.

The work area

This is roughly one-quarter of the floor space. Tables are needed. Two tables each one metre square, and two tables one metre by one-half metre, make a satisfactory and flexible combination. They are of infant or junior size, according to need rather than age, for some of the children are very big. The chairs, moulded bucket for stacking, are of a size appropriate for the tables. Otherwise there should be cupboards with shelves, provision for storage of books, work trays, etc., a plan chest for paper, a small movable whiteboard, and a display board. A wall clock is needed here or in the home area. A one-hour kitchen timer is useful for timing work, and as an incentive for persistence and controlled behaviour. Preferably in the work area, there should be a power point for a computer.

The computer

Few children in the group have the higher-order competencies required for the computer. They need to develop fine visuo-motor skills, and to see visually evident cause and effect in the real world, and to have a notion of symbolic representation before they are ready for this. It has a function for children who have consolidated this earlier stage, and need an introduction to the computer skills required in their mainstream classes. Children who have emotional and social needs at an early level but are cognitively better organized and competent, may have some expertise with the computer and want more. It is a requirement of the National Curriculum, but care must be taken to ensure that it does not become a barrier to social learning.

Materials, toys, games and equipment

Nurture groups cater for the classic nurture child who effectively may be at the 18-months level or less, and also for children who have emotional needs but are cognitively more competent. The equipment needed in any group is likely to vary from year to year but opportunities for baby and toddler experiences are always available. And no matter what the age of the children, animals are unlikely to be appropriate at first and are introduced only later, with preparation, when the group is established and the teacher feels that the children have developed a sense of caring.

Opportunities for the release of energy are needed, often in a runaround in the playground. Tricycles are useful if the classroom is fortunate enough to lead into a large outdoor play area, as are trucks to sit in and be pushed in. Otherwise it is sometimes possible to negotiate for occasional use of the nursery outdoor equipment.

The appearance of the room in relation to the needs of the children

The overall appearance of the room is influenced by the method of intake, the stage the group as a whole has reached, and the dominant needs of the children within it, but a comfortable relaxed home atmosphere is important. The equipment available covers the full range, but what is provided at any one time is determined by the needs of the children, and teaching style. At one extreme, in a school with widespread needs and many profoundly deprived children, all the toys except those in immediate use were kept hidden from sight in cupboards. Stimulation was reduced to a minimum, because the nurture group was intended to be basic and short term for children coming from the nursery or new entrants felt to be at risk. From there they moved on quickly to the mainstream class. This was run on nurturing lines but there was greater choice, and more creative activities were available. At the other extreme, in a school with similarly widespread and severe needs, the group was in a double-size classroom with an unusually rich variety of early-level toys and equipment on view. These were arranged in colour-coded areas according to their intrinsic value and interest for the child: touch, sound, water play, etc. In this school, as in most others, the children remained in the nurture group until they could manage in a relatively unmodified mainstream class, and so the experiences available for the children who could use them were extended to what are now Key Stage 1 activities. A variant in Enfield is to keep toys and resources for each developmental stage in separate large plastic boxes with lids. These are stored in a cupboard when not required and are brought out at the teacher's discretion to develop specific early learning skills with individual children, or to encourage waiting, sharing and taking turns.

Provision for outdoor clothing

If there is no separate cloakroom, the children's outdoor clothing may have to be kept in the classroom. Some schools have provided a small mirror on the wall and even individual towels, combs and toothbrushes.

It takes time to build up the resources needed

This is a composite picture, and even when money is available it takes a long time to build up the equipment needed and to create a classroom that 'works'. Many parents in the school generally are pleased to give toys and other things their own children no longer need, and occasionally major domestic items.

9

Deploying Resources

In ILEA schools with nurture groups, children with special needs were identified through a process of structured observation and discussion. The Developmental Screening Form (Boxall, 1974), an instrument specially devised for a broadly based developmental view of the entire school, was the starting point.

Screening provides a developmental perspective for a wide range of difficulties and an indication of the form of help needed. It alerts teachers to children who otherwise might be overlooked, and the process of screening also sometimes makes evident that many children need extra help. New structures and strategies within the classroom might be indicated, and possibly organizational changes and redeployment of resources in the school as a whole. A preliminary screening of the school is helpful also because initially class teachers often refer only those children with behaviour difficulties, and it is then difficult for the nurture teacher to form a balanced and viable group. Screening also gives some indication of the extent of stress in the mainstream class when the children in greatest need have been taken into the group. This information is important because there are special problems in 'weaning' a child from the nurture group into an unstable class, particularly if a number of children in the group are from this class. Staff attitudes, classroom practice and overall school organization also are relevant, and may be critical, and the implications have to be discussed and procedures negotiated. Other considerations centre on the physical characteristics of the school building and the nature of the accommodation available for the group.

The level of cognitive competence of children appropriately placed in the group is also a key factor in determining the type of group that is formed, particularly whether this is to be full-time or part-time. A further consideration is the range of competence in the mainstream class. Where the children in need of nurture-type help are a minority in an otherwise well-functioning class they are likely to need a full-time group and for longer, because a high level of achievement will be required of them if they are to be successfully returned to their mainstream class.

Schools new to nurture groups are strongly advised to start with a full-time group and modify their practice later, when they are more experienced.

Structuring the nurture group within the school

Most schools have a full-time group, but always with as much involvement as possible with the rest of the school from the beginning. Others have a morning group with support to the children in the afternoons in their mainstream class, or they run two half-time groups at different levels. Others function full time with varying numbers of children attending part-time. Whatever the pattern, nurture-level children need to be full time in the group. Others actively benefit from greater contact with the mainstream class, particularly those described as 'in need of nurturing', some of whom could be supported in the mainstream class with extra help.

Whether the group should be full time, half-time or even part-time is one of the first considerations, and is a particularly important issue in the junior school. This can be decided only in relation to the total school situation, and the proportion of children with special needs, and the nature of their difficulties.

Full-time groups

1 The full-time group, providing experiences at the 0–3-year level, was established for fundamentally deprived 'nurture' children whose overall development was markedly limited. It remains the logical and best provision for them, particularly in schools where most of the others in their age group are functioning adequately. They have not reached the minimal level of personal and social competence of the foundation stage and any time spent in their age-appropriate class is wasted and stressful for everyone. A period full time in a nurture group is appropriate also for a new school entrant 'at risk' and will greatly reduce the possibility of failure in the mainstream class. Where there is no special resource to help these children, the only alternative to exclusion, which happens increasingly at the infant stage, is to follow a learning support assistant about the school, or sit in the secretary's or headteacher's office 'helping' or playing inconsequentially at her feet. Children like this need close and continuing attachment and support within a carefully monitored and protected day, with satisfactions and learning experiences earlier than those of the foundation stage. This total nurturing environment is essential if they are to catch up with their peers in the mainstream class. But it is both rare and undesirable for a group to be made up entirely of children like this and usually, in a well-balanced group, one or two are very soon able to have some contact with their mainstream class, however minimal, and actively benefit from this. All are tried out, for carefully chosen periods, as soon as some degree of success is likely.

2 Many schools with nurture groups provide integrated support throughout the school and this enables certain children who would otherwise be full time in the nurture group to remain part time in their mainstream class from the beginning. Typically these children are able to

function to some extent at an age-appropriate level but they need the extra support of a particularly close relationship with an adult, and more intimate experiences and satisfactions, affection and reassurance than is possible in a large mainstream class. For some children, part-time nurture provision in conjunction with a modified mainstream class may be enough; others will need to be full-time in the nurture group.

3 In schools where severe deprivation and disadvantage are widespread the overall organization and orientation of the school inevitably changes, as already described, and implementing nurture principles becomes everyone's direct concern. It is usual for a full-time nurture group to be retained, but with considerable interchange of children on the periphery, and the other classes in the school, including the nursery, structure their day towards nurture principles and make nurture-level learning experiences a more explicit provision. The difference between the nurture group and the other classes is then largely determined by size, the smaller nurture class providing a more intensive input of earlier level experiences for the most profoundly deprived children.

Half-time groups

1 Half-time groups are appropriate for children who can manage to some extent in the mainstream class. It is then usual for the morning group to be for nurture children, and the afternoon group for 'children who need nurturing'. Any children who cannot cope at all in the mainstream class usually stay for both sessions. This is a very unsatisfactory compromise, as indicated in 'Part-time groups' 1, below.

2 Some schools run a morning group for a full range of 'nurture group' children, and in the afternoon the nurture teacher and assistant work in their mainstream classes giving direct support to the children in greatest need. This can be adequate for 'children who need nurturing' but is not satisfactory for nurture-level children and may be contra-indicated, and is not the most effective and efficient use of resources.

3 When a half-time teacher only is available.

Part-time groups

These have been introduced in four quite different circumstances, sometimes on the grounds of expediency. They satisfy only some aspects of a full nurture group experience.

1 Where problems of deprivation are general in the school, children in special need are in the nurture group for two or three sessions a week, together with one or two more competently functioning children, for the specially close relationships and domestic and play activities possible there. This method depends on the whole school being run on

co-ordinated nurturing lines. It has not been documented sufficiently well because of the large numbers of children involved, but anecdotal impression suggests that some children are sufficiently well organized and secure to relate to different people in changing situations, and benefit from greater involvement with the mainstream class. A major factor in making this possible is the early-level structuring and ambience of the school as a whole, but on the available evidence the total time spent in part-time provision is far greater than it would be in a full-time group.

This way of working does not meet the needs of children who cannot manage at all in the mainstream class. They need a full-time nurture group experience and the stable relationships inherent in this.

2 Where special needs cover a wide range, and there is only one person available to provide help, small groups have been formed according to the nature of the provision needed, and children with nurturing needs are in one of the groups, perhaps for one-third of the week.
3 Children whose difficulties centre largely on lack of trust and poor self-image, and who respond to reassurance and support, and sometimes verbalization of their feelings, usually make good progress in a part-time group.

The experience provided by part-time groups of these kinds is likely to be helpful for those children with better developed experience and personal control, and is preferable for others loosely described as 'troubled'. It cannot, however, provide the wealth of broadly based and integrated earliest level experiences that are essential for nurture level children, particularly if the numbers are small and there is no assistant in the group.

Advantages and disadvantages of full-time and half-time groups

The full-time group is essential for children who are without adequate basic foundations for the mainstream class, but all possible links there are fostered. They will then not feel excluded, will mix better at playtimes and will have more friends to invite in for birthday parties or other special events. The nurture group then slips into place as 'just another class' in a nurturing school, and the child's eventual integration with his peer group does not present a problem.

The half-time group has its own limitations and problems, but many issues that require special measures in a full-time group do not arise, thus:

● any absence of the nurture teacher and assistant is better tolerated, because the child already spends half the day in his mainstream class and is familiar with the teacher and children there;
● a run of bad behaviour is sometimes broken by a change of teacher at midday;

- there are more opportunities for the class teacher to reinforce behavioural expectations and management, and the child sees these standards as a more universal requirement. He also has the satisfaction of knowing that when he pleases one teacher his other teacher will know. This too, reinforces the 'approved' behaviour;
- aggressive behaviour in the mainstream class may be less of a problem than before because he becomes self-conscious about the consequences. He knows he can talk about his difficulties afterwards in the nurture group, and this helps him to contain his feelings;
- he benefits from being with children whose play and behaviour is more advanced;
- communication between the nurture teacher and class teacher is more easily maintained because both are fully in touch with the child's needs. Opportunities and management in the mainstream class are therefore more likely to complement and supplement the work of the nurture group. It does, however, require of the class teacher careful control of the child's experiences and meticulous acknowledgement of his achievements;
- a class teacher who is not greatly in sympathy with this approach has more opportunity to gain a developmental perspective on the child's difficulties in ongoing discussion with the nurture teacher;
- full integration of the child within the mainstream class later is not a problem because he is familiar with this class and the expectations there, and the class teacher knows what he can do. And he can cope with the loss of the nurture group because he knows he can go there if he needs to.

A half-time or part-time arrangement may therefore actively strengthen and consolidate the work being done in the nurture group. It presupposes, however, that experiences and controls have been at least minimally internalized and the child has some capacity for self-regulation, some ability to reflect and anticipate, and to share and so on. But although there are several advantages in a half-time group for such children, their academic needs pose particular problems, especially at the junior stage. The children are greatly in need of domestic and play activities, but formal work must be provided in the nurture group also. This is largely because much of it stems from the child's immediate experience and logically and naturally falls to the nurture teacher. Furthermore, if formal work is confined to the mainstream class the half- or part-time group would seem more like a special group. It is important, therefore, that the major responsibility for the academic needs of the child is with the nurture teacher, but wherever appropriate it is directly linked with that of the mainstream class. This requires the close co-operation of the nurture teacher and class teacher in planning their work. The considerations for the morning and afternoon groups are therefore different, particularly as the work of the nurture group and mainstream class tends to be more formal in the mornings, but in both cases there are problems in maintaining a balance between basic structured work and more general experiences.

Whether the group is full-time, half-time or part-time, sympathetic rapport and good communication between the nurture teacher and class teacher is of critical importance if the child is to be successful in the mainstream class. Whatever the arrangement, the children's progress is maximized if the approach to their difficulties throughout the school is consistent, and is informed by a 'nurturing' attitude.

Size and composition of the group

The size of the group is important. Teachers forming a group for the first time, particularly if many of the candidates are described as 'aggressive and disruptive', may well feel scared of building the number up to 10–12. This is generally thought to be a useful and viable number, though some of the ILEA groups, both infant and junior, ran successfully at 14 and 16. Contrary to what might be expected a group smaller than 12 does not necessarily function better, and it is undesirable for it to fall below 10. Small numbers are less satisfactory for many of the children, thus:

- there is less scope for contriving a 'balanced' group and for influencing the dynamics of the group;
- the children see, and are part of, a narrower range of interactions and so have fewer opportunities for personal and social learning;
- aggressive behaviour in a small group is more disruptive than in a bigger group;
- loosening the child's ties with the nurture group is more difficult.

The composition of the group is important. As a general guide, no more than two-thirds of the children should be 'aggressive and disruptive' when the group is being formed, and pressure for more than this is resisted, particularly as children whose functioning is very limited become assertive as they progress. The 'uninvolved' children are usually less readily referred, partly because the teacher feels they will be distressed by being with the more 'aggressive' children, but also because some may seem to be coping sufficiently well in their mainstream class. Resistance to referring children like this is usually resolved as the class teachers become more aware of the nature of nurture-work, and see the rapid and dramatic change in some of the children. Interestingly, such children occasionally attach themselves to the group of their own accord. There are advantages in having in the group children with difficulties of different kinds. Those who are timid and unventuring seem relieved that control is firm and gain security from the clear guidelines, routine and orderliness. They also benefit from being with children who more readily involve themselves and are more demanding and assertive. They become drawn into their play, at first in a following or passive role, but when they see that it is 'safe' they start to shadow their activities, and then begin to interact. They gain the confidence to assert themselves, and to test out the limits. With children like themselves they say little or nothing: there is little or no interaction between them, and to make progress they need a great deal of the adult's time. The 'aggressive' children also gain. They see the more productive interaction between the adults and the less forthcoming children, and the satisfactions that are part of this. They become aware of the kindness and caring, and begin to understand that the teacher's control is part of the caring, and begin to take over a caring and controlling role. Often they adopt the teacher's kindly supportive attitude to the 'unforthcoming' children, and with others more like themselves they assert the requirements and impose controls. Their experience with children unlike themselves helps them to be more aware of themselves and each other, and is part of the process of learning to care for each other.

Difficulties in forming a viable group

Not all the children referred are appropriately placed in the group at the same time, and it is then likely to get an unsuccessful image. To make a viable situation it is advisable to pick out from the referrals those children who will probably make a well-balanced group, taking into account their size and the proportion who are 'aggressive'. Some of the most difficult 'aggressive and disruptive' children can be helped in the group and should be included if they seem to have the 'nurture' features described earlier. Often they are the children who make the most striking progress. On the other hand, the group is not expected to take in children simply on the grounds that they present management problems, because they may not be suitably placed there. For these reasons it is important, when discussing referrals, to keep firmly in mind the basic principles underlying the choice of individual children as well as the ultimate composition of the group. The nurture teacher should try to convey, with tact and conviction, some idea of the rationale behind the work and what can be achieved, for there are likely to be many misunderstandings. The term 'nurture' was adopted because it conveyed the process of early development in all its aspects, but some people interpret it as indulgent permissiveness while others, less involved, expect it to provide an instant solution to their problems. A great deal of responsibility therefore falls on the nurture teacher at this early stage. Faith in the approach and an intellectual grasp of the concepts underpinning it is needed. In the words of teachers in the early 1970s: 'they must not think of us as misguided or as martyrs, nor must they think of the nurture group as a remedial class, a freak side-show, or a magic trick that will cause the problems to disappear overnight'.

Experience is clearly essential in handling these issues. Inevitably, before the group has proved itself and a productive way of working has evolved, it is usual for the nurture teacher to be very accommodating and to defer to the class teacher's views, largely to maintain good working relationships at this early delicate stage. This has resulted in unsuitable cases being taken in and children who could be helped being left out. These difficulties quickly resolve when the group begins to function well, for the children are unlikely to make progress in the mainstream class and some are a serious liability there. It is therefore in the class teacher's interests to refer them. A serious problem sometimes arises when a class teacher unloads onto the group a child presenting a major problem of management and abdicates from all further responsibility. This makes it impossible for the nurture teacher to foster adequate contacts with the child's mainstream class, and attempts to resettle him there as he makes progress are likely to fail. In cases like this the child might be left in the group until the end of the school year. More usually he is introduced to a different class but this depends on the goodwill of the other teachers in the school. Goodwill is forthcoming in ample abundance, negative attitudes change, but the pressures of contemporary school life require personal resources and strengths of an extraordinary order.

A talk from the educational psychologist may be needed initially to provide a broader context for the work of the group, and certain difficulties might then not arise, particularly if the teachers have been through the Developmental Screening Form for each of their children in turn. A further helpful step is for the nurture teacher to discuss, with the class teacher, the more detailed structured observations of the Boxall Profile. Although relevant information will already be on record, referral forms are sometimes a useful administrative hurdle because they draw the teacher's attention to the child's total situation, and to his strengths, and his difficulties are then within a broader perspective.

Reorganization and reorientation of the school

Not all schools need a nurture group, though many in deprived areas do. However, if the school is small or very few children need this form of help, it may not be feasible to form a group, and in other schools there may be too many children for the places available. In these circumstances, before any action is taken for the child individually, it is relevant to consider the extent to which developmentally appropriate structures, strategies and procedures could be built into the school as a whole in relation to the nature and incidence of special needs.

Organizational change within the school

Organizational change is easier to make when appreciable numbers of children have special needs, and in a large school it is sometimes possible to form a small class where nurture structures and principles can be implemented cohesively. A successful development, feasible in an infant school, is to regroup the whole school including the nursery, by developmental rather than chronological age, class sizes and learning needs arranged accordingly. In two junior schools with widespread needs, mostly at a 'nurturing' level, all the classes had access to a wide range of domestic experiences within close caring and supportive relationships. For new entrants there is the possibility of structuring and developing the reception class, which normally is small at the beginning of the year, along 'nurture' lines. The school nursery is bigger but it is sometimes possible, with relatively modest extra resources and some reorganization, to provide nurture level relationships and experiences there. This would be logical because the functional competence of children taken into nurture groups is less than that of the adequately able nursery child.

It might also be possible to deploy existing fragmented resources in a different and more cohesive and effective way. Many children for whom the nurture group is the most appropriate and effective resource have major difficulties. In schools where this form of provision is not available they are almost invariably referred for assessment, either immediately or in the course of time. They would be deemed to have special needs and would attract special help, either off-site or in a special school, or extra support in the mainstream class. For children who clearly need 'nurture' help it would be a more efficient use of resources if they were treated as a group, with all the advantages that accrue from this. Without early intervention the children's difficulties usually get worse and they will be increasingly difficult to help.

The nurturing school

All these are organizational changes, but it is possible, also, to build into the school certain structures, procedures and strategies that are enabling for the less developed child but do not unduly restrict the others. These follow in detail the principles underpinning the nurture groups. They arise from a changed perspective that implicitly acknowledges the complexity and confusion of school for some children, and makes no hopeful but unreal assumptions about their capacity to cope. It is a 'from the beginning' perspective, based on acceptance of the child's helplessness, and identification with his earliest level needs, and leads to positive action rather than baffled impotence in the face of the difficulties. It depends on analysis of every situation for its potential difficulty with all aspects of the child's behaviour, however difficult, treated as a learning need, rather than a problem for disentangling by a psychotherapist. This leads to well-organized school and class surroundings, clear routine and sequence with expectations clearly stated and all large group situations – assembly, playtime and dinnertime – predictable and manageable, with no child left unsupported. Relationships are warm and family-like; emotional, social and cognitive experiences within this include those appropriate for a 'nurture' child; earliest level needs are met as they arise; and structured help is provided.

But it is not enough to give special care only to the children. The staff, too, need to be cared for and acknowledged, and where there are nurturing relationships between the staff, the benefit to the children is immense.

10

Assessing Needs

The extent of special needs in the school as a whole influences the way the nurture group is structured within the school and the way it is organized and run, as indicated in the previous chapter. This inevitably affects the composition of the group. The first consideration, nevertheless, when selecting children to form a viable group is the nature of their difficulties.

Selection of cases: general considerations

School-based provision for disturbed and distressed children ranges from part-time individual support in the mainstream class to full-time help in a special group. This should reflect a continuum of need, from the insecure and poorly sustained child who is responsive to reassurance and support, to those who are functioning so inappropriately that they cannot make progress in the mainstream class. In-between will be children who need something special for themselves on a part-time or ad hoc basis. The different forms of provision developed to meet these different needs, however conceptualized, usually involve a closer relationship with the child, and more personally adapted activities than is possible in the mainstream class. To this extent they have elements of 'nurture'; and the children they provide for on a full-time basis could be found in a nurture group, though the rationale of the work is different.

The need for experiences normally gained in the pre-nursery years and the potential to 'catch up' are the basic criteria for a place in the nurture group. It is usual, however, for a wide range of children to be considered, broadly on the grounds of emotional, behavioural and learning difficulties in the mainstream class.

The best provision for the child is sometimes uncertain

The emotional and behavioural difficulties of many children referred for special help are complex and the most appropriate provision is sometimes equivocal. In different ways the nurture group provides something for most of them, for it is an organized, supportive and protected environment where clearly defined limits are set, attachments are made, trust is established and pressure relieved more readily than in the mainstream class. The learning experiences provided are broadly based, and so are relevant to a wide range of difficulties. But for some children the nurture group, although appropriate in concept, is too short term. For others it is unnecessarily general, for they need more intensive and circumscribed help. Among these will be better developed children whose early experiences and relationships are 'knotted up'. They may be more appropriately helped by psychotherapy, and a helpful first step would be discussion with the educational psychologist. In a few cases the nurture group is contraindicated. The decision made is based on the nature of the child's difficulties, and his strengths and advantages, in relation to all other available forms of provision that might be appropriate. If the nurture group seems indicated it is expected that he will make sufficiently good progress there within four terms, exceptionally more, to become established in a mainstream class before leaving his present school and subsequently will continue to prosper. Children who are likely to need special provision throughout their school years are appropriately placed in the nurture group only exceptionally, as a planned intermediate stage. When a place is offered for a 'doubtful' case it is usually for positive and clearly formulated reasons. Sometimes it is because referral elsewhere is not acceptable to the family, or the nature of the problem is not understood and further and continuing assessment is needed, or because no clearly better alternative is available. Occasionally it is for goodwill within the school. Although the reasons are not very positive in these cases, the decision is purposeful and, within the total context, is a relevant one.

Children for whom the nurture group is appropriate

The nurture group was designed for children whose needs were at the 0 to 3-year level. Their development in different ways has not progressed in a constructive organized way, sometimes from birth. Other children have needs at the 3–5-year level, and experiences that support the foundation stage are of primary importance. All are appropriately placed in the nurture group.

Nurture children

Nurture children are without the personal resources and autonomy needed for the nursery or reception class. No assumptions are made regarding their prior learning experiences, whether emotional, social or cognitive. Features seen to differing extents in children in the nurture groups:

- *They do not engage appropriately with adults.* Some function barely at all and make no acknowledgement of the adult, or they heed her and appear to be biddable but respond mechanically. Others are indiscriminate in their search for affection, or make dependent or immature relationships. Others again, disregard the teacher and may be overtly resistive and negative. Eye contact typically is not normal: the children look past, through, stare fixedly or their eyes dart everywhere, giving attention to nothing. Lack of trust is usual; they do not relate to adults or resist making a relationship. Others are immature in their approach and response.

- *They have limited resources; lack basic competencies.* They have limited resources for play and do not explore constructively. Their language and concept development, and gross and fine motor skills are often poor. Their attention is difficult to gain and sustain, and they do not involve themselves constructively and with persistence in class activities, or engage with the events of school. In the inappropriate situation of the mainstream class they show emotional and behavioural difficulties that are often severe and sometimes seem bizarre.
- *They have limited social skills and poor peer group relationships.* Many are not able to wait and share, their tolerance for frustration is poor and some have temper tantrums. Communication and relationships with other children are usually limited and unconstructive. Some are aggressive and are involved in fights, and may be resistive, destructive, explosive and violent, and in some cases deliberately antisocial.
- *They are depressed in their functioning or distressed in more overt ways.* Within this picture of general underdevelopment are children who are untrusting and insecure, lack confidence and have low self-esteem. Some are overtly distressed and may be self-destructive in different ways, or show disconnected fragments of obsessional behaviour.

These children are potentially more able than their level of functioning would suggest. Their limited competencies are assumed to be a reflection of their poor learning opportunities in the past. This is mainly limited or impaired attachment experiences at the baby stage, inadequate play and verbal interaction with the carer in later infancy and restricted or impaired opportunity to give purposeful attention and to investigate, explore and play. Intrusive negative experiences that disturb or distort the learning process are quite common, and in some cases early development has been disturbed or disrupted by sudden loss or bereavement or other trauma or crisis.

Associated or causally related perceptual-motor difficulties are more prevalent than in the general school population, particularly poor gross motor co-ordination. In the younger children there is also a higher than expected incidence of intrinsic, medically based difficulties, some directly relevant to formal learning in school, such as speech impairment and/or an intrinsic language delay, others such as epilepsy less directly so. Difficulties centring on poor gross and fine motor co-ordination, and on language deficit, sometimes improve dramatically in the nurture group, suggesting that their origin may lie in lack of developmental opportunities.

Whatever the nature of their additional specific difficulties, effectively all function at 3 years of age or less and need a global 'nurture' level experience. Following the model of early infancy this encompasses every aspect of development. These different aspects of development – 'developmental strands' – are tightly intermeshing at the earliest stage. As already indicated, they come to the baby as a unitary experience, mediated through a mutually sustaining relationship with the carer and cannot be treated separately. The children's specific needs come within this and get attention as part of the nurturing process. Physiotherapists and speech therapists are sometimes involved with individual children, or have an advisory role.

In spite of the complexities and severity of the difficulties, and the uncertainties in some cases, the decision to take the child into the group rests with the school in discussion with the parents. A psychologist's individual assessment is not usually necessary and is not a statutory requirement, though in extreme or equivocal cases where special school provision or psychiatric help may be needed, a formal psychological assessment and discussion with the parents helps to clarify the position. When the group serves a diagnostic function it is made clear to the parents from the beginning that the nurture group is not long-term provision, and a further assessment will be necessary later.

Intrinsic learning difficulties in the context of disadvantage

In selecting cases for the nurture group, special consideration is given to children from well-nurturing homes who have minor specific difficulties, sometimes multiple, in the context of overall limited functioning. Speech and motor co-ordination are the most common, and particularly for children from disadvantaged homes the total learning difficulty is considerable. Typically their opportunities to experience and explore have been restricted, either independently of a medical, physical or language difficulty or because of it, and the stress of their inability to cope in the mainstream class leads to secondary emotional and behavioural difficulties. The overall picture they present is sometimes very similar to the more classic 'nurture' child, particularly those with associated educational needs of a more specific kind. Although psychosocial stress may be no more than a subsidiary factor, the early developmental nature of nurture-work generates a broadly based 'curriculum' that meets their special educational needs and this is the criterion for their selection. Most of these children make considerable progress in the nurture group and integrate successfully in the mainstream class.

More extreme specific needs cannot be met in the nurture group, although a great deal of extra care and help can be given and reassuring progress made. A psychological assessment of cognitive functioning at the early referral stage cannot give a firm prediction and may be misleading. A more reliable guide is the child's progress in the nurture group. He is likely to be more relaxed and secure in this homely, supportive and more structured environment. The slower tempo, clearer routine and more appropriate domestic and formal learning experiences enable him to engage better with activities. He communicates more, is happier and his emotional and behavioural difficulties lessen markedly or are not evident in this setting. However, if he continues to have general learning difficulties in spite of more relevant help and opportunities, he is unlikely to transfer successfully to his mainstream class. Such children commonly reach a plateau after one or two terms and make only very slow further progress. As soon as the teacher's impressions clarify he is seen by the educational psychologist for an individual assessment as it becomes increasingly difficult for parents to accept that other provision is more appropriate. The decision to take a child like this into the nurture group clearly will be influenced by the nature of the difficulties of the other children.

Difficult diagnostic problems

Particularly difficult and controversial 'diagnostic' problems are presented by the small number of children whose emotional/behavioural and formal learning difficulties are attributed to 'Attention Deficit Hyperactive Disorder'. They are distractible, hyperactive, have a low tolerance for frustration, lack persistence and make very little progress. Some impulse-dominated 'nurture' children may seem very similar, and the underlying nature of their difficulties is not always apparent until they have been in the group for some time, and even then there may be doubt. Overall, the 'nurture child' shows greater variability in his behaviour and is likely to have periods when he is more settled and calm, particularly in an individual relationship with the adult. If his distractibility remains at a high level he is referred for a medical and psychological opinion. Here, again, parents have resisted alternative provision, particularly as their child seems comparatively well settled in the nurture group, and it is therefore important to make any doubts clear to them at the outset.

Children with multiple and complex intermeshing difficulties are extremely difficult to assess, but the nurture group or nurture-type provision is an ideal situation from which to do this. The teacher provides a clearly defined structure that supports them, her management of the group and individual children is appropriate, as are the experiences she makes available, and the relevance of her response helps to establish an attachment, a more constructive and confident attitude, and better functioning.

Cultural discontinuity

The families of these children often live in difficult and disadvantaged circumstances, are largely estranged from the mainstream culture and frequently are isolated within their own cultural group. They insulate themselves from their surroundings in bewilderment and fear, and lead unusually stressed, depressed and restricted lives. Many are from recently arrived immigrant families where for different reasons the ethos of the home is markedly at variance with that of the school, and in some cases customs, beliefs and expectations, and attitudes to authority are different. Occasionally these factors come together in indigenous families. Usually these children are well cared for within the resources of their parents and are secure within their homes, but have a very restricted life experience and are not able to bridge the emotional, cultural and environmental gap between home and the contemporary UK school. Typically they are unventuring and withdrawn, or frightened and bewildered in the mainstream classroom, and sometimes disorganized and resistive; some seem 'frozen' and function like automata. They participate minimally and without constructive purpose in the life of the class. Most of them are not 'nurture' children, in the strict sense of being without primary experiences and basic autonomy, and schools familiar with these difficulties usually can provide sufficient help. Where the difficulties are extreme, the children are usually well placed in the nurture group. They respond to the comfort and affection, accept physical contact and 'attach'; they are reassured by the clear expectations and manageable experiences and their progress is often dramatic, particularly when the school is a source of support for the parents.

Refugee children have suffered a traumatic severance from their community and cultural roots, and sometimes from their families. They come into the strange environment of the UK school from a barely viable, usually temporary home base and typically are not able to speak English. They, too, benefit from the nurture group.

In cases where English is the child's alternative language (EAL) and is the central difficulty, broadly based EAL help is more appropriate. And where the central difficulty is not disadvantage and seclusion, but firmly held parental attitudes and beliefs that are at variance with the ethos of the school, the nurture group may be counterproductive and is likely to be rejected. Help based in the mainstream class or in a formal, academically oriented group may be preferable.

Small-group 'nurturing' support: nurture group or appropriate alternative

Other children appropriately placed in the nurture group have better developed skills and concepts, and their level of organized experience may be adequate for supported work in the mainstream class. In some cases their organized experience is on a very narrow base and is sufficient for participation in formal activities but not for personal and social growth. Such children, for different reasons, are only loosely attached in homes that otherwise provide adequate nurturing care and basic opportunities for cognitive development. They do not usually cause concern in the nursery because they have sufficient competence to engage with activities of their choice. Their difficulties are more apparent at Key Stage 1 when the demands are greater and sustained on-task attention is required. The emotional and behavioural difficulties of these children are not primarily related to social stress and a general impairment of early nurturing care, and in this respect they are not typical nurture group children. They are not usually considered suitable for psychotherapy either, though some are known to the local child mental health services and may have been referred from there to a school-based support group. Their main need is for an educational environment where the tempo is slower than in the mainstream class, the pressure of events can be relieved, and their personal 'space' protected. Trust, security and attachment can be gently established and relationships more delicately attuned. They feel a sense of comfort and well-being, reassurance and approval, get pleasure from the relationships and activities, and have an outlet for both self-development and the expression of their difficulties in creative activities. Although some could manage with individual support in the mainstream class it is rarely possible, and is not cost-effective, to provide there the breadth of organized personal and social experiences they need.

Children who need nurturing

These children are considered under five broad headings. All the circumstances described may be additional factors in children under more general and chronic social stress.

- They are from families where there are no seriously limiting or distorting environmental factors, but for different reasons there is clearly defined long-term stress within the home. Typical examples are chronic illness in a parent, including severe depression, or a disabled or handicapped sibling. Such circumstances generate anxiety and stress in the whole family and limit the attention available to the others, who lose experiences they would otherwise have with and through the parents, and may well feel less valued. They blossom in the nurture group.
- Children who have experienced, or are experiencing, the loss of a key relationship, parent or sibling , through death or other traumatic event, typically do not take part adequately in the experiences and events of the mainstream class. They may be unresponsive, lack interest and initiative, seem traumatized, have impaired capacity to play and show marked symptoms of anxiety and sometimes obsessional behaviour. Some show more overt distress and, in some cases, anger. Such children have experienced the desolation of the loss of a primary attachment relationship, and with this a profound disturbance of personal identity.

They might also experience the mourning of the family in the case of bereavement as a withdrawal of interest and affection, and feel a sense of responsibility and blame. Particularly when the loss has been of a sibling, the surviving child might experience a damaging intensity of protective attachment from the grieving parents, and some might identify with the dead family member to a pathological extent.

- Although the difficulties and disturbances of children with a history of loss of different kinds are individual and complex, all have experienced a traumatic break in their development. The nurture group or other appropriate school-based support resource can be a healing experience that helps them connect with their roots and function again. A head-teacher, describing a child whose mother had recently died, said of her: 'She was tight and closed-in and never smiled, but in the nurture group she opened out like a beautiful flower.'

Children like this are usually discussed with the educational psychologist. If the nurture group is indicated, careful thought is given to the nature of the difficulties of the other children in the group and the overall stability and level of control, and a contra-indication is a high proportion of older 'aggressive' children.

- Some children are well cared for physically and their opportunities at home are often of a high order, but their parents are involved in time- and interest-consuming work. When the substitute or supplementary care they arrange is unsatisfactory and the transition negotiated too quickly and without adequate preparation, the children suddenly lose familiar support and direction, are confused, and often resentful and angry. They respond well to the concern and support of the nurture group, or other similar resource, and this would be on a part-time basis.
- Occasionally parents reluctantly accept the nurture group, having refused psychotherapy, and this would be on a half-time or part-time basis. Here, again, the group provides a sanctuary for the child, and an opportunity for him to express his feelings.

All the children described in this section could be equally, and sometimes more appropriately helped in an alternative form of 'therapeutic' group providing opportunities at a later developmental level. The choice made is determined by the relevance of the alternative provision available. For convenience of terminology, they are usefully termed 'children who need nurturing', though in other contexts would have a different though equally non-specific designation. This distinction between 'nurture' needs and 'nurturing' needs is based on cognitive competence largely because the nurture group is an educational resource in an educational setting. In some groups all the children have 'nurturing' needs and the content of the nurture group day is then more advanced, and it may be misleading to call it a nurture group. Attendance, particularly when such children are older, is usually on a half-time or part-time basis. A successful junior school pattern is a morning group for ' nurture' children and an afternoon group for 'children who need nurturing', each structured but with relationships and experiences at different levels.

Integrated whole-school strategies preferred

Some children are appropriately helped within the school generally:

- These children are part of an estranged and self-defined subculture and present considerable problems for the school. Their families have a lifestyle that often is well organized and loyal within itself but is delinquent to varying extents. They are not part of the mainstream of society, and although living physically within it they disregard its expectations and even behavioural norms. Their young are well established within their own culture and are brought up to adopt its attitudes. They are often well organized and competent within their own exclusive group but neither engage actively in school, nor relate positively to the teacher or even to the other children. Many are challenging and confrontational.
- Other children presenting somewhat similar but less serious difficulties for the schools are from families in adversity and estranged. They lack trust, expect nothing from others and give nothing, and are vigilant in protecting their own interests. They are tough survivors who treat school with suspicion and are challenging and self-asserting.

The nurture group is rarely appropriate for these children, and may be counterproductive, and is likely to be rejected by the parents. Whole-school strategies directed to helping the children to be more constructively involved in school are preferred, and the nurture teacher and assistant have a part in this, and sometimes the group itself may be useful on a part-time or ad hoc basis.

- A small but increasing group of children dominate and manipulate their parents and expect to do the same with the teachers in school. They seem unaware or unconcerned about the effects of their actions on others, but understand the mechanics of social interaction sufficiently well to control and dominate. They try to get what they want regardless of others. They make conditions, and deliberate defiance is not uncommon. Some parents collude with this and are resentful when their children are disciplined. The children need a clear and consistent demonstration of acceptable behaviour that is appropriately provided in the context of the mainstream class. Case-work with the parents is sometimes helpful.

- Other parents, who are concerned and caring and have the personal and material resources to provide adequately for their children, are indulgent and compliant or restrictive, or differ in their management to an extent which leads to difficulties for the child, particularly when he goes to school. The nurture group is not usually appropriate though the parents may ask for this, and are reassured by seeing the teacher's purposeful management. Case-work with an outside agency is preferred and the group may be useful in conjunction with this.

- A child who functions adequately well in all areas but has a limited behaviour difficulty, for example he cannot wait for his turn or share with the other children, is better placed in the mainstream class with stratagems devised for his specific needs. This approach would be supported, where appropriate, by occasional visits to the nurture group for breakfast and for planned interactive activities.

Special provision, other than the nurture group

- Children whose first language is not English, and where adequate EAL help will resolve secondary stress-related difficulties, are not appropriately placed in the nurture group. If they have 'nurture' needs as well, they are offered a place, and minor EAL needs would be met in the nurturing context, as already indicated.

- Children from supportive homes who have major sensori-motor impairment, other physically based difficulties, or primary learning difficulties need special provision directed to their difficulties or, in the less severe cases, special educational needs support in the mainstream class from peripatetic teachers. Where deprivation is a major complicating factor and the difficulties are severe, a special school may be indicated.

- Children for whom a formal assessment procedure has already been started, or those on a Statement who are waiting for a different form of provision, are placed in the nurture group only in exceptional and carefully considered circumstances, as a 'holding' operation.

- Children who appear to need long-term provision, but whose parents have refused a Full Assessment, are usually difficult-to-place children for whom the nurture group can be no more than short-term expediency. Often they are 'nurture' children, with a history of major loss and change, in homes that are intrusively destructive and sometimes punitive, or are disturbed by severe mental illness, often both. It is in everyone's interests for long-term more appropriate provision to be sought. Placing them in the group merely delays this, and reinforces the parents' reluctance to consider special provision. It also markedly reduces and may damage the opportunities available for the others.

All these are firm reservations, but there is some flexibility, based on consideration of the needs of the particular child concerned and the other children, and the best use of the nurture resource within the school as a whole. For children likely to need long-term provision there is an urgent need for objective criteria to be established so that they can be identified at an early stage.

The nurture group relieves stress, and is therefore a helpful resource for observation and diagnosis in complex cases. This would be available in conjunction with the educational psychologist, SENCO and other relevant services.

Referral, assessment, admission and monitoring procedures

The structures and procedures established at the beginning of the year are not only an essential precursor of the work itself, but they draw everyone into a learning experience and are the starting point of ongoing discussion between members of staff.

Preliminary observations

Some schools make home visits prior to school entry on all the children registered. This has inherent risks but is usually more acceptable than later as it is a positive and friendly contact with the explicit aim of easing the child's entry into school. A possible need for the nurture group is sometimes given by the stress and pressure on the adults and the extent and nature of their interaction with the child and his siblings. The mother may appear severely depressed and unresponsive to her child's needs when he clearly needs help, or is over-controlling, or gives an occasional indiscriminate slap. The organization within the home may be bewilderingly chaotic or repressively rigid. Play materials, not necessarily toys as such, may be lacking or unsuitable and there may be unnecessary restrictions on the freedom to explore. The child may be overactive and restless and settle to nothing with purpose, or may lack spontaneity and make no response. Where there are indications of these kinds that initial extra help might be needed, some schools take the child into the nurture group at school entry, for assessment.

Observations at the time of registration: children 'at risk'

Children in need of special help usually come to the notice of the headteacher when the parent registers the child. The headteacher is alerted by the child's behaviour, and his response to the simple toys offered. In other cases social workers and health visitors are involved with the family and have indicated that the child might be personally and educationally at risk.

Initial observations are usually made in the mainstream class

Exceptionally, a new entrant in extreme need is taken into the nurture group straightaway, but always has a designated mainstream class. For others a period of observation under normal school conditions for at least two weeks is important and is felt to outweigh the risk of failure. The class teachers then have a clear idea of the nature and extent of the children's difficulties and will have a more realistic appreciation of their progress in the nurture group. They are also likely to maintain a more personal contact and it will be easier, when the time comes, to restore him to his mainstream class. Most teachers feel that *all* children should be tried initially in the mainstream class, except those whose disruptive behaviour is unmanageable, particularly as some children settle sufficiently well in a new class to remain there. This period of settling in is especially important for children coming to the school from elsewhere. Some teachers prefer to transfer nursery children to the nurture group immediately on admission to the infant school as this is a more natural transition at this stage, and is acceptable and unthreatening to the parents. Similarly children coming to the junior school from the infants' are likely to go straightaway into the nurture group.

Older children

The difficulties of children suitable for the nurture group usually get worse as time goes on, and inevitably when a group is newly established it is these older children who are referred, for they present the most serious problems and there is anxiety about their move to the next school. When the group is well established the trend is to take in younger children. Logically the earlier they are referred the better, preferably as new entrants before a pattern of resistance and cumulative failure has set in. But even when the policy is to take in younger children there are always a few older ones whose problems exacerbate later, or who come from another school and cannot be contained in a mainstream class.

Consensus decisions

Discussion of any child causing anxiety is based on shared experience of the child in the classroom, in assembly and in the playground. Adequate observation and discussion at this stage provide the basis for regular and continuing discussion after admission to the group. It is useful to draw observations from everyone involved with the child, and the decisions taken are normally based on consensus, both then and later. A special note is made of situations that seem particularly stressful, and the possibility that immature, disorganized, disruptive, resistive or antic-ing behaviour might be a direct product of poor class management is considered. This is sometimes shown on the Developmental Screening Form as a limited set of difficulties recurring in a particular class. The nurture group is not for problems of this kind. Frequently this preliminary work is done towards the end of the summer term and the final selection is made in September.

This is partly because most of the children will be with a new teacher and one or two may unexpectedly settle down.

Hesitant class teachers

It is usually the class teacher who initiates discussion about a child who is not settling in the class and in different ways is causing anxiety. This will have been recorded at Stages 1 and 2 of the Code of Practice. Familiarity with the Developmental Screening Form and Boxall Profile helps to clarify any concerns about referral to the group, and some schools have found it of value to screen the nursery children and new intake to the school. A general discussion in the staff room about the rationale of nurture work is essential, and a handout to every teacher describing this is a personal reinforcement. In general, extreme reluctance to give up a child is accepted, but observation continues, and further discussion is initiated when this seems appropriate.

Older children, especially at the junior stage, are admitted to the group only if it seems likely that they will become full members of their mainstream class at least a term before transfer to their next school. This gives them time to feel secure in their mainstream class in a familiar school environment. Often they are latecomers to the school. Whether or not they are given a place in the nurture group rests ultimately on school policy and what is felt to be the best use of resources. Sometimes, however, a child like this is taken into the nurture group to relieve the stress on himself and on the school generally. Special thought is needed, too, in the case of an older markedly antisocial child who may be beyond the nurture approach. These situations are far less likely to arise when the nurture group is in the infant school.

New entrants needing extra support

Other children coming into school need help in organizing and widening their experiences, and in establishing routine and trust. They are not nurture children in the sense already described, but they profit greatly from a few weeks in the nurture group. One school took several such children into the nurture group for a term, including some who had been through the nursery. They seemed happier after this experience, and in the mainstream class were markedly advanced in their overall competence. The nurture teacher and assistant could not, however, fully meet the needs of nine nurture children and an additional 12 rising-5s, but the experiment pointed to the value of a more structured introductory term for children who are not well equipped for the requirements of school.

These are the usual ways in which children are considered for the nurture group. In cases of doubt, some schools take the child into the nurture group, others into the mainstream class, but feel that the decision can be quickly reversed if within the first few days it seems that a mistake has been made.

Initial discussion

It is usual for children under consideration for the nurture group to be made known during the course of informal discussion in the staff room at playtime or dinnertime, and during the special time set aside for this.

Decisions are made for positive reasons

Children are placed in the nurture group in the expectation that they are likely to gain sufficient resources to be assimilated into a mainstream class within a year, or two years at the most. The reasons are always positive and clearly formulated, and are not usually based on short-term expediency. For a few children, not necessarily the most worrying from the class teacher's point of view, it is important to seek for more relevant long-term provision. Placing them in the nurture group is not in their interests, and could lead to a damaging imbalance in the group. Even when individually the children are appropriate referrals, it is important that a proper balance of cases is maintained. Not all children with difficulties at a particular level can be accepted if this negates the possibility of progress for the group, though children not given a place initially might be taken in later, or visit from time to time. Where siblings are concerned it is usual for the one who is older or more in need to be taken in first, but the composition of the group is relevant and there may be other factors. It may be preferable to admit twins together but this is a matter for individual consideration. Discussion takes into account everyone's views, but as the composition of the group and the timing of admission are important, the final decision rests with the nurture teacher and headteacher.

When the function of the nurture group is understood, children whose behaviour disturbs the class or who are unduly fearful and apprehensive, or who barely function, are usually referred quite readily. Discussion otherwise may need to be purposefully directed to the difficulties of those children who are secure in the attachment they have made to their class teacher, but relate to no one else.

Most of the children taken into the nurture group need intensive continuing help. Others may be in difficulties temporarily and extra comfort and support is enough to tide them over, while a few manage well in the mainstream class if they start the day with the warmth of a 'family breakfast'.

When a preliminary list of children has been drawn up their needs are discussed at a staff meeting, the proposal is discussed with the parents and the final selection is influenced by the headteacher's perception of stress in the school generally.

Approaching the parents

Discussion with the parent/s precedes any action taken for special needs help, and their permission is mandatory. Typically the headteacher or the class teacher makes the initial contact, either when one of the parents is in school or more commonly by letter, inviting them to call in. Some new entrants may have been seen at home already, or are known because an older sibling is in school, or through a mother and toddler's club, and a place in the nurture group is suggested as a precautionary measure. Exceptionally, the suggestion of the nurture group is made by or through an outside agency, that is, social services, the local child mental health services or the health visitor. When there is doubt about the provision needed, a short time in the nurture group helps the children to bridge the gap and settle in, and pay attention and concentrate better. This is acceptable when the group is for infant children but there are special difficulties at the junior stage because the nurture group is so obviously unlike the other classes. In schools that have become a focal point for the local community, and where the nurture group is known and accepted, an approach to the parents is easier than it would otherwise be. Many of them welcome an opportunity to discuss their children's difficulties and leap at the offer of a place in the nurture group. Most of the parents, sometimes after initial resistance or distress, accept the group with positive feelings. A small minority, particularly those who are not familiar with UK schools, are concerned about the informality of the surroundings and find it difficult to accept that formal work is done there, and that play in the group is purposeful and has educational content. Occasionally the parents refuse, but accept the nurture group later, after further discussion, when it is clear to them that the child's difficulties still persist. Sometimes, when psychiatric help is felt to be more appropriate and has been suggested and refused, the nurture group is accepted as the lesser of two unwelcome alternatives. Other parents are driven by desperation to accept the nurture group, too disturbed and fraught to understand or even care. Occasionally there are considerable difficulties in contacting parents. Letters are not answered, 'medicals' are not attended, and persistence and a great deal of pressure may be needed to get a minimal response.

The resistance some of the parents initially feel when the group is suggested does not stem from its nurturing orientation. Not all of them recognize and understand the process at an intuitive level. Those who do understand are grateful. They realize that something has gone wrong and mind deeply. Most of them are desperate about the reported problems and see the group as helpful and constructive. Some initially insist that there are no difficulties at home, and sometimes this is so. Any resistance usually centres round what appears to them to be permissiveness, though others focus on the structure and control, and like it.

Sympathetic discussion is usually reassuring, and a visit to the nurture group can dramatically change their views. They see the wide range of children taken into the group, not just the ones whose difficulties are immediately apparent, and realize that the teacher requires a great deal of the children and has high standards. They become aware of the many links that are made with the other classes, and the fluid arrangements within the school, and the way that children not in the group sometimes casually attach themselves to it. Reluctance to accept a place in the nurture group arises less often when the school has a productive relationship with the parents from the beginning, before major difficulties are evident. It is extremely unusual when the group is an established part of the school. The group is held in high regard and parents welcome the opportunity of a place for their child, and some ask for it, occasionally for a child who does not need it. If the place offered is refused by the parents, the child remains in his mainstream class.

Referral procedure: a summary

- Concern is expressed by member/s of staff and/or parents. Commonly the class teacher voices anxiety to the SENCO initially, following the Code of Practice for England and Wales, but usually this will have been recorded already at Stages 1 and 2. Discussion is based on any pre-school information available, earlier recorded concerns, contact with the parents and their concerns, the class teacher's observations, and the baseline assessments that are in use in the school generally.
- Further observations of the child in his mainstream class are made by the nurture teacher and SENCO, and if possible by the headteacher also. There is further discussion at a staff meeting. Everyone in the school is involved.
- Where appropriate the educational psychologist makes an individual assessment, but this is not a statutory requirement and is rarely necessary. However, as the nurture group is Stage 3 provision, s/he would have been involved when the child moved from Stage 2 to Stage 3 of the Code of Practice.
- The class teacher completes the Boxall Profile, in discussion with the nurture teacher if she is unfamiliar with it. This gives an initial assessment of the nature and extent of the child's early developmental learning needs.
- The class teacher and the headteacher meet the parents, with the child there if this is appropriate, to seek their views, and to discuss the school's concerns and a possible place in the nurture group. The observations made in school, often focusing on poor attention to school work, are discussed in relation to this. They visit the nurture group to see how it runs and to talk to the staff, and they consider how their child can be helped there.

- A decision is made by the headteacher, nurture group teacher, SENCO and class teacher in conjunction with the parents who, if still doubtful, are given time to think it over.
- If it seems that the nurture group is appropriate provision, there is a general discussion in the school about the child's needs within the group, and likely progress.
- A review date is arranged, e.g. at half-term for a full-time group, with the main review within a year. The aim is to monitor adequately the child's progress to eventual integration within his mainstream class.
- Between one and four terms in the nurture group is usual when this is full-time provision. Where a longer period than this is anticipated, it is because there is good reason to believe that the child will eventually become a full member of his mainstream class.

In schools where a substantial number of children need special help, the screening procedure is undertaken for the whole school as this may give pointers to useful reorganization within the school, and possible redeployment of resources.

Nurture by definition comes before nursery, and so ideally children are transferred to the group as soon as it is clear that their difficulties persist. Logically, too, the nurture group should be an induction-to-school class for all new school entrants felt to be at risk in the mainstream class, and should precede nursery. This is the long-term aim.

Induction to the group

The policy concerning admission of the children to the nurture group varies. The usual practice, when the group is being newly formed, is for the children to be introduced in ones, twos and threes over the first few days, for relatively short periods no matter what the nature of their difficulties. If the group is continuing from the year before, any newcomers then are admitted slowly. At this stage the nurture teacher is the sole focus of the group. This is logical and appropriate because she already has considerable knowledge of the children and is responsible for the overall organization of the group and for giving the lead in the behaviour expected. The assistant, however, quickly gets involved, freeing the teacher to introduce the next one, two or three children. They become familiar with the room, are introduced to simple activities and are given all the help they need to cope with these. Trust and confidence develop. They become used to each other and are brought in different combinations. Their time is gradually built up and they are asked if they would like to stay. The procedure varies with the child and circumstances in the nurture group and in the mainstream class. One practice is for the new child to be brought into the nurture group for breakfast and to stay for the first part of the morning and eventually for the whole day.

This slow induction is particularly helpful for children who are markedly inexperienced and unventuring, or are functioning at an immature nursery level. They are usually biddable in this restricted situation and with reassurance readily make an attachment, and quickly become familiar with the layout of the room, and the toys and materials put out for them. They learn what the teacher and assistant are like, and what to expect and what is expected, and that they can turn to them for help when they need it, or when things go wrong. They also become familiar with the basic routine, for example, when they arrive in the morning they go straight to the home area and look at a comic or play with certain specified quiet toys that are kept in a particular place. Other basic requirements are made clear at this stage, for example 'no fighting', though it is not expected that this injunction will influence the children's behaviour straightaway. During this introductory period the children have the concentrated attention of an adult and are introduced to activities that are developmentally appropriate, enjoyable and satisfying. They are therefore likely, far more than in the mainstream class, to give concentrated attention to the adult and to their activities.

Most groups have a wide range of children and over the first few days it is possible to bring them together in small groups, making new combinations as they gain increasing confidence and become more used to each other. This leads up to the formation of the full group. The general guideline now is that aggressive and disruptive children, who need tight organization and firm control and limits, are taken in first on the new permanent basis; the more withdrawn children are brought in next, and the children whose main need is for extended experiences last of all. The process is quite rapid and it is usually possible to establish a typical group of 12 children over a period of two or three weeks. Children in a group continuing from the previous year are likely to be well settled by then and can be reassured about the admission of new children; and the newcomers can be given quite easily the extra help and attention they need with their individual activities. With support and guidance from the adult, and the example of the other children, they are able to follow the routine and take part in simple directed group activities.

Latecomers to the group

Special problems arise when there are latecomers to a group that has settled in and is functioning well. They are usually new admissions from another school. They come into an organized situation where they are the only ones who do not know what to do. They are not part of the happy activities and relationships they see all about them and inevitably they react with worsening behaviour or become inhibited and immobilized. Fortunately the other children seem to expect that the newcomers will get extra attention. Clearly the most difficult situation of all is created by the arrival of a new entrant to a group that is still unstable.

Special efforts are needed to settle the newcomers in and they put a brake on the group at first. They have not been through the early stage of meticulous structuring and controlled experiences, and the need for this is easily overlooked. Most schools prefer to give individual help in situations like this, but others feel it is useful and appropriate to take all the children through the early basic organization and routines again, as this saves time in the long run. The crucial issue then may be the provision, or not, of a lengthy and formal breakfast. Breakfast is very important, particularly for children who are not able to wait and share, but takes up valuable time from others who are beyond this stage and could profit from a wider range of experiences. By and large the policy adopted is determined by the level of need of most of the children in the group, with adaptations for the others. Occasionally, the difficulties of a child already in a group that has stabilized exacerbate when under sudden and severe stress and here, again, the overall organization of the group may need to be modified to contain the disturbed child.

At any one time therefore some of the children will need immediate support and help, others will be able to do more on their own, while one or two in an established group will be almost ready to move on to their mainstream class. Newcomers to the group will need a great deal of help in grasping the routine and acquiring basic skills, but even if three or four children are admitted together it is usually possible to provide this, and within a few days most of the children understand what is expected.

The need for flexibility

An important point is the need for flexibility. As the year progresses and the children develop, the nurture teacher becomes increasingly like a class teacher, and when she starts the next year with a new group of children may forget the need for a nurture-level approach. The result can be disastrous and salutary. And the groups themselves vary a great deal from year to year. One year the cooker might be needed for breakfast every day, while the following year it would be used only for the weekly bake and for an occasional special event.

Monitoring procedures

These vary and sometimes incorporate assessment procedures that are specific to the school, but are not part of general nurture group practice. Typically, however, all or most of the procedures set out below are followed. Planning is linked to desired outcomes, targets are set in each child's IEP and these are broken down into small progressing steps and evaluated regularly. The information from the Boxall Profile contributes to the targets set for each child.

- The nurture teacher has frequent ad hoc discussions about the children with the class teacher, and with teachers with special areas of responsibility where their expertise is needed (EAL, language development, etc.). One practice is for the nurture group to run in the mornings only, and for the nurture teacher and assistant to provide support in the mainstream class in the afternoons for all special needs children, not just those in the nurture group. In this way, all children in the school with special needs are better catered for and, in conjunction with the SENCO are under constant review. Whether such an arrangement is feasible depends on the level of need of the children in the nurture group, and the extent of unmet needs in the school as a whole.

- Meetings are arranged more formally with the headteacher, class teacher and SENCO, usually at the end of each half-term, to discuss the well-being and academic progress of all the children in the group. If other agencies are involved with specific children a date is arranged for an inclusive review. Depending on the child's special needs, this might include the speech therapist, occupational therapist, EWO, school nurse and perhaps the school doctor, and sometimes a psychiatric social worker or psychiatrist is involved. A contribution from social services is sought and wherever possible agreed lines of communication are established.

- Daily notes are kept of academic work, social relationships, participation in project work, and the child's activities for first and second choosing. 'First choosing' is made from a selection of quiet basic structured activities offered by the teacher. 'Second choosing', later in the day, is less restricted and involves more action and noise, and requires space. In the ILEA, a specially devised Weekly Record Form was completed regularly.

- The Boxall Profile will have been completed for the child when in the mainstream class, and the nurture teacher usually chooses to repeat this, with the assistant, after three weeks or so in the group, to provide a baseline for his progress in the group.

- Initial assessment otherwise follows the overall procedures of the school. In the ILEA, on admission to the group and at the end of each half-term, any child for whom this is appropriate is asked to draw a person and a picture. He writes or copies his name, copies geometric shapes and colours in a simple outline picture or geometric shape. The teacher keeps a sample of his first piece of written and number work, and records his reading level.

- Thereafter the teacher keeps an ongoing descriptive account of progress, and usually, in the ILEA, the Weekly Record Form on a nurture-level child, and the Profile at intervals on particularly difficult or instructive cases. A note is made of any changed or particularly stressful circumstances, and a comment on any contact with the parent(s).

- Preferably at the end of each term, but always on leaving the group, a final description of the child and the progress made is recorded, and a

Profile is completed. This is in addition to any academic records required by the school.

- Towards the end of each term, the nurture teacher invites the parents for a chat about their child's progress, though many will have been regular visitors to the group and will be well informed already. A record is kept of the discussion.
- A major review is made before the end of the year, or at Easter if the child is a year 2 infant. If necessary, and in full consultation with the parents and staff, the child is referred to the educational psychologist for assessment. In most cases, however, the child's formal work and general progress and interests will suggest that he is ready to be tried in his mainstream class. Wherever possible, the situation is discussed with the parents in general terms two or three weeks before the 'integration' process is anticipated.

Return to the mainstream class

The child has had his other class from the beginning, albeit notionally in a few cases, and as much contact as possible will have been built in already. His progress is known to the receiving class teacher through ongoing discussion and regular contact, and from the beginning s/he knows that eventually he will return to this class. S/he also knows that the nurture teacher will continue to have a responsibility for discussion and support, and usually will monitor his progress for at least a year.

The process of return to the mainstream class – the time of day, the work he will do there – is negotiated with the class teacher. It varies from child to child and from school to school but is always discussed and carefully planned. Very occasionally a child does not have another class. In this case, the class to which he will eventually return will have been negotiated well in advance of the time when he will take up full membership, and his difficulties and progress will be known to the teacher concerned.

Transition to the mainstream class

Most of the children in the nurture group have come from another class in the school and so have a class to which they can return. Others will have been admitted from the nursery and a few from another school. They have no prior links with a mainstream class and have to be assigned to one. Consideration is given to the likely compatibility of teacher and child, and any earlier positive contact. Sometimes a child, for apparently capricious reasons, develops an attachment to a particular member of staff and assumes that he will go into that class. Interest of this kind is fostered, for example by inviting the teacher in for breakfast. Any existing peer group attachment would be a further consideration, and also the level of maturity of the receiving class. Occasionally the teacher in the child's mainstream class resists being involved and when this is so, nurture teachers try to introduce him to a different teacher. If no way round the problem can be found it is sometimes necessary to keep the child in the nurture group for the whole year. There are particular difficulties when several children in the nurture group are from the same class, but as far as possible this is avoided, and if it does arise the children are re-settled in ones and twos. A further problem is the stability of the receiving class. Ideally it provides an example of more mature behaviour, but in reality the behavioural requirements there may be less rigorous than in the nurture group. Frequently the noise level is higher and many nurture group children have complained about this. Finally, the organization of the school is of relevance. Many schools have the same broad time structure and the same pattern of activities in all classes. This eases considerably the process of integration, because when the child goes from the nurture group to his mainstream class at a chosen time he finds a situation that is of the same general type as the one he left.

Transition to the mainstream class begins only when the child is advanced enough to grasp that the nurture class is one of several, and has improved enough for his other teacher to have noticed his increasing awareness. It is a delicate process and requires a sympathetic acceptance of the child by the receiving teacher and an interest in discussing his needs in detail. This interest is usually there because the child has had continuing contact with this class from the beginning. The aim of the teacher and assistant is to help the children develop the necessary personal resources for successful participation in the mainstream class. It is not enough, however, that they have made progress in the nurture group and have adequate continuing support from the nurture teacher and assistant during this critical period. They need adequate and continuing co-ordinated support planned in conjunction with the receiving class teacher, and carefully controlled contact with this class. The stratagems planned are the outcome of detailed discussion in the context of a sympathetic shared understanding of the child's difficulties and needs. This is a vitally important aspect of the work and hinges on adequate liaison and communication with everyone concerned. It presupposes that the receiving class teacher is positive and constructive in her attitude to the nurture group and wants to have her children back.

Support for the nurture group is normally sufficiently positive for the children to be tried in their mainstream classes as soon as this is feasible, and for all but the most undeveloped and poorly organized children some involvement there is built in almost from the beginning. This is usually as soon as they are able to manage on their own, if only for a short period of time and for a carefully selected activity, and the expectations are gradually increased as they become increasingly able to cope. This transition is possible because the nurture group is not a separate unit within the school. It is an integral part of the school and is a flexible resource with give and take fostered on both sides. Easy contact is therefore possible and is achieved in different ways. In some schools the children give in their dinner money and register with their mainstream class but this is realistic only if most of them can manage this. It is an accepted routine and provides a natural daily encounter. It is a brief encounter and so is likely to be trouble free, and if not, the end is in sight and the nurture teacher will soon arrive. The class teacher is therefore more likely to maintain interest in the child and feel continuing responsibility for him, and to give a positive welcome. It is a useful way of working when the group is in a junior school or where informal contact is not easy to arrange.

In groups functioning at a 'nurture' level the children register with the nurture group. In this case the mainstream class teachers try to visit the nurture group from time to time and might join them for a birthday event. In most established groups, whether infant or junior, one or two children from the child's 'other' class come in for his birthday party, or perhaps for Friday afternoon tea. This, too, helps to make links with the mainstream class. Some children, otherwise full time in the mainstream class, go to the nurture group regularly to play, or from time to time when under particular stress, or simply to have the comfort and caring of the 'family' breakfast. Other groups, particularly those in junior schools, are on a half-time basis for most of the children. This is because at the junior stage the nurture children are more likely to be seen as 'different', and it is more difficult to get them back into their mainstream class. Usually they have two groups running at different levels, and are able to help more children. Whatever the organization of the school, and the nature of the contacts that are made, it is important that the nurture teacher is a familiar person about the school, and for everyone to feel that she is fully part of the school. Nevertheless, without continuing effort on her part, the supportive involvement of other members of staff may begin to fade away. But it is vitally important to maintain this interest if the child is to become fully part of his mainstream class, and determined contact with it relieves the anxiety felt by some parents about the long-term outcome for their child.

Indications for return to the mainstream class

The class teacher, nurture teacher and assistant sense that the time has come for disengaging the child from the nurture group. Eagerness in a young child to be part of the mainstream class is sometimes a good indication that he is ready to move on, provided he has adequate formal attainments, and often he signals this by seeming to be bored in the nurture group. This is a useful pointer, especially in the case of older children. Information is also picked up from other people in the school, including the 'midday staff' whose observations are important from the beginning.

Although some of the children make the transition from the nurture group with very little direct help, and may take the initiative to go, the loosening of ties is more difficult for others, and the step forward into the mainstream class is a very big one. It is as big as the normally developing younger child takes when he goes to school for the first time. It is indeed bigger, because the security the nurture child gets from the nurture teacher and assistant is against a background of insecurity, and so leaving the nurture group may be particularly difficult.

The process of return to the mainstream class

The child has already had as much contact as possible with his mainstream class, and it is usual for him to have taken good work to show his class teacher, sometimes every day. A relationship is fostered, also, with one to two visitors to the group from his 'other' class, and the teacher arranges for these children to be with him in this critical trial period. He may also have been involved in outings with his mainstream class, sometimes for a whole afternoon. One procedure when the group is stable is for all the children to be in their mainstream class for one morning a week with support from the nurture teacher and assistant, but this is not usually feasible. A variant is for the nurture children to be in their mainstream classes for the first hour of each afternoon, and a wider range of children can cope with this, though some will not be able to manage any kind of regular contact.

Support to the child

A child in the nurture group who is venturing into his mainstream class needs the same kind of help that supportive parents intuitively provide when their child first goes to school. He will be familiar already with the inside of the classroom and will have an expectation that enjoyable things happen there. He knows the teacher, and he knows that she is expecting him and wants to have him. The nurture teacher and class teacher choose the time of day when the mainstream class is most settled, and a class activity that is familiar and where sufficient support will be possible. He takes with him work prepared by the nurture teacher, something that he has accomplished successfully in the nurture group and has enjoyed. At first this is a structured task that requires little initiative on his part, and can be completed quickly and successfully before problems arise. The class teacher gives him what attention she can. She keeps an eye on him and is alert to acknowledge his effort and success, or to provide help in good time if he appears to be struggling. Other children may not have the competence to persist with a task on their own, but can manage storytime in their mainstream class, even though there are far more children there. They will have had lots of stories in the nurture group, have learned to attend to the teacher's face and can follow what she is saying with interest. For other children storytime would be catastrophic. Each child needs individual consideration, and a successful outcome depends on the close liaison of nurture teacher and class teacher. When the child has completed his task, or has had enough, he is taken back. He tells the nurture teacher what he has done and shows his work and would probably have a drink. The class teacher makes it clear that she wants him to come again soon. Even if the situation has gone wrong she is positive in her comments and might suggest that he tries again tomorrow, but the situation would be reviewed and modified, and extra supports would be built in.

He is tried for up to one hour, or even one half-day initially, perhaps two or three times a week, and this is gradually increased. The situation becomes more complex and fluid, and requires more competence, confidence and self-control. If he seems to be coping, and at registration time one or other teacher senses that he seems settled, he is tried for a full day and is eventually full time. But he goes back to the nurture group for visits at times of stress if he seems to need this, or by arrangement at the end of the day. This relieves the stress and is a gesture that they are still there for him. At this stage he is no longer a visitor to his mainstream class; he is a full member of that class, and responsibility for his formal work now rests entirely with the class teacher.

In general these planned ventures into the mainstream class are successful, though mistakes are sometimes made and a situation might be misjudged. There are special difficulties if the school community generally is unstable but, even so, many of the children manage to maintain a satisfactory and even high standard of behaviour in their mainstream class. The extra effort they have to make is sometimes released in restless, excited and immature behaviour when they return to the nurture group, but the advantages are felt to outweigh the possibility of a humiliating tantrum in front of the other children.

'Letting go'

It is important that 'letting go' is not too long delayed. The children need the experience of being with others who are more mature than they are, and there seems to be a critical point when they are able to respond to the expectations of their mainstream class and make better progress there, even though their problems are not fully resolved. This is a matter of fine judgement, and entails risk. The children for the most part enjoy these ventures into their mainstream class and often seem able to maintain a higher level of behaviour there than in the nurture group, and their concern to behave well suggests that they experience this as an achievement. This is very much like the achievement of the normally developing child when he goes to school: he functions at a relatively high level in school but may be immature and babyish when he returns home. Some children, however, need the special sheltering of the nurture group for a long time, and any visit to their mainstream class, however brief, would be counterproductive. They may protest that they want to go, not knowing what is going on there but wanting it all the same. Their pleas are resisted and they are easily diverted with a different form of 'treat'.

Some of the children have built up a very close relationship with the nurture teacher or assistant, or both, and particularly like going back to the nurture group to visit, though they very soon begin to refer to the mainstream class teacher as 'my real teacher'. The tie with the nurture group is maintained for as long as the children need it, but is gradually loosened as they become less dependent on immediate support and reassurance. Some infant children look in on the nurture group after they have transferred to the juniors, and some secondary school children, and children who have left school have called in on a junior group for a friendly chat, or when in trouble, and have sent Christmas cards. These long-term contacts are of a mature order. The children look around the class, notice changes, recall events and like to exchange news. It is tremendously rewarding for the nurture teacher and assistant to see the children again and to know that they are making good progress.

During the transitional phase, for some time they seem very close to the nurture teacher and assistant at one moment and very dependent, and then suddenly are very independent. The nurture teacher and assistant sometimes feel rejected and a group of them expressed this ruefully at one of our meetings. Most of them were mothers and they commented with considerable feeling about themselves as mothers in relation to their own children: 'Teacher is everything in the world for 6-year-olds. They don't stop to kiss you goodbye when they are going to school, don't even look over their shoulder.'

References

Bennathan, M. and Boxall, M. (1998) *The Boxall Profile, Handbook for Teachers*. Maidstone: AWCEBD.

Bennathan, M. and Boxall, M. (2000) *Effective Intervention in Primary Schools: Nurture Groups*. revised edn, London: David Fulton.

Boxall, M. (1974) 'Developmental Screening Form'. Unpublished (being re-trialled 2001).

Department for Education and Employment (DfEE) (1994) *The Code of Practice on the Identification and Assessment of Special Education Needs*. London: HMSO.

Department for Education and Employment (DfEE) (2000) *Curriculum Guidance for the Foundation Stage*. London: Qualifications and Curriculum Authority.

Goldschmied, E. and Jackson, S. (1994) *People Under Three: Young Children in Day Care*, ch. on Treasure Basket. London: Routledge.

Lucas, S. (forthcoming) *The Discovery Basket: A Curriculum Resource for Nurture Group Children*. In preparation.

Rutter, M., et al. (1999) 'Quasi-autistic patterns following severe early global privation', *Journal of Child Psychology and Psychiatry*, **40**(4): 537–49.

Winnicott, D.W. (1971) *Playing and Reality*, Ch. 1. London: Routledge.

Bibliography Specific to Nurture-Work

Bennathan, M. (2001) 'How we think about children', *AWCEBD Newsletter*, Summer: 1–3.

Bennathan, M. et al. (2001) 'Nurture group news', *AWCEBD Newsletter*, Summer: 9–13.

Cooper, P., Arnold, R. and Boyd, E. (1999) *The Nature and Distribution of Nurture Groups in England and Wales*. Cambridge: Cambridge University, School of Education.

Cooper, P., Arnold, R. and Boyd, E. (2000) 'The Cambridge research. Reasons to be cheerful . . . ?' in *Nurture Group News, AWCEBD Newsletter*, Winter: 9–10.

Cooper, P. and Lovey, J. (1999) 'Early intervention in emotional and behavioural difficulties: the role of nurture groups', *European Journal of Special Educational Needs Education*, **14**(2): 122–31.

Department for Education and Employment (DfEE) (1997) *Excellence for all Children: Meeting Special Educational Needs*. London: HMSO.

Henson, S. (1993) 'Nurture groups as a resource for children with special educational needs: an investigation into how the nurture group aims to meet children's needs and provides support at a whole school level', M.Sc. dissertation in Educational Psychology, Tavistock Clinic and Brunel University.

Holmes, E. (1982) 'The effectiveness of educational intervention for pre-school children in day or residential care', *New Growth*, **2**(1): 17–30.

Holmes, E. (1995) 'Educational intervention for young children who have experienced fragmented care', in J. Trowell and M. Bower (eds) *The Emotional Needs of Young Children and their Families*. London: Routledge.

Holmes, E. (2000) 'Nurture groups: a therapeutic intervention', *Educational Therapy and Therapeutic Teaching*, **9**, March (see Outcome Table p. 62).

Iszatt, J. and Wasilewska, T. (1997) 'Nurture groups: an early intervention model enabling vulnerable children with emotional and behavioural difficulties to integrate successfully into school', *Educational and Child Psychology*, **14**(3): 63–70.

Jaffey, D. (1990) 'An evaluation of the work of nurture groups: an analysis of teacher and child verbal interaction in the nurture group and mainstream classroom' unpublished M.Sc. dissertation in Educational Psychology, Tavistock Clinic and Brunel University.

King, P. (2001) *Curriculum Guidelines for Nurture Groups*. Maidstone: Nurture Group Network AWCEBD.

Lucas, S. (1999) 'The nurturing school: the impact of nurture group principles and practice on the whole school', *Emotional and Behavioural Difficulties*, **4**(3): 14–19.

General Bibliography

The following is a list of mostly recent publications of more academic interest.

Acredolo, L.P. (1980) 'Development of spatial orientation in infancy', *Developmental Psychology*, **4**(3): 224–34.

Alvarez, A. (1992) *Live Company*. London: Tavistock; New York: Routledge.

Ainsworth, M.D.S., Blehar, M.C., Waters, E. and Wall, S. (1978) *Patterns of Attachment*. Hillsdale, NJ: Lawrence Erlbaum Associates.

Balbernie, R. (1999) 'Infant mental health: how events wire up a baby's brain', *Young Minds Magazine*, **38**: 12–15; **39**: 17–18.

Barnes, P. (ed.) (1995) *Personal, Social and Emotional Development of Children*. Milton Keynes: Open University/Blackwell.

Barrett, M. (1999) 'The development of language', *Studies in Developmental Psychology*. Hove: Psychology Press.

Barrett, M. and Trevitt, J.V. (1991) *Attachment Behaviour and the School Child: An Introduction to Educational Therapy*. London: Tavistock/Routledge.

Bennathan, M. (1997) 'Effective intervention in primary schools: what nurture groups achieve', in P. Cooper (ed.), *Emotional and Behavioural Difficulties*, **2**(3): 23–9.

Bennett, P.L. and Gamman, R. (2000) 'Whole school behaviour policy: reviews and projects', *Educational and Child Psychology*, **17**(1): 20–32.

Berry Brazelton, T. and Greenspan, S.I. (2000) The irreducible needs of children. What every child needs to grow, learn and flourish. Cambridge, MA: Perseus Publishing.

Blackford, P. and Sharp, S. (1994) *Breaktime and the School: Understanding and Changing Playtime Behaviour*. London: Routledge.

Blatchford, P. (1998) 'The state of play in schools', *Forum on Play, Child Psychology and Psychiatry*, **3**(2): 58–67.

Blenkin, G.M. and Kelly, A.V. (eds) (1996) *Early Childhood Education: A Development Curriculum*, 2nd edn London: Paul Chapman Publishing.

Bloom, L. (1993) *The Transition from Infancy to Language*. Cambridge: Cambridge University Press.

Bornstein, M.H. and O'Reilly, A.W. (eds) (1993) 'The role of play in the development of thought', *New Directions for Child Development*, **59**, Spring, San Francisco: Jossey–Bass.

Bray, M., Ross, A. and Todd, C. (1999) *Speech and Language: Clinical process and practice*. London: Whurr, Ch. 6.

Bremner, J.G. (1994) *Infancy*. Oxford: Blackwell.

Brown, A. (1987) *Active Games for Children with Movement Problems*. London: Harper and Row.

Cameron, R.J. (1998) 'School discipline in the United Kingdom: promoting classroom behaviour which encourages effective teaching and learning', *Educational and Child Psychology*, **15**(1): 40–5.

Chapman, R.S. (2000) 'Children's language learning: an interactionist perspective', *Journal of Child Psychology and Psychiatry*, **41**(1): 33–54.

Chrisholm, K. (1998) 'A three year follow-up of attachment and indiscriminate friendliness in children adopted from Romanian orphanages', *Child Development*, **69**(4): 1092–106.

Clarke, A. and Clarke, A., (1998) 'Early experience and the life path', *The Psychologist*, September: 433–6.

Clarke, M. (1999) *Managing the Difficult Child: A Practical Handbook for Effective Care and Control*. Resources in Education. Devon: Northcote House Publishers.

Clay, M. (1991) *Becoming Literate: The Construction of Inner Control*. Portsmouth, NH: Heinemann.

Crandell, L.E. and Hobson, R.P. (1999) 'Individual differences in young children's IQ: a social-developmental perspective', *Journal of Child Psychology and Psychiatry* **40**(3): 455–64.

Crawley, S.B. Parks Rogers, P., Friedman, S., Iacobbo, M., Criticos, A., Richardson, L. and Thompson, M.A. (1978) 'Developmental changes in the structure of mother–infant play', *Developmental Psychology*, **14**(1): 30–6.

Cummings, E.M. and Davies, P.T. (1994) 'Maternal depression and child development', *Journal of Child Psychology and Psychiatry–Annual Research Review*, **35**(1): 73–112.

Cunningham, C.E., Bremner, R. and Boyle, M. (1995) 'Large group community-based parenting programs for families of preschoolers at risk for disruptive behaviour disorders: utilization, cost effectiveness and outcome', *Journal of Child Psychology and Psychiatry*, **36**: 1141–59.

Docker-Drysdale, B. (1990). *The Provision of Primary Experience: Winnicottian Work with Children and Adolescents*. London: Free Association Books.

Eisenberg, N. and Mussen, P.H. (1989) *The Roots of Prosocial Behaviour in Children*, Cambridge Studies in Social and Emotional Development. Cambridge: Cambridge University Press.

Farran, D.C. (1986) *Risk in Intellectual and Psychosocial Development*, Developmental Psychology Series. London: Academic Press.

Farrell, P. (ed.) (1995) *Children with Emotional and Behavioural Difficulties: Strategies for Assessment and Intervention*. London: Falmer Press.

Fergusson, D.M. and Woodward, L.J. (1999) 'Maternal age and educational and psychosocial outcomes in early adulthood', *Journal of Child Psychology and Psychiatry*, **40**(3): 479–89.

Fitzherbert, K. (1997) 'The work of the Pyramid Trust', in P. Cooper (ed.), *Emotional and Behavioural Difficulties*, **2**(3): 30–5.

Forum on Play (1998) *Child Psychology and Psychiatry Review*, **3**(2); **3**(3), various authors.

Gallaway, C. and Richards, B.J. (eds) (1994) *Input and Interaction in Language Acquisition*, Chs 1, 5, 6 and 7. Cambridge: Cambridge University Press.

Gardner, F.E.M., Sonuga-Barke, E.J.S. and Sayal, K. (1999) 'Parents anticipating misbehaviour: an observational study of strategies parents use to prevent conflict with behaviour problem children', *Journal of Child Psychology and Psychiatry*, **40**(8): 1185–96.

Garton, A.F. (1992) *Social Interaction and the Development of Language and Cognition*. London: Lawrence Erlbaum Associates.

Garvey, C. (1990) *Play*. Cambridge, MA: Harvard University Press.

Gerhardt, L. (1973) *Moving and Knowing: The Young Child Orientates Himself in Space*. Englewood Cliffs, NJ: Prentice Hall.

Glacer, D. (2000) 'Child abuse and neglect and the brain – a review', *Journal of Child Psychology and Psychiatry*, **41**(1): 97–116.

Goldschmied, E. (1986) *Infants at Work: Babies of 6–9 Months Exploring Everyday Objects*. VHS video: National Children's Bureau.

Goldschmied, E. and Hughes, A. (1992) *Heuristic Play with Objects: Children of 12–20 Months Exploring Everyday Objects*. VHS video: National Children's Bureau.

Goleman, D. (1996) *Emotional Intelligence: Why It Can Matter More than IQ*. London: Bloomsbury.

Goswami, U. (1998) *Cognition in Childhood*. Developmental Psychology. Hove: Psychology Press.

Greenberg, M.T., Speltz, M.L. and Deklynen, M. (1993) 'The role of attachment in the early development of disruptive behaviour problems', *Development and Psychopathology*, **5**: 191–213.

Grusec, J.E. and Goodnow, J.J. (1994) 'Impact of parental discipline methods on the child's internalisation of values: a reconceptualization of current points of view', *Developmental Psychology*, **30**(1): 4–19.

Grusec, J.E. and Goodnow, J.J. (1994) 'Summing up and looking to the future', *Developmental Psychology*, **30**(1): 29–31.

Harris, P.L. (1994) 'The child's understanding of emotion: developmental change and the family environment', *Journal of Child Psychology and Psychiatry–Annual Research Review*, **35**(1): 3–28.

Hay, D.F. (1994) 'Pro-social development', *Journal of Child Psychology and Psychiatry – Annual Research Review*, **35**(1): 29–71.

Hodes, M. (2000) 'Psychologically distressed refugee children in the United Kingdom', *Child Psychology and Psychiatry Review*, **5**(2): 57–68.

Hoffman, M.L. (1994) 'Discipline and internalisation', *Developmental Psychology*, **30**(1): 26–8.

Holmes, J. (1993) *John Bowlby and Attachment Theory*. London: Routledge.

Jennings, S. (1999) *Introduction to Developmental Playtherapy: Playing and Health*. London: Jessica Kingsley.

Johnson, M.H. (2000) 'How babies' brains work', in *The Psychologist*, **13**(6): 298–301.

Kochanska, G. (1994) 'Beyond cognition: expanding the search for the early roots of internalisation and conscience', *Developmental Psychology*, **30**(1): 20–2.

Levy, T.M. (ed.) (2000) *Handbook of Attachment Interventions*. London: Academic Press.

Main, M. and George, C. (1985) 'Responses of abused and disadvantaged toddlers to distress in agemates: a study in the day care setting', *Developmental Psychology*, **21**(3): 407–12.

Marsh, J. and Hallet, E. (ed.) (1999) *Desirable Literacies: Approaches to Language and Literacy in the Early Years*. London: Paul Chapman Publishing.

Maughan, B. (1988–91) 'School experiences as risk/protective factors', in M. Rutter, (ed.) *Studies of Psychosocial Risk: The Power of Longitudinal Data*, Ch. 11. Cambridge: Cambridge University Press.

Meadows, S. (1996) *Parenting Behaviour and Children's Cognitive Development*. Hove: Psychology Press.

Meadows, S. (1998) 'Children learning to think: learning from others? Vygotskian theory and educational psychology', *Educational and Child Psychology*, **15**(2): 6–13.

Meins, E. (1997) *Security of Attachment and the Social Development of Cognition*, Essays in Developmental Psychology. Hove: Psychology Press.

Nind, M. and Hewett, D. (1988) 'Interaction as curriculum: a process method in a school for pupils with severe learning difficulties', *British Journal of Special Education*, **15**(2): 55–7.

Oates, J. (ed.) (1979) *Early Cognitive Development*. Buckingham: Open University.

Oates, J. and Sheldon, S. (eds.) (1987) *Cognitive Development in Infancy*. London: Lawrence Erlbaum Associates/Open University.

Perry, D.G. (1994) 'Comments on the Grusec and Goodnow (1994) model of the role of discipline in moral internalization', *Developmental Psychology*, **30**(1): 23–5.

Power, T.G. (2000) *Play and Exploration in Children and Animals*, (esp. Chs 3, 5, 7 and 8. Mahwah, NJ, and London: Lawrence Erlbaum Associates.

Puckering, C., Pickles, A., Skuse, D., Heptinstall, E., Dowdney, L. and Zur-Szpiro, S. (1995) 'Mother–child interaction and the cognitive and behavioural development of four-year-old children with poor growth', *Journal of Child Psychology and Psychiatry*, 36: 573–95.

Richer, J. (ed.) (1994) *The Clinical Application of Ethology and Attachment Theory*. Association of Child Psychology and Psychiatry – Occasional Papers, 9.

Rutter, M. (1975) *Helping Troubled Children*. Harmondsworth: Penguin Books.

Rutter, M. (1993) 'An overview of developmental neuropsychiatry', in 'The brain and behaviour: organic influences in the behaviour of children', *Educational and Child Psychology*, **10**(1): 4–11.

Rutter, M. (1995) 'Clinical implications of attachment concepts: retrospect and prospect', *Journal of Child Psychology and Psychiatry*, **36**(4): 549–71.

Rutter, M. and the English and Romanian Adoptees (ERA) Study Team (1998) 'Developmental catch-up and deficit, following adoption after severe global early privation', *Journal of Child Psychology and Psychiatry*, **39**(4): 465–76.

Rutter, M. and Smith, D.J. (eds) (1995) *Psychosocial Disorders in Young People: Time, Trends and their Causes*. London: John Wiley.

Rutter, M., Giller, H. and Hagell, A. (1998) *Antisocial Behaviour by Young People*, particularly Chs 7 and 11. Cambridge: Cambridge University Press.

Schaefer, C.E. (ed.) (1993) *The Therapeutic Powers of Play*. Northvale, NJ, and London: Jason Aronson, Inc.

Slater, A. and Muir, D. (eds) (1999) The *Blackwell Reader in Developmental Psychology*. Oxford: Blackwell.

Smilansky, S. (1968) *The effects of Sociodramatic Play on Disadvantaged Pre-School Children*. New York: John Wiley.

Snow, C.E. and Ferguson, C.A. (eds) (1977) *Talking to Children: Language Input and Acquisition*. Cambridge: Cambridge University Press.

Sroufe, L.A. (1996) *Emotional Development: The Organisation of Emotional Life in the Early Years*. Cambridge: Cambridge University Press.

Stoker, B. (ed.) (1998) 'Discourse between academics and practitioners: cognition, attribution and reading'. *Educational and Child Psychology*, **15**(2): 6–66.

Sylva, K. (1994) 'School influences on children's development', *Journal of Child Psychology and Psychiatry–Annual Research Review*, **35**(1): 135–70.

Webster-Stratton, C. (1999) *How to Promote Children's Social and Emotional Competence*. London: Paul Chapman Publishing.

Weinberger, J. (1996) *Literacy Goes to School*. London: Paul Chapman Publishing.

Whitehead, M. (1997) *Language and Literacy in the Early Years*, 2nd edn. London: Paul Chapman Publishing.

Williams, L.M, O'Callaghan, J. and Cowie, H. (1995) 'Therapeutic issues in educational psychology: can attachment theory inform practice?' in D. Indoe and A. Pecherek (eds) 'Therapeutic Interventions' *Educational and Child Psychology*, **12**(4): 48–54.

Wood, D. (1998) *How Children Think and Learn: The Social Contexts of Cognitive Development*. Oxford: Blackwell

Wood, E. and Attfield, J. (1996) *Play, Learning and the Early Childhood Curriculum*. London: Paul Chapman Publishing.

Woodhead, M., Carr, R. and Light, P. (eds) (1991) *Becoming a Person*. London: Routledge/Open University.

Index